RECEIVING GOD'S KINGDOM BY JOYFUL REPENTANCE

BARRY HALL

RECEIVING GOD'S KINGDOM BY JOYFUL REPENTANCE

VOLUME 1:
HOLINESS, PROTECTION, AND FIGHTING EVIL –
By Directing Our Heart Toward Childlike Faith and Love for God's Presence

God

MANIFEST | PUBLISHING

www.GodManifestPublishing.com

This book and all other God Manifest Publishing books are available on Amazon.com.

Cover designed by Jonnathan Zin Truong
Cover Photo by Marie Dehayes on Unsplash
Interior designed by Uyen Vu

For more information on foreign distributors, email publishers@godmanifestpublishing.com

Reach us online: www.godmanifestpublishing.com

ISBN: 979-8-9920028-1-2
eBook: ISBN: 979-8-9920028-2-9

Printed in the United States of America.
Copyright © 2024 Barry Hall.
All rights reserved.

TABLE OF CONTENTS

RECOMMENDATIONS

"I have known Barry Hall for almost half a century. He is my son-in-law, and we have taken the opportunity to share on the deepest spiritual level. Barry is a competent and serious biblical scholar. He is a precious friend, and I love exchanging ideas with him.

Before Barry's book was complete, he offered me and a close friend a central idea in the book relating to spiritual warfare and the protection God gives believers. This material profoundly affected my friend and helped her feel secure and sense the presence of God."

BL Fraser, professor and biblical teacher living on Camano Island, Washington. He taught the Bible, trained pastors in the Belgian Congo, and was a Baptist pastor in the US until he was ninety-two years old.

✝

"I have known Barry for more than twenty-five years. What he has taught me about repentance (turning to God) has been instrumental in shaping my walk as a follower of Jesus, and I am incredibly grateful for the time we have had together.

There are several things I have learned through Barry's teaching and through my own experience that I would like to highlight for the reader of this book:

- Our hearts, rather than our intellect, are the drivers for our motivation and actions. So, even if we intellectually believe something, it will not change our behavior if that truth isn't also accepted at a heart level.

- Our hearts are not rational and need to be 'trained' to change deeply held beliefs (a simple one-time explanation will not do the trick).

- Training our hearts requires repeated exposure to the truth about God. Declarations of joy are a very effective way to accomplish this.

- Reading these truths silently can help, but it is much more effective to read/say them out loud.

- Even more effective is to speak them—declare them—aloud with a joyful, enthusiastic voice. This can feel very awkward to many people, but it really is more effective and worth pushing through those initial feelings of reservation.

- Because, going through life in a fallen world, we are constantly bombarded with pressure to glory in many different earthly things, we must continually (daily) counter this pressure with the message we want our hearts to hear: to glory in God.

- Training your heart this way leads to greater humility and trust in Him, and opens you up to experiencing His presence and glory in ways that you may not even be able to imagine right now.

- We have a tremendous hope of glory in Him, and He freely offers us the opportunity to draw near, drink of His glory, and be satisfied in Him.

I have gone through periods of neglecting this kind of heart training and periods of being faithful and diligent with it, and the diligent periods have been much better! Through the practice of humbling my heart and redirecting my thirsty desires to be satisfied in God, I have experienced much greater freedom from temptation, greater personal holiness, deeper relationship with Jesus, and the healing of deep emotional traumas. It really does work, and although it takes time and effort, there is a definite reward that makes the investment worthwhile.

My prayer for you is that God will help you identify the parts of your heart and deeply held beliefs that will lead to the greatest transformation in your life, and that you will experience the abundant riches of the glory He offers to each of us."

Bryan Beck, consultant to the forest products industry from Oregon City, Oregon

1

WHAT IN THE WORLD IS GOD DOING?

TO THOSE WHO MAY BE NEW TO CHRISTIANITY

This chapter jumps right into the deep end. If you lack Bible knowledge, you might want to read chapters 3 and 4 first and then come back here. Those chapters are also heavy, but they give background you will find helpful for this.

THE SHORT VERSION

God wants to heal our land, but that hasn't happened yet (2 Chron. 7:14). Jesus came to "destroy the works of the devil" (1 John 3:8). But evil is still rampant and not yet destroyed. God wants us to turn away from sin and toward Him. He also wants us to receive His justice and righteousness to earth so He can finish the task of destroying evil (Amos 5:24; Rev. 5:10). How can we align our thinking and application of the Bible more fully with what God wants to do with us and in our world?

Early in the Bible, God made an "everlasting covenant" that He would be God to us (Gen. 17:7; Gal. 3:29). God wants to be our God with emotional benefits that keep us coming back to Him (Deut. 32:37–39; Jer. 17:5–8; 2:11–13). But idolatry and sin have broken the everlasting covenant God made so that He is unable to be God to us at the level He desires (Isa. 24:5; 43:12; Jer. 11:10).

How can we recognize heart-level idolatry and turn away from it practically? Is it realistic for us to turn away from idolatry and sin so we can depend on God as our God in a pure and childlike way?

Later in this book, we will consider what God considers idolatry and how He wants to be God to us. Directly related to this topic are verses about experiencing God's presence more fully by drinking from the radiance around Him. But how does that work, and what does it look like in everyday life? When you pray and study these things long enough, you eventually see puzzle pieces from all over the Bible that fit together perfectly.

The most common forms of idolatry are well-hidden and easily ignored. But idolatry of any kind damages our ability to receive God's presence so we can abide in Him well.[1] What if we combine the puzzle pieces of Scripture, consider the big picture, and take God at His Word? Is opening up to God and drinking from Him related to receiving His kingdom like a child (Ps. 36:7–9; Mark 10:15)? If it is, what if we use joyful declarations that direct our hearts away from idolatry and sin (1 Sam. 7:3) and into a more significant place of childlike faith that enables us to freely drink from God as the Scriptures say (John 7:37–39)? These questions and more are answered in this book.

WHO THIS IS FOR

This book is not for people who want to stay comfortable with holding back from God. This is for people willing to humble themselves enough to boldly use the Word of God and their emotions as fuel for declarations that break up hardness in their hearts and propel them toward God, holiness, and significance from spiritual power.

Unwanted behaviors, reactions, idolatry, and sin are damaging ways of filling our emotional needs and avoiding emotional pain. Emotions can also motivate positive and healthy behaviors.

In this book, I give reasons why you should listen to yourself making audible declarations that joyfully humble you into embracing a childlike perspective that you are unable to have consistent purity of heart and protection from evil without cutting off worldly ways of finding refuge, strength, and glory. Your declarations need to help you boldly cut off every other option until all you can do is let your heart believe truth about seeking the kingdom of God (Mark 10:15) and receiving Heaven around you so you can abide in Him twenty-four seven (Heb. 12:22–24, 28; Matt. 19:14). This book also shows where to focus your repentance for deep and long-lasting effectiveness, without getting run over by guilt and shame in the process.

The Bible speaks of God as "covering [Himself] with light as with a cloak, / Stretching out heaven like a tent curtain" around you here (Ps. 104:2). It also tells us to "walk in the Light as He Himself is in the Light" (1 John 1:7). The implications of combining those two verses are staggering! Even though it might seem a long way off for you to literally "walk in the Light" as He is in Light, I want to help you with a joyous kind of repentance that helps you change your mind step by step until it becomes practical for you to go even from a place of idolatry and sin to one of freely receiving from the radiance around God so you can apply these things yourself. This book shows the Scriptures and reasoning that led me to these conclusions and practice.

IT WASN'T ENOUGH

On the surface, I had everything going for me. I grew up in a Christian home. We had a good church and a wonderful youth group. I was never abused sexually or emotionally. For a year or so, I memorized large portions of Scripture. I even went to a Christian school for part of my college years.

---

[1] I will show the Scriptures about this later in this book.

But these things were not enough. I was frustrated and failing as a Christian. Sin had weakened me to where I would fall in my private life even at the slightest temptation. Eventually, deep depression and despair became the norm for me—even for months and years at a time. I didn't like to think about it, but something was missing, and it hurt. As best I could, I tried to believe that Christ was my savior, but something was desperately wrong inside, and I didn't know what it was.

> Deep inside, I was feeling the pain of Heaven because I was trying to drink from the glory of the world instead of the glory of God (Jer. 2:11-13).

I longed to be closer to God, but my heart was hard. All the failure and pain made me want to hide and stay far away from Him. Deep down, I knew the solution had to do with repentance. But the pain worsened when I couldn't find anyone to tell me how.

Did Jesus die to save us from sin, or did He not? I could see why the gospel is good news for eternity, but what about the present? What makes the gospel good news for this life?

The integrity and holiness I longed for compared to reality in my heart were vastly different. I figured either God is horrible, disconnected, and not good because He is asking too much of us or that His goodness is beyond anything we know. Could there be something vitally important we didn't yet understand? If God is perfect and good, there must be more to the Christian life than I knew.

Often, I wanted to give up and run away. But I still wondered, "What if God wants me to give my life to trying to understand what we Christians are missing?" If that were true, I would have to be extremely careful to observe what the Bible says so that I would not miss something important or be misled.

But how could I observe the Scriptures skillfully without an underlying belief about the goodness of God? It made sense that if I were even to begin to see and understand God's solution, I would have to start with an idealistic assumption about God's goodness beyond the prevailing Christian paradigm (Isa. 42:19–23).

To stay motivated and have even a slight possibility of arriving at the truth, I would need a perspective about God's goodness that would allow me to study the Scriptures consistently and with hope. The most difficult part would be that I had to study without dismissing something important because I did not yet understand how to live it. If I could not study honestly and with a belief in the overwhelming goodness of God, I was sure I would miss what God offers and never even begin to understand.

Eventually, the prayer of my heart became that God would teach me in a way that would help me to live what He says and then also that I would be able to teach others. Now, after many years of tears and struggle, I am pleased to be able to share with you what I have learned.

Photo by Zac Durant on Unsplash

YOU DO WANT GOD!

I do not agree with those who tell you that you don't want God enough! You do want God. This book will help you better recognize your practical desire and need for God and His presence with you in everyday life. It will also help you to use the evidence of your need for God as motivation to direct your heart toward childlike openness to receiving His presence with freedom, gratitude, playfulness, and praise.

God is seeking true worshipers (John 4:23), so He designed all of us with needs that drive our behavior, reactions, longings, and pursuits are need-driven. Filling our needs makes us depend on and worship something. But what is the most accurate way to describe our human emotional needs? Some psychologists say that we do what we do out of a need for significance and security. Others say it is power and pleasure. Still others say respect and relationships are what we want most.

It hurts when these needs go unmet. But these are only symptoms of a stronger and much deeper need. Saying our behavior results from emotional, psychological, or self-esteem needs doesn't get at the heart of the matter. It is more accurate to say that we want God. My view is that we need to feel secure and confident because our falling short results in a great and driving need for the presence of God's radiant glory upon and around our physical humanity here (Ps. 84:11). Cooperating with how God designed us brings His presence. Understanding this requires the explanation that comes later in this book.

Let me be clear before I go further. This book will help you understand the hidden idolatry we all need to be vigilant to continue repenting from. But this book and the series do not stop there. We must also consider more deeply what we are repenting toward. Our repentance is incomplete if it only helps us turn away from idolatry and reoccurring sin. True repentance brings the presence of God or we haven't taken our repentance far enough (Acts 3:19)! Sin and idolatry are evidence of our unmet need for God's presence as what reassures us; makes us confident, strong, and worthy; and becomes armor around us. More explanation about that comes later also.

The Bible calls our need a thirst for God's presence. King David wrote, "O God, You are my God; I shall seek You earnestly; / My soul thirsts for You, my flesh yearns for You, / In a dry and weary land where there is no water. / Thus I have seen You in the sanctuary, / To see Your power and Your glory /...My soul is satisfied" (Ps. 63:1–2, 5).

Did you see that? Seeing by faith the greatness of God's power and glory while inside the sanctuary is what satisfied him both spiritually and emotionally. The path I want you to take is one of directing your heart away from idolatry and into a place of faith for receiving the sanctuary of Heaven around you here like a child. Once inside, you can apply your faith to believing the abundance and closeness of God's great power and glory while enjoying Him as the God who satisfies you just as He did for King David. The practical benefits to you are great because you feel secure, significant, powerful, and worthy. The benefits to God and His kingdom are that your practical holiness increases. You love and praise God more. The demonic realm also gets crushed.[2]

> To avoid confusion, let me emphasize that there is a glory God gives and a glory He does not give. The glory God does not give away to anyone is the glory that rightly goes to Him through our worship and praise (Isa. 42:8). The glory that God does give freely is the glory that is the substance of His tangible presence (Ps. 84:11; James 4:8; Ex. 33:18–22). It is right for us to seek and receive the glory that comes from God and not from the world or other people (John 5:44). The key is that we must avoid turning His presence into pride. We must praise and glorify God for what we receive from His radiance and not ourselves.

DOES ABIDING INCLUDE OUR PHYSICAL BODY?

Jesus said to abide with Him in us and us in Him (John 15:4). But is doing that purely spiritual, or should our abiding include our physical body? Should we consider it strictly spiritual when the Bible says, "He who dwells in the shelter of the Most High / Will abide in the shadow of the Almighty" (Ps. 91:1)? We should not.

Christians are kingdom priests (Rev. 5:10), and priests are told to stand before the Lord (2 Chron. 29:11). How do we do that? King David said he was secure when abiding by standing before the Lord, "I have set the LORD continually before me; / Because He is at my right hand, I will not be shaken. / Therefore my heart is glad and my glory rejoices; / My flesh also will dwell securely" (Ps. 16:8–9).

> If we take God at His Word, the unshakable kingdom we receive here like a child is the mountain of God and Heaven itself (Heb. 12:22–24, 28). When we believe God's kingdom is coming down to us from above, the mountain of God comes as a heavy rock, His peace comes as Heaven comes, and evil gets crushed in the process (Dan. 2:35, 44–45; Matt. 21:42–44; Rom. 16:20; 14:17; James 1:17). What if you coached your heart into believing these Scriptures enough for you to live them powerfully?

If you are like me, your first response would be to dismiss these things as impractical and untrue. But what would change if you took steady and practical steps to teach your heart to joyfully turn toward God until you can believe and apply the Scriptures in ways that enable you to receive the kingdom like a child and abide in God's presence twenty-four seven?

This book explains abiding as a continual process of presenting our body to God by receiving Heaven here with the faith of a child so we can stand in the radiance around God as kingdom priests (Rom. 12:1; Mark 10:15). There is a sense in which we abide because of salvation (1 John 4:13; 1 Cor. 6:19). But with God, it is always possible to experience His presence more fully (1 Kings 8:11). It is not enough to occasionally soak in the presence of God! Being practical about abiding requires us also to consider what we can do to transform our mind so we can believe these Scriptures in our hearts enough to apply these things well (Rom. 12:2).

The battle we face on earth is with the influence of evil. To fight well, we need more of God's kingdom here. Receiving the presence of God and His kingdom so we can abide by presenting our physical body before God fits perfectly with what God is trying to do in our world.

When you confront your disbelief and joyfully direct your heart to believe the Scriptures on these topics (1 Sam. 7:3; Rom. 12:2), God's presence and kingdom come much more easily (Matt. 6:10; Mark 10:15).

CLEANSING AFTER SALVATION INCLUDES OUR PHYSICAL BODY

Cleansing for salvation is vital (Titus 3:5–6). We received Christ for salvation by faith in God to come and save us (John 1:12; Eph. 2:8–9). But after salvation, how do we deal with the shame from the idolatry and sin we still see in our hearts?

After salvation, God's cleansing presence continues to come upon and around us by the radiant Spirit of glory that shines through Jesus because of His sinless life, death, resurrection, and glorification (Heb. 4:15; John 7:39; 1 Peter 4:14; Titus 3:5–6). But walking in the cleansing light that shines from God is not automatic just because of salvation (1 John 1:5, 7)! Just as with salvation initially, we continue to receive the promise of the Spirit by actively believing we are receiving His Spirit in an ongoing

---

[2] In this book, I talk about the crushing being done by the mountain of God and His kingdom coming down. The Word of God also crushes evil (Jer. 23:29). I emphasize Heaven coming down because when His spoken word comes to us, it comes through the Holy Spirit inside us, but it also comes down like snow and like rain (Isa. 55:10-11). By emphasizing Heaven coming down and crushing evil, I am trying to also include the spoken Word of God.

away (Gal. 3:14; Col. 2:6). After the cleansing we receive for salvation, cleansing is still needed for conscience and our physical body (Heb. 10:19–22). Intervention is needed before we can abide in the fullness of what the Bible describes.

Because God does not want to be forsaken as a "fountain," the radiant glory of God should be central to the everyday experience and faith of Christians worldwide (Jer. 2:11–13; Jer. 17:13; Ps. 84:11). More will be said about this ongoing cleansing later in this book.

WHAT IS GOD DOING IN OUR DAY?

From God's unlimited perspective of time, the earth is already filled with His glory (Isa. 6:3). From our limited standpoint of time, the earth is in the process of being filled with God's glory by what we receive from the radiance around Him (Num. 14:21; John 5:44). When we take it literally that our God is a radiant fountain of glory and grace, God can use what we freely receive of the shine around Him to help fill the earth with His glory (Ps. 84:11; John 7:37–39).

At the end of the Bible, the outcome of everything is that the tabernacle of God is coming to be with us here on earth (Rev. 21:3). But is this something that will happen suddenly, or is it something God is doing progressively? In Psalm 27, God's tabernacle is where God protects His people (vv. 1–6). What if we are to receive Heaven here like a child so that the dwelling place of God progressively comes to earth and protects us during end times (Ps. 91)?

Our promised land as believers is to stand before the Lord as priests in the throne room before we die (Heb. 3; 12; 2 Chron. 29:11; Rev. 5:10). Showing gratitude about receiving Heaven here helps us to open up and enter by receiving Heaven around us here with the freedom and joy of a child (Heb. 12:22–24, 28; Mark 10:15)! Early in the Bible, it says of God, "You will bring them and plant them in the mountain of Your inheritance, / The place, O Lord, which You have made for Your dwelling, / The sanctuary, O Lord, which Your hands have established" (Ex. 15:17).

We must see that verse as something God is doing before we die. We are temples for the holy Spirit. But God is also building us together into a dwelling place for His presence (Eph. 2:21–22). In the Old Testament, God was inside the temple. He was also upon and all around it. God is doing that in our day also. Of course, He is including those who have gone to Heaven by their physical death after salvation, but God's grand plan is to establish Heaven on earth progressively. Before we die, we enter by receiving Heaven here like a child who can only rest after they wrap themselves in their favorite blanket. To do this, we must believe we are entering with a heart full of childlike faith, freedom, and joy about the greatness of having God draw near to us in this way. Great change is required.

Jesus came to destroy the works of the devil (1 John 3:8). He accomplished that when He died on our behalf. But the story doesn't stop there. He wants to use us to help increase His rule and reign on earth because He tells us to "let justice roll down like waters / And righteousness like an ever-flowing stream (Isa. 9:7; Amo. 5:24).

How can we avoid mere head knowledge? How can we go from holding ourselves back to embracing the Scripture enough to apply what it says joyfully? You have to listen to yourself as you reassure your heart about the truth until you believe that God wants to come to you so He can accomplish His purposes on earth!

DECLARATIONS CAN BRING FAITH FOR DEEPER THINGS

When speaking of salvation, the Bible says that if we confess with our mouth and believe in our heart, God saves us, resulting in righteousness (Rom. 10:9–10). When applied to repentance, we can change our minds by listening to ourselves make declarations that direct our hearts away from treasuring idolatry and into greater faith in God (1 Sam. 7:3). Explaining that is one of the main topics in this book. But in short, if you listen to the confessions of your mouth as a way to get your heart to believe and depend on God as your God, righteous behavior comes much more naturally than is otherwise possible.

My story began with a longing for heart-level righteousness and holy living. Initially, I would have rejected the idea of receiving Heaven here like a child. But while changes brought by listening to myself make joyous declarations of repentance and faith[3] took effort and time, my declarations brought a humility that helped to turn my faith away from earthly sources, sin, and pride and opened me to faith in God at much deeper levels. Declarations of repentance with joy took my blinders off. I am much more childlike in my faith and worship.

While I have not fully arrived, I am much better at taking God at His Word and believing I can do what the Bible says.

What if we were to use gratitude and praise (Heb. 12:28; Ps. 100:4) to direct our hearts into trusting by faith that the blood of Christ is cleansing our physical hands and our hearts as we enter the holy place through the torn veil, by receiving Heaven upon and around our body here? (See Ps. 24:3–4; Heb. 10:22–24; 1 John 1:5, 7; and Heb. 12:22–24, 28.) What if the torn veil is like a gate above us that we can easily swing open so the King of Glory can come freely to earth and battle evil on our behalf (Ps. 24:7–8)?

It isn't natural to live these Scriptures well, but if you turn your heart away from believing that the world's glory fills your longings for God, your childlike faith has much greater freedom to grow. The presence of God increases, you love God more, and your purity increases. You live a more profound and significant Christian life when you direct your heart into joyfully believing the truth of these Scriptures for you personally.

How would your life change if your heart were to believe you can enter and stand before the Lord, where God is crushing evil under your physical feet because you are receiving Heaven upon and around you here like a child (Rom. 12:2; 16:20; 2 Chron. 29:11; Mark 10:15)? Would Heaven come down to you from above (James 1:17), and would God protect you (Ps. 91)? Would God's will be done on earth as it is in Heaven (Matt. 6:10) because of what you are receiving here?

Jesus said, "Whoever does not receive the kingdom of God like a child will not enter it at all" (Mark 10:15). Speaking of children, Jesus said, "The kingdom of heaven belongs to such as these" (Matt. 19:14).

Later, we are told to present our bodies to God (Rom. 12:1). What if these verses aren't talking about salvation? Are we to enter before the Lord so we can present our bodies to God by receiving Heaven here like a child? If so, then the significance of our role in receiving Heaven here is huge! The more we become childlike in our faith, the more we are able to receive and the more the will of God can be done on earth as it is in Heaven!

---

[3] Making declarations of repentance and faith is a descriptive phrase for what I call *heart training*.

Can adults become childlike enough to receive the kingdom of Heaven easily? Is receiving God's presence and the kingdom of Heaven something you can realistically improve? You can because listening to yourself make audible declarations removes obstacles to greater faith for a deeper Christian life.

A FORMULA?

Christians consider our relationship with God as something we can't put into a formula. I agree with that. This book does not give a formula for a relationship with God. It provides repeatable steps for turning away from worldly things and presenting our bodies before God (Rom. 12:2; 2 Chron. 29:11) by receiving Heaven here like a child (Mark 10:15; Matt. 19:14).

> Scriptures about idolatry explain that God wants to be God to us in practical ways that benefit us emotionally. In that context, the vehicle that helps us to stay in His presence fills our emotional needs by receiving and enjoying instead of what we receive from other things. Doing so brings greater holiness and makes us more spiritually powerful.

Some Christians learn to receive and soak in God's presence during church services or their alone times with God. But few understand receiving God's presence in ways that let them abide. Abiding twenty-four seven requires that we make God our one God so that our hearts don't get drawn away and enticed by the world (James 1:14). You won't understand this at first, but let me say it anyway.

Jesus said that we receive glory from other people when we should be receiving the glory that shines from God (John 5:44). The reason we receive glory from other people is that our emotional needs get filled this way. Our faith and the loves of our hearts need to be turned toward God. By the glory God gives, He becomes a shield around us, and we are enabled to "walk uprightly" (Ps. 84:11) and in "newness of life" (Rom. 6:4).

Since God's glory never stops pouring out from Him, why don't we receive more, and why do we later stop receiving? Our hearts are bent on receiving from the world much more than we realize. Christians need to repent much more deeply than is apparent on the surface. But our repentance must also change what we believe and how much we can believe it.

Receiving God's presence has a series of steps that can be understood, duplicated, and improved. But central to what improves our receiving is that we must turn our hearts away from the world and more fully toward God. When you understand how you open up and receive from the world, you can use declarations of repentance and faith that redirect your heart's affections toward God until His kingdom comes to you quickly and easily. As you continue on this path, you learn to stay open before God and keep receiving so His presence stays with you here!

Does this sound like a formula? The receiving part of it is a repeatable formula, but after you turn your heart more fully away from the world and your heart learns to apply the steps to God's presence and kingdom as an ongoing process, your relationship with God takes over, and there are no formulas. This book explains how to direct your heart toward God so you can easily enter by receiving, but there is a lot involved in applying these things consistently.

Salvation begins the Christian life by providing God's acceptance that continues into eternity (Rom. 15:16; Lev. 19:5; John 1:29; 1 John 2:2). What about after salvation? This book gives practical direction to Christ's command that we should "seek first His kingdom and His righteousness" (Matt. 6:33). Because of how God defines idolatry, this book is about a joyous kind of repentance that helps us draw near to God by receiving the kingdom of Heaven upon and around us here like a child (James 4:8; Mark 10:15). By this, we can make God the one God who is our refuge of security, our strength that makes us confident, and our glory that gives us identity and worth in everyday life. Depending on God to be God to us in this way becomes like glue that helps us want to abide in Him more steadily.

PARADIGM CHANGERS

Let me make some statements that will not make sense until after you begin making declarations of repentance and faith as described in this book.

Jesus said that because we receive glory from one another, we make it difficult to believe we can receive the glory that shines from God (John 5:44; Ps. 84:11). One example is that we are told to seek and receive the kingdom here like a child (Matt. 6:10, 33). Even though this is a familiar phrase to Christians, because

WHAT IN THE WORLD IS GOD DOING?

most don't know how to do it, we hesitate to allow ourselves to believe it is a literal thing we should be doing after salvation. Even if you aren't aware of receiving "glory from one another," you should take it by faith that your faith suffers because of it. What is the result? Even when our head is convinced that we all are to receive the kingdom like a child, doing it can sound impractical, complicated, and maybe even wrong.

For reasons I will discuss later, we receive glory from one another because it is easier to have faith in the glory we earn than to trust God that we can receive by faith in His grace the radiance that never stops pouring out from Him.

As you read through this book, it is vital that you keep in mind that it will be unnatural for your heart to believe what you know in your head is right for you to do. It is in this place that we all begin. If you are like I was, you will have to repent by speaking to your disbelief and self-protection with bold and joyful declarations of faith before the hardness in your heart can be broken down and you can believe the truth your head becomes convinced about.

> Our heart doesn't always believe what we know in our head is true, and behavior follows what our heart believes and treasures. Without intervention that directs our heart toward God, paradigms in our thinking and behavior that are misaligned with the Word of God result (1 Sam. 7:3). The repentance that changes paradigms requires proactive declarations that boldly change the deeply seated thinking patterns in our hearts, from self-protection and holding back to unreserved faith. We must listen to our declarations with the intention of getting our hearts to hear, believe, and love the truth in God's Word, especially in regard to receiving the kingdom of Heaven here. We must say with King David that "my soul will make its boast in the Lord," and I will "hear it" until I "rejoice" (Ps. 34:2).

Let me give you another example. We are also told to come to the Lord (Matt. 11:28), but because we are not to ascend into Heaven in order to bring Christ down (Rom. 10:6), we must come to believe that we draw near by trusting God to draw

near to us here (James 4:8). There are many Scriptures that support this view. The way I see it, the advancement of the kingdom of Heaven on earth depends on our willingness to believe these truths with childlike delight and faith.

This book gives a practical and effective path for cleansing your hands and purifying your heart by entering before the Lord so that He can draw near and wash you here (Heb. 10:19–22). When you boldly go down the path of joyously directing your heart away from even the possibility of idolatry, your faith will grow and you will find the freedom you need to ascend to the hill of the Lord by receiving the mountain of God and Heaven coming down to you here (Ps. 24:3; Heb. 12:22–24, 28).

I will show you how to remove obstacles of idolatry and sin (Isa. 57:14) with joyous zeal (Rev. 3:19), so you can make a highway for God (Isa. 40:3–5) where you learn to easily flop open the gates of the torn veil above you so that the King of Glory can come freely to earth because of what you receive (Ps. 24:7–8; Heb. 10:19–20; 12:28). By receiving upon and around you what you abide in and take refuge inside, the presence of God and the kingdom of Heaven coming down (James 1:17) around you become your protection and strength in the battle against evil (Ps. 91).

We must direct our hearts into a place of greater childlike faith, but the key is in taking refuge in the Lord until we possess His holy mountain (Isa. 57:13). The mountain of God and Heaven are inseparable because the dwelling place of God is on His holy mountain. When we receive the kingdom with childlike gratitude, the mountain of God drops down from above and we go through the middle of it. As it comes down quickly, the mountain of God brings Heaven and angels with it here (Heb. 12:22–24, 28).[4] When we repent of idolatry and sin enough to also become childlike in our faith, we can more easily open up and receive until we possess the mountain of God and Heaven belongs to us here (Matt. 19:14).

PARADOXES AND FULL DISCLOSURE

This book is full of paradoxes. The explanations in this book sound technical because we must honestly consider many

---

[4] In his book *The Final Quest*, Rick Joyner calls this "going up through the middle of the mountain." I don't apply the Scriptures as our "going up" because God wants to dwell in us and among us here (2 Cor. 6:16). We are to seek the kingdom and to receive it like a child (Matt. 6:33; Mark 10:15) until Heaven belongs to us (Matt. 19:14).

Scriptures as puzzle pieces of a bigger picture. Yet applying my detailed descriptions is simple enough for a child to do. The tricky part is that we, as adults, are not childlike in our delight and the simplicity of our faith in God. We are also often disconnected from what is happening in our hearts.

I give extensive details about the heart-level activities of opening up so we can easily receive the presence of God and the kingdom of Heaven and rest in Him here. Many will be grateful for these descriptions, but these explanations will seem like too much detail to some. To apply these things, you will need to observe your heart without condemnation while trusting the radiance of God is coming onto you, washing you clean (1 John 1:5, 7). While receiving Heaven here like a child is a simple activity, you must remove the obstacles to your childlike faith for doing these things or applying these things will seem entirely impossible for you.

We must fight the battles within us, but we dare not ignore the battle that rages around us. Most of the time, the cleansing I talk about is more for the outside of you than the inside. Many of the obstacles to your faith are not from you. Often, the shame you feel before God is being put on you by the demonic outside of you to keep you away from Him. You don't have to know for sure whether the shame you feel is from you or from outside you.

If you make your behavior the focus of repentance, you will only make yourself feel guilty and ashamed. You must learn to enjoy the ongoing cleansing of God while continuing to focus your repentance on changing what your heart believes and treasures (Heb. 10:22; Matt. 13:44). Obedience comes from faith (Rom. 1:5). Freedom from sin comes from what we treasure about the truth in the Word of God (Ps. 119:11). True repentance changes what you believe and love. By this, your main focus won't be on disciplining your behavior. The focus of your effort will be on making declarations that increase your faith and hope so that your behavior gets pulled toward God by your increasing delight and love for Him.

But to deal with it, you must teach yourself to present any shame you feel, inside or outside, before God so that He can wash it from you. You can turn your thinking patterns away from shame toward yourself, but if the shame is not from you, then you need to take the fight to another level. Jesus came to destroy evil (1 John 3:8), so the thinking patterns in your heart need to change to include faith that lets you enjoy taking refuge in the Lord to the point that the holiness of God is coming down hard enough upon and around you that God is crushing and burning the demonic because of what you love receiving as cleansing.

In this book, I talk a lot about repentance with joy, and this too will seem paradoxical because to be effective, your repentance must be celebrative, and the focus of your repentance must stay on changing your thinking patterns and not your behavior directly.

Sometimes, it might seem like this book is changing your heart-level thinking patterns. It is not! I can only teach your head. After that, you will have two options. You can wait years before your heart catches up to believing what your head learns is true here. Or you can fight the status quo by taking assertive steps that lead your heart into the place of hearing and believing the truth about what God offers freely.

The court system in the USA says innocent until proven guilty. Here, I ask you to do the opposite. Will you embrace your humanness by assuming heart-level idolatry is true of you and then joyously make declarations that turn your heart away from the possibility of idolatry without wallowing in guilt and shame?

Photo by Lina Trochez on Unsplash

The bottom line is that you need more of God's presence, and God wants His kingdom here so that His will can be done on earth as it is in Heaven (Matt. 6:10). For this, your repentance can't be something that closes you off from the kingdom because of heaping condemnation on yourself! You have to become more childlike in your faith and love for God.

This book will teach you to make declarations that help you joyously turn away from idolatry and sin. But I will not be asking you to determine the specifics of idolatry in your heart. I will ask you to embrace that you are human and expect the possibility of idolatry without condemnation and then make joyous declarations that cut off and direct your heart away from earthly sources as idolatrous options for you.

Will you direct your heart into joyously trusting God to cleanse you of idolatry and sin while you are using declarations to assertively direct your heart away from idolatry that is typical for people and do this without having to decide for sure whether that form of idolatry is a problem for you?

I am asking you to make joyful declarations about what you don't have to depend on and about the God who wants to be God to you here. If you make a declaration and suddenly realize that what you are turning from is an idol for you, don't stop to wallow in condemnation or remorse. Agree with God about it as sin and present it before the holy radiance of God while trusting He is washing you clean.

Are you willing to courageously consider and turn away from the subtle ways you might be manufacturing shame in order to keep yourself at a safer distance from God? If you can take it by faith that these things might be an issue and boldly cut them off as a possibility by declarations of joyous repentance, your delight toward God will increase, and God will have more freedom to draw near intensely and be the one God whose presence and kingdom become your security, hope, and courage.

Applying these things in everyday life feels easy, comforting, powerful, and significant, but not until after you boldly remove the hidden obstacles in your thinking that keep you treasuring earthly and human glory as your comfort and significance. Just be warned at the start that you will have to cut off faith in self-protection to enable explosive faith in God for receiving the kingdom of Heaven here like a child. Before you joyously cut off earthly sources and pride, your first reaction to my descriptions will be to doubt and even protect yourself from believing the many Scriptures I give.

Are you willing to listen to yourself as you make declarations that direct your heart away from treasuring how much you punish yourself for your human lack of perfection? Are you willing to embrace the presence of God coming to you and touching your skin as holiness and perfection, even for your humanity? The more your heart learns to love staying in the holiness of God around you, the more holy living becomes practical.

It will take courage on your part to keep reading. You will have to get through my many descriptions. You must also direct your heart away from a lifetime of thinking patterns that prevent childlike freedom and delight toward God.

The disclosure here is that before you courageously change your thinking patterns and joyfully redirect your dependencies toward God, you may only be able to read this book as information for your head without wholeheartedly embracing it as truth in your heart. To avoid wasting time and effort, it will help to soften your heart if you pause as you read this book so you can courageously thank God that He is good and that the Scriptures and what I write are doable for you. Your thinking has to change, but repentance that happens this way will take time, and you must be patient with yourself.

> Am I done cutting off pride so I can joyously become more childlike? I have gone a long way down this path but am far from reaching the goal because the goal is not a destination. Because the world never stops trying to conform us to its mold, the goal for us is continuous improvement.

HOW DO I KNOW HEAVEN COMES?

When trusting that Heaven is coming down from above, I know I am receiving Heaven here like a child because I can often feel when Heaven envelops me with a sudden increase of peace (Rom. 14:17). It feels like I am inside an open heaven that extends under me and where the roof above me is entirely off. When I make declarations that build my faith about the power of the holiness of God and playfully love His closeness to me, all torment from the enemy and witchcraft stops.

I know that I am receiving Heaven around me because I have also had several experiences with physical healing while trusting that Heaven is near. Most of the healing I experience comes after extended times of thanks and praise when looking at the Lord and rejoicing about the power of His presence for physical healing touching the ailment. It is a lot easier when I am going after healing for myself than for other people. I no longer have heart palpitations. At more than seventy years old, my knees and hip joints have no pain. At thirty-five years old, I couldn't kneel and get up without horrible pain.

Over the course of my life, four or five people have been healed of significant sickness when I prayed for them, including one with stage 4 cancer and another with decades-long diabetes.

Photo by Nate Rayfield on Unsplash

Only one time when I didn't do any prior extended time of thanks and praise have I prayed for someone who was healed. At a Christian meeting, I met a guy in his early twenties who had scoliosis from birth. Several of us gathered around him to pray for his healing, but after a few minutes, when nothing happened, everyone else left. That didn't seem right to me, so I stayed and asked if I could quote some Scripture and continue praying. I spoke some Scripture and then thanked God that we can enter before Him by receiving Heaven here. As I was thanking God that His healing power was coming and touching this young man, he joined in with me, agreeing and thanking God with me.

While we were both joyfully thanking God that Heaven was surrounding us, I had my hand on his upper back and thought I could feel things moving around, but I wasn't sure, so I continued. Because I am a "more is better" kind of guy, I would have gone on for a lot longer. But after maybe fifteen minutes, his girlfriend came up to rescue him from me and said, "I think you look taller. You should go look at yourself in the mirror." He went and came out with a huge smile saying it was gone. Later, the doctors cleared him for military service, and he is still doing that today.

I freely admit that it seems like I should have seen a lot more healings like this. But at this point in my life, to see others healed, I seem to need to be in worship constantly for a few days, thanking God for His healing power and looking at Him before me here, and the older I get, the harder it is to stay focused like that.

It may be that if I focused more on the power of the Holy Spirit in me, I would see more healing happen when I pray for other people. But Heaven around me as protection is important for consistent holiness, and I can't seem to do well at focusing on the greatness of God in me and around me at the same time. Putting on the armor of light in order to avoid lust is paramount for my purity. The unexpected power in spiritual warfare has also been a great blessing.

Aside from physical healing, there are other ways I am assured that I am receiving Heaven here. God often gives brief pictures of people I don't know, and I sense He wants me to receive on their behalf. So I bind the power of witchcraft and the demonic in their situation. I then open up to Heaven above me while trusting that because the veil has been torn (Heb. 10:19–22), the gates above us are easily swinging open (Ps. 24:7–8), the mountain of God is coming down with Heaven onto them, and angels are working in their situation (Heb. 12:22–24, 28). I thank God that angels are working and that His will is being done on earth as it is in Heaven (Matt. 6:10). I will often also praise God that His lovingkindness, justice, and righteousness are coming into their circumstances and that God is working these things as needed on their behalf (Jer. 9:24; Amos 5:24).

I look forward to finding out what God will do when large numbers of people begin to apply these things together.

QUESTIONS WE MUST ANSWER WELL

God is holy and wants us to be holy (1 Peter 1:16). We know we need to repent and turn away from sinful behavior, but how can we be more consistent with holiness in our private behavior and hearts? How can we look honestly at the condition of our hearts without holding back from God because of shame and guilt?

Beyond stopping the destructive behaviors, what about the more profoundly spiritual things we know God wants us to do? God promised, "[If] My people who are called by My name humble themselves and pray and seek My face and turn from their wicked ways, then I will hear from heaven, will forgive their sin and will heal their land" (2 Chron. 7:14). God wants to heal our land. How can we free ourselves from the distractions that keep us from seeking the face of God more fully?

We live in desperate times. Christians should not shy away from asking difficult questions!

Salvation is vital because that is what assures us that we will spend eternity in Heaven after we die. But most people have yet to respond to our message of good news. Would a combined gospel message of salvation, the kingdom of God, and the glory of Christ be more practical and relevant both for us as individuals and for the big picture of what the world needs (Rom. 1:16; 2 Cor. 4:4; Matt. 4:23; 24:14)? I believe it would.

Let me repeat that at the end of the Bible, the outcome of everything is that the tabernacle of God is coming to be with us here on earth (Rev. 21:3). God's grand plan is to reunite Heaven with earth so that He can dwell with us here.[5] What if God wants to use us to make that happen in a progressively increasing way? What would that look like? This book answers these questions in practical ways. It also makes the big picture of good news in the Bible profoundly relevant to everyday living.

TO WHERE SHOULD WE EXPECT THE KINGDOM TO COME?

I have found it helpful to believe what the Bible says about where we should expect the kingdom of Heaven to come. I first need to put it in context.

God's power is inside us because it talks about "the Spirit of Him who raised Jesus from the dead dwells in you" (Rom. 8:11) and "the power that works within us" (Eph. 3:20).

Consider also these verses:

- "Jesus said, 'Someone did touch Me, for I was aware that power had gone out of Me'" (Luke 8:46).

- "I am in the Father, and the Father is in Me...
  the Father abiding in Me does His works" (John 14:10).

But God's power should also be around and on us!

Jesus told us, "I am sending forth the promise of My Father upon you" (Luke 24:49). He said that what He sends will clothe us "with power from on high" (Luke 24:49). Another place it says that "you will receive power when the Holy Spirit has come upon you" (Acts 1:8). When the Holy Spirit comes upon us, He is on the outside of us all around.

When speaking of God's power coming onto us, we have to talk about the kingdom of Heaven coming onto us here. When the Bible talks about the kingdom of God or receiving the kingdom like a child, we need to think about it as being Heaven because these two things in Scripture are spoken of interchangeably (Matt. 13:11; 18:3; Mark 4:11; Luke 18:17).

Jesus said He would come again and receive us "to Myself, that where I am, there you may be also" (John 14:3). Jesus was with His disciples when He said that, but notice that He was also talking about His being somewhere in that moment that the disciples didn't understand. In those verses, Jesus was referring to standing before the Father, in His radiance, as where He was spiritually at that time (John 14:10; 2 Chron. 29:11).

Having that context, we can now talk about where the kingdom of Heaven comes when it comes. Jesus said that Heaven had come to where He was because He was in the Father at that very moment. To abide with Him in the Father and the Father in Him, Jesus Himself was applying what He told us to do when He said to enter by receiving Heaven upon and around us here like a child (Mark 10:15; Matt. 19:14).

It was because Jesus had received Heaven upon and around Him that He was able to say that Heaven was at hand (Matt. 3:1–2; 4:17). At other times, Jesus was receiving on behalf of others around Him because He said, "The kingdom of God has come upon you" (Matt. 12:28; Luke 11:20) or that "the kingdom of God has come near" (Luke 10:9, 11). In still another verse, it talks about the kingdom being "in your midst" (Luke 17:21).

The word *midst* can mean "within," as in the middle of a person or in the middle of a group. The context of the other gospels suggests the word *midst* in the Luke 17 verse means in the middle of the group of people present. What if we think of the meaning as "within"?

---

[5] The first time I heard someone else talk about Heaven being reunited with earth was through The Bible Project, which does teaching videos online.

Because of salvation, we do have something of the kingdom of Heaven inside us. And even if you want to believe that the Luke 17 verse should be translated "within," we still have six other verses saying that when Heaven comes, it comes upon, near, and around us here. The way I see it, the emphasis in the Bible should be the emphasis in our application. All seven verses in the gospels agree with each other. When God's heavenly kingdom comes, it comes upon us and surrounds us here.

Even though the NASB and the most recent NIV translate this phrase as "in your midst," some versions (KJV and the 1988 NIV) translate the Luke 17 verse by saying the kingdom of God is "within you." But in context, Jesus was talking to the Pharisees, who Jesus said were not of God and would not have the kingdom inside them because of that (John 8:44).

When we are thinking about abiding in Christ, the most helpful way of thinking about where the kingdom of Heaven comes is to think of it coming upon and around us so that we can be in Him, present our bodies to God (Rom. 12:1), and stand before Him as a priest (2 Chron. 29:11).

Yes, there are times in Scripture when God says to us, "Come up here" (Rev. 4:1). There are some in the body of Christ who are taken up into Heaven regularly. But for practical everyday abiding in Christ, we are to trust that both the mountain of God and Heaven are coming down around us here (Dan. 2:35, 44–45; Matt. 21:42–44; Heb. 12:22–24, 28). The advantages of thinking of it this way are powerful for holiness and spiritual warfare.

From God's perspective, we are to come to Him (John 14:6). From our viewpoint, He comes to us here (Mark 10:15; Heb. 12:28). We draw near to God by trusting Him to draw near to us (James 4:8). We must trust that Heaven comes to us because that is how we find protection for our physical body. King David said, "I have set the LORD continually before me," and because God was close, David said his flesh would "dwell securely" (Ps. 16:8–9).

When we draw near to God by trusting He is drawing near to us, we receive Heaven here like a child, and Jesus receives us to Himself as He comes with His kingdom to us here (Matt. 6:33; Heb. 10:19–22; 12:22–24, 28). When we receive the kingdom of Heaven near us here, the kingdom of Heaven comes upon and near to everyone else around us also! Holiness becomes practical. Protection during and after spiritual warfare increases exponentially. It also brings Heaven to earth so that the will of God can be done here as it is in Heaven (Matt. 6:10).

Directly related is that before we die, we are to praise God while inside His heavenly sanctuary (Ps. 150:1). The protection we need is found by taking refuge and abiding inside the shelter of the Most High God (Ps. 91:1). In Psalm 91, the shelter is sometimes referred to as the dwelling place of God or the secret place. To take refuge in the dwelling place of the Most High God is to make our physical bodies refuge in the kingdom of Heaven itself.

But "who may ascend into the hill of the LORD? / And who may stand in His holy place?" (Ps. 24:2–4). Here is another example where we have to fit the puzzle pieces together! When we draw near to God by trusting that He is drawing near to us here, the conscience in our hearts is "sprinkled clean" (Heb. 10:22), and our physical body is washed because of the holy place coming down to us here (James 4:8; Ps. 24:3–4; Heb. 10:19). When we enter the throne room, our physical body doesn't leave the earth. Because we "receive the promise of the Spirit through faith" (Gal. 3:14), we have to apply faith to the kingdom of Heaven coming here when we enter or our conscience and our body won't get washed.

God wants to accomplish His purposes for you and the earth. Draw near to God by expecting Heaven to come to you freely and in abundance (Isa. 55:1–2). By trusting that Heaven comes to you here intensely, God comes to you to keep you holy and protected from the touch of evil upon you in this earthly realm. You can enter by receiving Heaven here with bold confidence because the Spirit of God draws near to wash your physical humanity as Heaven touches your body here (1 Cor. 6:11).

WHY WOULD GOD FREELY GIVE US HIS GLORIOUS PRESENCE AND KINGDOM?

The following reasons are not shown in order of their importance. If there is something in this list that you need help understanding, please keep reading because it will make more sense as you go along.

Consider thoughtfully that God gives His kingdom and His glorious presence to us freely:

1 Because receiving from the radiance around God helps us with practical purity and protection from the demonic (Rom. 13:12–14; 6:4)

2 Because we are trading in earthly glory for an abundance of His glory given to us freely (Isa. 55:1–2; Ps. 84:11)

3 So that we can have power and be His witnesses (Acts 1:8; Isa. 43:12; Matt. 10:8)

4 In order for us to stay protected spiritually and physically by what we receive from Him (Ps. 91; 16:8–9; 36:7–9)

5 Because the Spirit of God coming to us is what purifies us and makes the atmosphere around us holy (Rom. 15:16)

6 Because Jesus is a military leader whose aim is to conquer evil by what we receive from Him (Rev. 6:2; 5:10; Eph. 6:12; 1 John 3:8; Isa. 9:7; Luke 18:17; Rom. 16:20; Dan. 2:35, 44–45)

7 Because receiving His presence and kingdom freely is how we can present our bodies acceptable to God and stand before Him as priests (Rom. 12:1; 2 Chron. 29:11; 1 Kings 17:1; 2 Kings 3:14; Ex. 17:6)

8 Because continuing to receive the Spirit of Christ after salvation is how we can walk in Him here and how we can bear fruit that glorifies the Father (Col. 2:6; Titus 3:5–6; John 15:4, 8)

9 Because God is love and He wants to fill the earth with His glory by what we receive. So we can love others with what we receive from God on their behalf (Num. 14:21; 1 Peter 4:14; John 7:37, 39; Hos. 6:3).

10 Because God wants us to receive His lovingkindness, justice, and righteousness here so that HE can exercise these things in the earth (Jer. 9:24; Amos 5:24)

⓫ Because we cause God to feel pleasure when our faith trusts that He is rewarding our seeking Him by His coming to us here (Heb. 11:6).

⓬ Because receiving the holy mountain of God and Heaven around us here results in further change. We can build our faith by boasting in the greatness of God's closeness, release angels who we commission to fight on Heaven's behalf, and reverse the demonic backlash onto the demons for trying to hurt us.

Because of salvation, we have God's acceptance (Rom. 15:16). Because of our faith (defined in Heb. 11:1), we have His approval (Heb. 11:2). Because of faith that believes God is rewarding us with His presence when we seek Him, we have His pleasure (Heb. 11:6). We will never earn or deserve God's presence. All we will ever be able to do is to draw near to God by being utterly dependent on God to be drawing near to us (James 4:8; Mark 10:15). So be intentional to enjoy that your childlike faith and dependence on God to draw near to you is causing Him to feel pleasure simply because you believe Him to be coming to you here. Let your active faith in the pleasure God feels because of your childlike faith become an often-used source of motivation, joy, and fun for you.

THE ONE THING

Learning to ride a bicycle is confusing because there are so many things happening all at the same time. Once you know how to ride, you see all of it as one thing. Similarly, there are a lot of related ideas in this book. I am fitting them together as "one thing" so that you can apply them together more completely and practically. The more you read in this book, the more it will make sense why what follows is the all-inclusive one thing.

God defines idolatry in terms of the emotional benefits we gain as we depend on the idol. Very subtly, emotional benefits are the reason sin and idolatry become attractive to us. Idolatry damages our faith in God and our ability to apply His Word with simplicity.

Feeling secure and finding a sense of approval are not idols. But how we find security and acceptance can quickly become idols. We need to learn from a child who wraps themselves in their favorite blanket to feel comforted and safe. When a child receives a smile, they wrap themselves in the acceptance.

What children do with the emotional benefit they gain from a smile is what we as adults have to learn to do to easily receive and abide in the presence of God and the kingdom of Heaven with us here. The problem is that we are not children. Years of living have hardened us, so being childlike in our faith and love for God is challenging.

This book will teach you to make joyous declarations that transform your thinking away from dependence on the emotional benefits you gain from idolatry and sin. The declarations will also help you to build momentum in being more childlike in your reliance on God and faith. Eventually, your faith will let you believe that your act of opening up to God moves the torn veil aside so that the kingdom of Heaven—together with God's love and radiance—can easily come down, peel the demonic off of you, envelop you with His holiness, and then crush and burn any surrounding evil under your feet.

The life we now live as believers is by faith (Gal. 2:20). The feeling of being loved by God may not always be present, but that does not mean we are to avoid believing the truth! Jesus told us to abide in His love (John 15:9). The more you put these things into practice by making declarations that build your faith, the more God will reveal His heart to you. More and more, you will have a sense of what is wrapping around you here (Ps. 84:11).

This book will teach you to become more childlike in your receiving by the way you learn to delight yourself in the abundance God offers freely because of your faith that He is giving it (Isa. 55:1–2; Rom. 4:16). I will provide you with verses of Scripture you can use as a foundation for your faith. I feel compelled to be complete, but I will also do my best to keep it simple enough that a child can do it.

Let me repeat. The difficulty with applying the Word of God with simplicity is that we are not children. Most of us have learned to protect ourselves with an intentional kind of disbelief and cynicism. So on my website,[6] I will also give you tools to break down the hardness and direct your heart toward God. If you struggle with believing God would give you His presence and kingdom abundantly, or if you want to apply these things with an increasingly more significant impact, this book is for you.

AN EXAMPLE OF CHILDLIKE FAITH

The true gospel is good news that is simple enough for children. But how can receiving Heaven here be simple for us as adults?

It is loving the presence of God and the kingdom of Heaven around us as our protection and security that makes it simple and childlike. When you receive the kingdom of Heaven around you before you fall asleep, you love the closeness of God and His kingdom like a child loves their blanket as protection. That is what will keep you staying in the throne room all night long even while you sleep. It is how

you playfully love the closeness of God in the way a child loves wrapping themselves up in a blanket that will keep you in the presence of God so that when you wake up, His presence will still be all over you.

It was beautiful when I had a chance to explain these things to a child in a Sunday school class. The little girl was crawling around the room's edges, being disruptive by meowing loudly. Later, she was in my small group, and I wanted to help her, so I asked if she wanted to play a game.

I only had a small cloth covering available, so I asked her to curl up in a ball. I then covered her with the little blanket and asked her to think of it as protecting her from everything bad around her. I asked her to hold the corners of the cloth down onto the floor around her and then asked her to wait until she could tell me she believed it was protecting her. Doing that took only a little time.

I then explained that when the presence of God comes to us, He comes down from above by our believing that He is coming as the Bible describes (Gal. 3:14; James 1:17; Hos. 6:3). Next I asked her to think of the presence of God coming down onto her and settling on her all around like the little cloth. Like before, I asked her to tell me when she believed the presence of God was there enough to protect her. Trusting for the presence of God took a little longer, but she could also easily say He was there and protecting her.

I then asked her to wait until she could take the little blanket off and still believe the presence of God was on her as protection. I wanted her to be sure God was close to her as protection instead of the blanket. So I asked her to slowly remove the cloth covering her only after she could believe that God was all around as protection. Soon, she was taking the blanket off.

---

[6] My website is hearttrainingministries.com. The plan is to have it up and running by the time this book becomes available.

Her smile was beautiful! The transformation was so sweet. She freely believed the presence of God had come down upon her and was wrapping her all around. Before our little exercise, she looked tormented. Now, she was all smiles, was attentive to the class, and looked free.

I love that children can freely open up and believe that God is coming to them and He is surrounding them, and that they accept it without question. As adults, we need to use the Scriptures to build a stronger foundation so we can nurture being more childlike in our faith.

WHAT IN THE WORLD IS GOD DOING?

We must use Scripture to interpret Scripture. Therefore, verses in the Bible are like puzzle pieces; only when we fit them together can we understand the big picture of what God is doing. Fitting the puzzle pieces together has been a hugely complex and rewarding undertaking for me.

Let me repeat that God is leading us all to the same place: "You will bring them and plant them in the mountain of Your inheritance, / The place, O Lord, which You have made for Your dwelling, / The sanctuary, O Lord, which Your hands have established" (Ex. 15:17). Bringing the sanctuary of Heaven to earth has been God's plan right from the start. By leading us into the sanctuary of Heaven, God fulfills His everlasting covenant (Gen. 17:7) by becoming the one God who is our protection, strength, identity, and worth.

Central to the premise of this book is that because God is seeking true worshipers, He designed us so that our humanity falls short of His glory. Because we fall short, we feel insecure before God, and our resulting emotional neediness drives us to depend on the glory of something else. By observing what we rely on for glory in this life, God sees who and what we will worship.

Will your heart remain set on earthly and human glory? Or will you take assertive steps to direct your heart into depending on God and praise Him for the radiant glory that shines from Him freely?

We are at war with evil. So the more we set our hearts on God's glory and learn to abide in the tabernacle of God around us here, the more we do our part in helping to crush evil and reunite Heaven with earth.

When Christians come together with understanding and application about receiving Heaven here as their glory and strength, God will become the one God whose presence with us is our security, strength, courage, and worth. By this, Heaven will come in a much more significant way than we have ever seen on earth before. When Heaven comes to earth, the nations will know about it (Ezek. 37:26–28).

Let me repeat. At the end of the Bible, the outcome of everything is that the tabernacle of God is coming to be with us here on earth (Rev. 21:3). Everyone is different, yet God is building all of us into a dwelling place for His presence (Eph. 2:19–22). It is through His leading us into the sanctuary to stand before Him as kingdom priests that Heaven comes to earth and the tabernacle of God is more fully established (2 Chron. 29:11).

What in the world is God doing? The more people learn to enter the sanctuary of God by receiving Heaven here so they can present their body to God and abide before the Lord in this life before they die (Rom. 12:1; Ex. 15:17), the more the holy place of God will be established on earth (Rev. 21:3; Isa. 2:3; Hos. 11:10; Heb. 10:19).

We put on the bright white wedding dress of God's presence and prepare ourselves as His bride when we come to a place of believing we can and should tabernacle ourselves in God's presence and kingdom here. We as believers must align our thinking and the practice of our Christian faith with this truth because both God's ultimate end-times goal and our physical protection are at stake.

On the one hand, God will not give to anyone the glory that comes to Him by our worship and praise (Isa. 42:8). On the other hand, God freely gives the glory of His presence that shines from Him by His grace (Ps. 84:11). The glory that God gives is His Spirit of glory that pours out from all around Him because of His glorification (1 Peter 4:14; John 7:39). Like the verse in Psalm 84 says, giving us His glory is how He becomes a shield around us here.

2

THE BIG PICTURE OF GOOD NEWS

THE PROBLEM AND THE SOLUTION

This book uses Scripture to show the direct connection between our human emotional needs and idolatry in our hearts. Directly related is how God wants to be God to us. Here, you will learn to use your emotional needs as the motive and means of turning your heart more fully toward God so that you can better enjoy Him as your God and do your part in helping Him accomplish His purposes on earth.

After searching the Scriptures about repentance and change, I became convinced it is not enough to repent from sinful behaviors. Since repenting means changing our mind, and since behavior flows from our hearts, we must repent in ways that help us believe what the Bible says enough to be able to live what it says consistently.

To apply the Scriptures more fully, you will learn how to listen to yourself making declarations of repentance and faith. These will help transform your mind in ways that will remove the obstacles and enable you to receive the kingdom of Heaven here like a child. But the declarations you learn about here are not typical of those used in most churches today. What you

will learn here is not to help you believe in yourself. The declarations I will teach you to make are not for helping you to believe who you are in Christ. They are for helping you to make God your "I Am" instead of having to depend on yourself. The declarations will help you to more fully believe God, what He is doing, and what He offers freely to all of us.

All God's people need to repent in practical, effective, and boldly joyous ways that redirect our love and dependencies away from earthly sources and into increasingly greater alignment with God and His purposes.

WHAT IS THE EVERYTHING WE ALREADY HAVE?

Why talk about receiving more when the Bible says we already have "everything pertaining to life and godliness" (2 Peter 1:3)? The answer is in what the Bible says we already have.

Most churches today emphasize the death, burial, and resurrection of Jesus without also stressing His glorification and the resulting radiance that shines the Spirit of glory out from all around Him (1 Peter 4:14; John 7:39). The lack of emphasis on this glory is a mistake with far-reaching consequences (2 Cor. 4:4). Without the glorification of Jesus, we wouldn't have salvation because it is by the Holy Spirit being poured out through the glorification of Jesus that He washes us for salvation: "He saved us...by the washing of regeneration and renewing by the Holy Spirit, whom He poured out upon us richly through Jesus Christ our Savior" (Titus 3:5–6; see also 1 Cor. 12:13).

We drink from God for salvation (1 Cor. 12:13). The Bible says, "All who forsake You will be put to shame. / Those who turn away on earth will be written down, / Because they have forsaken the fountain of living water, even the Lord" (Jer. 17:13). God wants to be God to us instead of idols, and you will see later in this book that for us to experience Him being God to us here, we have to drink from the radiance around Him so that He can draw near and be God to us in practical ways. Therefore, in our everyday Christian practice of the Scriptures, we must include that our God is a radiant fountain as central to our faith, or we should ask ourselves, "Am I missing out? Am I forsaking the fullness of help God offers for practical Christian living?" If we ignore the glorification of Jesus after salvation, is it the same as forsaking the living water that is the "Helper" whom Jesus wants to send to us for practical holiness and a stronger testimony after salvation (John 15:26)?

After the ascension, the Father glorified Jesus, and He is still the radiance of the Father's glory to this day (Acts 2:33; Heb. 1:3). Even now, the Holy Spirit still "proceeds from the Father" (John 15:26) and from Jesus—and Christians should not ignore this wonderful truth in our everyday application of the Scriptures! Without the glory of the Father that pours out from Jesus, we would not be able to glory in Christ and then confidence in ourselves would remain our only option (Phil. 3:3).

The "everything" we already have for godliness includes salvation that gives us the right to receive the radiance of His glory that He wants to pour out onto us as a shield around us here (2 Peter 1:3; Ps. 84:11).

The Bible refers to receiving more of the Holy Spirit after salvation as drinking from God (John 7:37–39; Eph. 5:18). When speaking of salvation, it says we were "all made to drink of one Spirit" (1 Cor. 12:13). We began with God by drinking from Him for salvation; we walk inside the Spirit of God after salvation by continuing to drink from Him (Col. 2:6; Gal. 3:14).

The Bible explains the reason why we can drink from God when it says, "But this He spoke of the Spirit, whom those who believed in Him were to receive; for the Spirit was not yet given, because Jesus was not yet glorified" (John 7:39). We can drink from God because Jesus is a radiant fountain of the Father's glory (Heb. 1:3; Ps. 36:7–9; Jer. 2:11–13).

The more we direct our hearts to drink from the radiance around God instead of glory from the world, the more we will see that His Word comes true where it says, "In the last days...I will pour forth of My Spirit on all mankind" (Acts 2:17). God is waiting for His people to break up the hardness in our hearts and plant the truth of God so we can have faith for opening up to drink from the radiance around Him while actively believing that God is also pouring out the rain of His Spirit on everyone around us here (Hos. 6:3; 10:12). When we receive Heaven here, the heavens open around us, and there are fewer barriers between God and those around us who have yet to believe.

The Bible talks about our being "armed in the presence of the Lord" (Num. 32:32). It also tells us that we should "let justice roll down like waters / And righteousness like an ever-flowing stream" (Amos 5:24). When we drink by faith from the radiance around God and when we trust we are receiving His presence and the kingdom of Heaven here, what we receive from God becomes the ammunition that fights evil in the earth! More explanation about this comes later.

We must receive more of God's Spirit after salvation or all we can fight evil with is the sword of the Spirit (our words of declaration). This is vital because the sword cuts through demonic enemies, but it doesn't do well at crushing them. We need more than our sword in the spiritual battles we fight.

People need God for salvation. People need God after salvation as well. To the woman at the well, Jesus said that the water He would give would make her so she would never be thirsty again (John 4:14). Why then should we want to go after experiencing more of God after salvation? The answer is in being more careful to observe what the Bible says in that passage.

RECEIVING MORE AFTER SALVATION

To the woman at the well, Jesus said we would become "a well of water springing up." Think about that. A well cannot keep springing up if it stops receiving from the spring that supplies it! To become a well of water springing up, we must keep receiving from a never-ending, continuous supply (John 4:14; Jer. 17:13). In other words, after we drink from God for salvation (1 Cor. 12:13), Jesus wants us to keep drinking from Him so we will never be thirsty again, as He promised. The glorification of Jesus is the reason our thirst for God can be satisfied after salvation (John 7:37–39; Ps. 63:1–2, 5).

But we will not lose our salvation if we have stopped drinking and didn't know to continue.

Drinking from God is how we find and maintain purity after salvation because when we open up and receive with faith that the radiance around Him is drawing near, we can enjoy the greatness of His closeness instead of sin and He becomes the spiritual armor we need (Rom. 6:4; 13:12–14). Drinking from God after salvation is how we cooperate with God so that He can accomplish what He wants to do on earth.

But drinking from God is not automatic after salvation. Drinking from God in ways that keep you springing up requires that you direct your heart away from the many ways you are drinking from idolatry and sin (Jer. 2:11–13; 1 Sam. 7:3). It also requires that you remove the obstacles of fear and disbelief so you can stand before the fountain of God with your physical body and drink from Him before you here.

The Bible says, "Do not call to mind the former things, / Or ponder things of the past. / Behold, I will do something new.../ To give drink to My chosen people" (Isa. 43:18–20). The new thing God wants to do requires that we keep on drinking and receiving from Him instead of glory from other people, ourselves, or the world.

The good news about the glory of Christ (2 Cor. 4:4) is that Jesus died for us, but He was also raised and has been glorified so that He can continue receiving the glory of the Father and release it to us (John 15:26; Heb. 1:3; Acts 2:32–33).

The more fully we joyously turn from earthly and human glory, the more we find the freedom to turn to God and drink from Him. The better we get at joyfully turning our hearts toward God, the more Heaven can come.

Photo by Priscilla Du Preez on Unsplash

When Peter wrote that we already have everything pertaining to life and godliness, he was including our birthright as believers about freely receiving more from the radiant fountain of God after salvation.

PEOPLE NEED FREEDOM TO MAKE UNHINDERED DECISIONS ABOUT JESUS

Yes, we must actively tell people about Jesus and the good news about salvation. The practical problem is that the demonic has lied to them so much that having the freedom to decide about Jesus and salvation is difficult. Like Israel in bondage in Egypt, they need to be set free so they can go and worship God.

The most courageous and loving thing we can do for people is to receive the kingdom of Heaven here in a way that brings greater freedom to the lost so they can better make decisions about salvation. But the prerequisite is that God's people will have to much more courageously turn from well-hidden pride so that we can become more childlike in our faith and more easily believe what God says in His Word about receiving the kingdom of Heaven here.

In the book of Revelation, the "holy city, new Jerusalem" comes down out of Heaven (Rev. 21:2–3; see also vv. 9–11). In the book of Hebrews, it is the same "city of the living God, the heavenly Jerusalem" that we are to show gratitude about receiving here (Heb. 12:22–24, 28).

Just like we receive salvation by faith that we are receiving Christ, we, as God's people, must become more childlike so we can better believe we are receiving God's heavenly kingdom here (Mark 10:15). Doing that expands Heaven's influence over evil on earth. Only by this will people be free from demonic influence in their ability to make decisions about salvation.

Evil has been allowed far too much freedom to mess with people unhindered. I think this is true even of people in churches. I get angry when I have a sense of the demonic bothering Christians in church. In that situation, I trust by faith that the mountain of God and the kingdom of Heaven are dropping down hard onto the demonic and any witchcraft in the room. Often, I notice that when I remind myself to focus more on receiving Heaven into the room during worship, the level of worship among the people suddenly increases. When the peace of God comes into the room, I often feel the joy of the Lord about what He is free to do with people.

Thinking back, I was playing pickleball the first time I remember God asking me to receive the kingdom on behalf of people outside the church. Since then, I have woken up many times with a picture of someone or a situation I am to receive the kingdom for. Often, I have a strong sense that God wants me to receive the kingdom of Heaven on behalf of people around me in a grocery store.

A BIGGER PICTURE OF GOOD NEWS

The good news of salvation is that Jesus died on our behalf to make us acceptable to God for eternity (Eph. 2:1–2; John 3:16; 1:29; Rom. 15:16; Lev. 19:5; 22:29; 1 John 2:2). Salvation is good news because we get to spend eternity in Heaven instead of in hell and because it meets an emotional need for acceptance. Sadly, many people who profess to be Christians have yet to believe that God accepts them. I was like that. Directing my heart about what to believe changed me. It can change you also.

The big picture of good news is that God also wants His presence with us to be our basis for security, confidence, boldness, protection, worth, and identity in THIS life. For most people, that statement seems impractical for everyday living. It is not. Many Scriptures go together to make this message clear: the big-picture gospel is profoundly relevant to everyday living. God wants to be God to us here.

Early in my journey, I saw that the good news is primarily intended for the afflicted and needy (Isa. 61:1–3). I also saw where the Bible says, "The afflicted and needy are seeking water.../ I, the Lord, will answer them Myself" (Isa. 41:17). These verses seemed related, and the verses in Isaiah 41 seemed to talk about something more important than physical water.

The gospel in the Bible means good news. But salvation has always seemed like good news for the future after we die. So I wondered: since God is good, and the gospel is primarily for the afflicted and needy, shouldn't the gospel also be good news for the present before we die?

Deep inside, it felt like there was something big that I didn't understand about the gospel. So I asked God for years and with many tears to help me understand why the gospel is good news for the afflicted and needy in this life before we die. I pleaded with Him to help me understand and be able to communicate why the gospel is relevant for everyday living.

It was many years later that I found this verse: "He pled the cause of the afflicted and needy.../ Is not that what it means to know Me?' / Declares the Lord" (Jer. 22:16). When I saw that verse, it struck me that I was on the right path. So I continued to pray and study the Bible for answers.

In the early days of DOS computers, I had software that would let me print out verses in the Bible topically. In doing that, I learned the Bible talks about the good news in three ways: the gospel about salvation (Rom. 1:16), the gospel about the glory of Christ (2 Cor. 4:4), and the gospel about the kingdom of God (Matt. 4:23; 24:14).

I am writing to share the results of my more than forty-five year attempt at fitting all three gospels together so we can live them in a practical way for this present life. The gospel must be relevant to this life, or the attractiveness of our message fails at being good news for this life. I desire to present the good news in a big-picture way to avoid the pitfalls of secret sin and hurtful interactions that are far too common in the church today. A fully integrated gospel message is also my way of ensuring more significant big-picture outcomes as we live out our Christian faith.

Because my books are an integrated big-picture look at the good news, what you read here is not limited to the milk of the Word of God. It also includes "solid food...for the mature" (Heb. 5:14).

To me, it is only when all three gospels are fit together in a context of intentionally aligning our thinking with the Scriptures that living these things well becomes profoundly relevant and practical in everyday Christian living. The way I see it, if we aren't explaining the practical side of why and how we can live the good news consistently, we aren't fully communicating the big picture of the gospel in the Bible. It doesn't make sense that it would be good news if we can't live it consistently.

A REFORMATION BRINGS GOOD NEWS

In the first Reformation, Luther brought a message about the grace of God for salvation. Salvation by God's grace is good news because even though we must receive the Spirit of Christ for salvation, God does the work that accomplishes it. The second great reformation will be like the first but will be more encompassing. The second reformation will be about the grace of God allowing us to continually receive His Spirit's presence after salvation so that He can be God to us in practical ways. He can be God to us instead of us staying in bondage to earthly sources, self-effort, idolatry, and hidden sin.

God wants us to be as perfect and holy as He is (Matt. 5:48). When we trust God to draw near so we can make Him our God, we receive His holiness onto us, and the pressure to live holy lives is on Him and not on us. Read the verses that follow and thank God that the pressure of performance is on Him, not on us. Our responsibility is only to change our thinking, fears, and loves to the place where we can freely receive His presence and treasure His closeness so He can be God to us as He desires.

- "The nearness of God is my good" (Ps. 73:28).

- "I have no good besides You" (Ps. 16:2).

- "You, O Lord, are a shield about me, / My glory, and the One who lifts my head" (Ps. 3:3).

- "The Lord is our righteousness" (Jer. 33:16).

- "He loves righteousness" (Ps. 11:7).

- "He is a shield to all who take refuge in Him" (2 Sam 22:31).

- "O Lord God, You are my confidence" (Ps. 71:5).

- "I love You, O Lord, my strength" (Ps. 18:1).

It is because God wants to be God to us that it is practical for us to "glory in Christ Jesus and put no confidence in the flesh" (Phil. 3:3).

Did you notice that the pressure of performance in those verses is on God? These things are not practical until God draws near to us here. The good news is that all we have to do is stay open to God and keep receiving. The real pressure is on God because of His covenant to be God to us here (Gen. 17:7; Gal. 3:29).

WHAT IS THIS INTEGRATED GOSPEL MESSAGE?

The big-picture gospel in the Bible includes salvation, but it is more. The good news is also that God wants to be God to us where His presence and kingdom draw near and become our basis for confidence, security, reassurance, worth, and identity. Then we don't have to depend on enjoying what we gain by receiving from worldly things, ourselves, other people, or sin. The bad news is when we try to be our god by self-effort, that, at best, only temporarily feels like it is enough. The good news becomes practical when we learn to enjoy depending on God as our God.

A shorter way of saying it is that the kingdom of Heaven with us can be our greatest treasure, and joyfully bold declarations of repentance and faith make it practical!

The big picture of good news includes the significance and the meaning we feel from being able to freely receive and enjoy God's presence and kingdom with childlike faith, where our receiving increases the government of God on earth (Isa. 9:7; Matt. 6:10). The gospel is good news to us because of the eternal significance we gain from being able to help fill the earth with the glory we freely receive from the radiance around

God—while also receiving from Him the peace of God that crushes Satan under our feet (Num. 14:21; Rom. 16:20).

John's gospel message was that we should "repent and believe in the gospel" (Mark 1:15). The way I see it, presenting the big-picture message of the gospel must include a practical message about a joyous repentance that helps people to take steps toward aligning their thinking with the gospel message of salvation, the kingdom of God, and the glory of Christ.

If pastors communicated the good news presented in this book—and people applied it widely throughout the church—love, understanding, and patience for one another would significantly increase. Christian men would humble themselves from pride and find their sense of worth and power because of Heaven with them, and they wouldn't ever have to be mean and put their wives down to feel good about themselves! Practical behind-the-scenes holiness and even heart-level purity would soar. The government and the influence of God over evil on earth would increase greatly. God would be honored in more significant ways because of the increased love, faith, and passionate childlike praise central to the joyful, naturally motivational, and beneficial process of applying these things well on an everyday level.

By declarations of repentance and faith, your heart can learn thinking patterns that help you react to demonic attacks by putting on increasingly strengthened armor in playfully childlike ways to fight back and punish the devil for trying to hurt you. When the kingdom of Heaven becomes your greatest treasure, you only have to receive Heaven here like a child and love the closeness of God and His holiness to shut down demonic attacks completely.

FORCED TO TAKE THIS PATH

Growing up in the church, my pastor taught me that Jesus died to save us from sin. But as a young man, that part of the gospel wasn't working for me. My desire to understand the gospel's relevance in this life was for other people, but it was mainly a prayer of desperation for myself.

For as long as I can remember, holiness on a practical level has been a must-have for me. But rather than try harder and keep failing, I figured there was something I didn't understand.

After many years of prayer, I realized that I needed to repent in ways that would remove the obstacles keeping me from seeking and receiving God's kingdom and righteousness (Isa. 57:14; Matt. 6:33; Mark 10:15). I had to change how I was trying to repent by directing my heart away from using anger about my sin as a way to achieve the righteousness of God (James 1:20). I also had to become more childlike in the purity of my love for God (Matt. 19:14; 18:4). It became clear that I needed to "put on the armor of light...and make no provision for the flesh in regard to its lusts" (Rom. 13:12, 14). But it took years for me to understand, even with my mind, how to do these things practically and effectively. After that, I still had to make the effort to get my heart to believe it enough for me to put it into practice.

Photo by Ali Abdul Rahman on Unsplash

Let me clarify that I see two main sides to purity. Part of the problem is that the patterns of thinking and dependence in our hearts draw us away from God and toward brief moments of enjoying our sin instead of enjoying the nearness of God consistently as a way to prevent the sin (James 1:14). The other part has to do with making no provision for lust by humbling ourselves into faith until we are literally putting the armor of light on around our physical body in a way that is strong enough to keep the demonic and temptation away. I will explain more about these things later.

In the early days, applying the Bible with childlike faith seemed impossible. I couldn't bear to walk away from my faith. But I couldn't stay where I was. It seemed my only option was to stay determined about applying the Scriptures and prove to myself that the will of God is good (Rom. 12:2). But this meant that I had to turn away from my most natural tendency to hold back so I could change in other areas as well.

> I had to embrace faith in things I knew were right in the Scriptures, but I was terrified to allow myself to believe. The possibility of failure was overwhelming to me.

At times, all I could do was listen to myself thanking God for His goodness—and that did help, but I needed more. So I kept studying everything I could find in the Bible on how to repent by transforming my mind. I studied what I had to transform my mind away from and toward.

After about ten years of studying almost nothing else, I ran out of options. It was time to stop studying and start applying what I had learned. My pain from failure as a Christian forced me to have no other option except to repent in ways that would change my mind, reduce my fears, and help me to believe. It has been difficult, but intentionally repenting and building my faith by listening to my joyous declarations has helped me so much that I have no intention of ever stopping.

Without me knowing how it would all work at the time, my repentance became a process of making ongoing declarations of joyous thanks and praise to cut off my dependence on earthly sources and of building faith in God as my refuge, strength, and glory (Deut. 32:37–39; Hab. 1:11; Jer. 2:11–13).[7]

It was much easier for me to cut off glory from earthly sources than to turn to God and allow myself to open up and receive from Him. I knew I should drink from God, and I understood in my head some about how to do it. I couldn't get my heart to cooperate until after I began listening to myself reading Scriptures about drinking from God and then thanking Him that I could actually do what the Bible says. Thanks and praise that I could apply the Scriptures were instrumental in helping me to find freedom and ease my fears so I could open up to God and believe with confidence that He would draw near.

You have a significant advantage over me. Your advantage is that I will explain how to drink from God in this book. You don't have to endure years of hopelessness and pain while figuring it all out for yourself.

Faith that I was able to receive Heaven here like a child is not where I started. The armor of light was necessary for me to avoid temptation in the area of lust successfully. I also had to receive God's presence and rest in Him instead of reaching out for beauty, power, and reassurance apart from enjoying His closeness to me here. Consistent purity was a must-have for me. I knew in my head that because of Jesus's death, I should not have to go on living in bondage to sin. If a path to consistent and practical holiness was not available to me personally, how could I believe in the goodness of God? I was terrified to let myself have faith that He would come to me freely. But my failure as a Christian nagged at me. Through much study, trial, and a lot of error, I had no choice except to speak the truth to my fears until I could have faith to apply the truth in the Bible.

---

[7] I did this because these are the words God uses to define idolatry in the Bible. I will talk more about this later in this book.

My relentless pursuit of practical righteousness brought me to use joyous declarations of both repentance and faith to take one small step after another so that I could move forward. Today, it is just like Jesus said. The kingdom of Heaven close to me has become my greatest possession and treasure (Matt. 13:44).

A WRONG ROAD TAKEN

To be consistent with the idea of this book being a detailed overview, let me tell you a long story as briefly as possible. It is a story about the most difficult and painful change I ever had to make.

After I felt I understood repentance from idolatry, I was faithful to keep turning my heart from earthly sources and sin. I also sought to change my mind by preaching the Scriptures to my heart in ways that built up my faith in God as my refuge and strength. But even with that, living these things didn't make sense to me in the early days of my journey. So, to hurry things along, I started by applying what many Christians call *pressing in.*

I knew I needed to put on the armor of light and the Lord Jesus Christ to avoid temptation and lust (Rom. 13:12–14). Still, I thought that if I focused on pressing into the radiance around God enough, God's presence flowing through me would become the armor around me that I needed. The sense of God's presence was strong, but the harder I pressed into the Lord, the more I wondered if what I was doing was based on self-effort and my works. I could feel God's presence, but God's power wasn't there. My freedom from sin only seemed present when I kept myself so busy pressing in that I wasn't as likely to reach out toward sin.

At times, it felt like I was almost turning myself inside out to press into Heaven before the Lord. I couldn't shake the feeling that the benefit of purity was only due to how hard I was pressing in. I still couldn't be consistent with heart-level purity. I could fight off lust and avoid private sin, but the only way to keep it away was to press myself into Heaven and onto God more

forcibly. Was I walking in the Spirit so that the living Spirit of God was my armor? I couldn't find evidence of that because it was often easy to go from pressing into God to pressing myself out there toward lust. I was doing my best to put on the armor of light by pressing in, but it wasn't helping me to "put on the Lord Jesus Christ, and make no provision for the flesh in regard to its lusts" (Rom. 13:14). It didn't seem like God was helping me to live a holy life. It seemed utterly dependent on the force I put into pressing in.

During the years of my pressing in, I had two different prophetic people tell me they saw me chest-to-chest with Jesus; at the time, that is precisely how I was trying to abide twenty-four seven. I did that because pressing in was my only hope for avoiding sin, so please trust me when I say that I worked hard at pressing in. Even though I could feel God's presence when pressing in, and everything I was doing seemed deeply spiritual, I couldn't see any supernatural power in it.

Eventually, I observed that pressing into the Lord was similar to the reaching we do in lust. I could be pressing myself onto the Lord and worshiping Him one moment, and then the next moment, I would find myself reaching out in lust! Eventually, it was clear that the similarity between reaching and pressing in made it difficult to be consistent with purity. My prophetic friends kept hearing from God and telling me I needed to learn to rest in the Lord. I was frustrated.

The Bible talks about the throne room and Heaven being the third Heaven (2 Cor. 12:2–4). If we follow that logic, then the atmosphere we breathe is the first heaven. The spiritual realm in the air where demons operate might be called the second heaven. If you can accept those three heavens as accurate, it explains what I was doing wrong.

After years of almost turning myself inside out to press in, I began to understand the problem. When trying to abide by pressing in, there were times when I got spiritually tired and, without realizing it, was only pressing into the second heaven, where Satan and his demons function (Eph. 2:1–2). Other times, I entered before the Lord, got slightly distracted, and then very subtly slipped out of being before the Lord and back into the second heaven. The second heaven was where the attacks came, and I failed again. It was like I suddenly found myself in a boxing ring with demons and lost every time.

I knew that Jesus died to save us from sin, but for all my effort at pressing in, I wasn't even close to putting on the living Spirit of Jesus around me as armor. What was wrong? God wasn't fighting on my behalf to keep the demonic and temptation away!

> I was frustrated that my battle with the demonic seemed less than a decisive win. Despite all my pressing in, the phrase "more than conquerors" seemed untrue of me (Rom. 8:37 NKJV). It saddened me that my Christianity still seemed broken on so many levels. Even though the sense of God's presence was strong, pressing in only helped me experience an impersonal force and not a personal God. More changes were needed.

Eventually, I learned I was violating three critically essential verses in Scripture. One verse is explained further down in this section. I will give you the other two verses here, but I will fully explain how they relate to reoccurring sin later in this book. The first one is: "If we had forgotten the name of our God / Or extended our hands to a strange god, / Would not God find this out? / For He knows the secrets of the heart" (Ps. 44:20–21). The second one says, "Like a city that is broken into and without walls / Is a man who has no control over his spirit" (Prov. 25:28).

Part of my recurring sin problem was extending something out from within me to reach toward the sin so I could benefit emotionally from it. I was trying to relieve boredom and find power, pleasure, and reassurance from the sin. The result was that I became an unprotected city without walls. Over a long time, I learned to be painfully honest with myself. Pressing in was helping me to feel God's presence pouring through me, but when I tried to abide in Him that way, the strength of my protective armor was based on self-effort. Even though I could

feel the presence of God, I wasn't putting on the armor of light as God intended. God wasn't fighting on my behalf to crush evil under my feet.

The presence of God pouring through me because of pressing in only pushed the demonic away temporarily. Eventually, my self-effort would lessen, I would reach toward sin, my protection would drop, and evil would immediately attack me with temptation and sin (Prov. 25:28).

I had to learn two things. One was that the thinking patterns in my heart had to change about reaching toward sin to find temporary emotional benefits like reassurance and a sense of power or pleasure from it. I had to learn to find those emotional benefits in a pure way from God instead. I also had to learn that instead of pressing my way out into Heaven toward God, I had to learn to believe the Scriptures enough to freely open up so I could easily receive God's presence here and rest in Him for protection. I had to stop believing I could close the gap between me and God, and I had to trust that Jesus died so that Heaven could come to earth. This book explains these things in detail, but you must read the whole thing to understand.

CORRECTION ABOUT PRESSING IN

Throughout the years of pressing in, I kept making declarations that helped me cut off and direct my heart away from earthly sources and toward God as my God. I also kept praying for answers about how to make God my refuge, strength, and glory, as the Bible describes.

Eventually, God corrected my pressing in by reminding me that the "righteousness based on faith" does not say "who will ascend into heaven" to "bring Christ down" here (Rom. 10:6). Even though I was pressing myself chest-to-chest with Jesus way out there in Heaven, the attack of the demonic was on my physical humanity here. I needed faith that would let me receive the armor of God's presence coming upon me instead of putting the armor on by the presence of God I could feel pouring through me.

Photo by Dale Nibbe on Unsplash

I was seeking God's righteousness, but God's correction clarified that I had to completely change my entire way of being close to the Lord. I would also have to change how I was trying to abide. Doing that was painfully difficult because it felt like rejection from God.

Through the correction of God, I learned that righteousness by pressing in isn't righteousness that comes from faith. I had to put on the armor of light by faith that my receiving like a child would let me put on God's presence as armor onto my physical body here. Honestly, it would have been much easier if I had never gone down the path of pressing in. But having to stop pressing in so I could receive the kingdom here like a child and rest in God's presence was a vitally important change for me to make!

The thick veil between Heaven and earth was torn apart when Jesus died. Pressing in goes through the torn veil but ignores the wonderful truth that only God can close the gap between us.

We can't do that for Him. The purposes of Heaven are at stake. We must believe God wants to draw near and that He must do that to accomplish His will on earth. The beautiful thing for us is that we get to participate.

We have to align our thinking enough with the purposes of Heaven to believe like a child that our only job is to remove the obstacles and build a highway for God so that we can receive His presence and then love resting in the radiance of His glory upon us

---

[8] Being dizzy like that can feel spiritually dirty, almost like something demonic is trying to cling to my head. These are times when I believe that, in some subtle way, I am trying to reach out from inside toward God and have found my way into the second heaven. The solution is to rest in the Lord again by receiving Heaven upon and around me while also praising Him for the power of His holiness that is burning the evil off of me.

here (Isa. 57:14; 40:3–5). When trying to abide in Christ by receiving Heaven here, even slight amounts of pressing in can get us into trouble because it lowers our protection against the demonic. Now that I am trying to rest into receiving, I still find sometimes that my reaching out to press in can be very subtle. If I am trying to receive and press in, I can get very dizzy.[8] To avoid that, I have to look at the ground or my physical hands and remind myself to receive without reaching toward God. My declarations have to repeatedly remind me to draw near by trusting Him to draw near to me here. I have to remind myself to receive and enjoy the holiness and power of God's closeness to me here instead of trying to press way out there.

FAITH ABOUT RECEIVING IS NOT NATURAL

It is much more natural for us to believe we should have to earn God's presence. To believe God's grace is enough for Him to want to draw near—instead of me having to achieve it—I often have to reassure my heart about the truth until my thinking changes and simplicity returns. Let me be more specific.

To make the change to faith that God is bringing Heaven here, I repeatedly keep preaching the Scriptures to myself to align my thinking and application more fully with the Word of God. The benefits of going down this path have been profound. I will never want anything less because it feels like I have found the consistency I have longed for in heart-level purity. "More than a conqueror" is a fitting description now. If I have a sense of the demonic in a room, I take refuge in the Lord by receiving Heaven here like a child. Then I love His presence close to me, and when the peace of God comes, everything goes quiet and pure again.

Don't get me wrong: I still have to fight to stay playfully confident in my faith. It

takes a lot of effort. But the fight has more to do with the disbelief and pride in my heart that makes me want to earn or work somehow to deserve God drawing near.

The demonic makes it hard at times. The disbelief among Christians about receiving the kingdom is also profoundly influential. I have to fight against being drawn into that disbelief constantly.

If you go down this path with me, you will have to fight to avoid losing the simplicity of childlike delight, love, and faith in God. The truth is that God wants to draw near to us, and He does so the moment we trust that He is coming to us here. The only thing we can do is till the hard ground in our hearts until our faith can grow and we can open up with freedom and trust in God to come to us abundantly. Going down the path of humbling myself from pride and disbelief—and being intentional to playfully enjoy the closeness of God drawing near—has made living these things consistent and practical.

THE ANCIENT PATH

We are told to "ask for the ancient paths" (Jer. 6:16). The way I see it, the ancient paths converge into one path that is summarized way back at the start of the Bible: "You will bring them and plant them in the mountain of Your inheritance, / The place, O Lord, which You have made for Your dwelling, / The sanctuary, O Lord, which Your hands have established" (Ex. 15:17).

Walking the ancient path cleanses your hands and purifies your heart so you can ascend the hill of the Lord (Ps. 24:3–4; Heb. 10:19–22; Isa. 57:13). The ancient path took Elijah and Elisha to find their identity by standing before the Lord (1 Kings 18:15; 2 Kings 3:14). Enoch walked with God on the ancient path (Gen. 5:24). Walking this path will lead you into the throne room to stand before the Lord as a kingdom priest (2 Chron. 29:11; Rev. 5:10; Rom. 12:1).

The book of Hebrews describes the supremacy of Jesus in context with a description of the ancient path that runs through the entire book. The eventual goal of the ancient path is to build all of us together as a dwelling for God that reunites Heaven with earth (Eph. 2:22; Rev. 21:3).

It is time for God's people to build a highway for God (Isa. 40:3–5). To do that, we must remove obstacles (Isa. 57:14) because they are glory substitutions (John 5:44) that keep us from freedom, faith, and joy needed for freely receiving the kingdom of Heaven and drinking from the radiant glory of God here like a child (Mark 10:15; Matt. 19:14; Ps. 36:7–9; Heb. 12:22–24, 28).

The Bible says that people are unwilling to walk the ancient path (Jer. 6:16). But, the way I see it, Christians are unwilling because they don't understand what it is or how to walk it practically and consistently. Even though the ancient path requires great honesty and effort, and even though it requires that we humble ourselves from idolatry in our hearts and turn more fully to God (1 Sam. 7:3), many Christians would walk this path with great joy if they understood how!

The benefits are great because walking the ancient path prepares the bride of Christ, restores families, and brings unity to the body of Christ (Rev. 19:7; Mal. 4:6; John 17:22). Walking the ancient path opens the ancient doors and gates above us so that the King of Glory and His angels can freely come to earth, crushing evil as they come down (Ps. 24:7–8; 100:4; Rom. 16:20; James 1:17).

While I freely admit that I am not perfect in understanding these things, God has been preparing me to teach about this path for many years. This book is my best attempt to share what I have learned along the way.

ARE YOU READY FOR A PARADIGM CHANGE?

The prevailing Christian paradigm is the averaged sum of our thinking and views about God and about ourselves held by Christians in the church today. The Christian paradigm is important because the average quality of our collective spiritual life directly results from the paradigm commonly held in the church.

Spiritual and social norms and expectations are upheld and limited within the brackets of our paradigm. The current levels of holiness and love in the church today are examples supported and held back by our collective paradigm.

But it should be obvious that Christians are not living as God desires in many areas. To improve the quality of love, holiness, and spiritual life in the church today, the paradigm of how we view and think about God and ourselves needs a drastic shift.

Are you a leader in the church who wants to see improvements in how Christians live? If so, you must not think you know the best way Christians should live to function at the highest level within the current church paradigm. If you think that way, you are only a maintenance man and are not helping prepare people for something significantly better.

Over the years, I have seen many Scriptures that have seemed far beyond the quality of where we currently live. But I have not considered myself an engineer who needs to design a new paradigm. God is the engineer. The best role any of us can take is to be technicians whose job is to understand God's design and live it ourselves.

If you have only been a maintenance man trying to help people live their best within the current paradigm's confines, you must lift your vision higher. Your view of God must be that He is good enough to have already included an effective solution in His Word that will drastically improve our currently existing conditions. The key is in aligning ourselves with the everlasting covenant God made that He would be God to us (Gen. 17:7).

> Your job as a Christian leader is not to help people live their best life within the currently existing Christian paradigm. You must want more. You must also live that more. You must consider what your head knows to be true about God and His Word. Then you must listen to yourself making declarations that align the thinking in your heart with that truth. As a Christian leader who shepherds people, you must help others to direct their hearts toward God so that He can feed them instead of them feeding on what comes from you (Ezek. 34).

You can be confident that what I write will work for you because I have done my best to go before you and apply what you will read here. I have made many mistakes and have had to backpedal and change my understanding of these things many times. But I made the adjustments and grew. After over forty-five years of this journey, I have tested these things thoroughly enough to believe I have proven by living these things that the will of God for all of us in this is good, acceptable, and perfect (Rom. 12:2).

3

JESUS CHRIST ON EARTH AND GOD IN HEAVEN

IN THIS CHAPTER

I recognize that some who read this book will have little or no previous Bible knowledge. I have written this chapter for those readers, but it is important for all.

In this chapter, I start by introducing the person of Jesus Christ. Then, I talk about God in Heaven. I cover these topics to connect what we have covered so far with how to drink from God. This chapter is important because it helps build a foundation for explaining why the topic of this book is practical.

Photo by Bruno van der Kraan on Unsplash

JESUS CHRIST WAS NOT AN ORDINARY MAN

Jesus was and still is God's Son. He was sent from God in Heaven with a message to bring and a job to do.

About two thousand years ago, Jesus was born as a baby to a woman named Mary—without her having had any sexual relations with a man. The Bible says,

> The angel Gabriel was sent from God...to a virgin engaged to a man whose name was Joseph...and the virgin's name was Mary. And coming in, he said to her, "Greetings, favored one! The Lord is with you." But she was very perplexed at this statement and kept pondering what kind of salutation [greeting] this was. The angel said to her, "Do not be afraid, Mary; for you have found favor with God... you will conceive in your womb and bear a son, and you shall name Him Jesus. He will be great and will be called the Son of the Most High; and the Lord God will give Him the throne...and He will reign...and His kingdom will have no end." Mary said to the angel, "How can this be, since I am a virgin?" The angel answered and said to her, "The Holy Spirit will come upon you, and the power of the Most High will overshadow you; and for that reason, the holy Child shall be called the Son of God" (Luke 1:26–35).

Jesus was no ordinary human being. Jesus was God's Son because "His mother Mary... was found to be with child by the Holy Spirit" (Matt. 1:18). He didn't have an earthly father. His Father was God Himself.

As Jesus grew up, "Jesus kept increasing in wisdom and stature, and in favor with God and men" (Luke 2:52).

When He was about thirty years old, the Bible says, "Jesus arrived...at the Jordan [river] ...to be baptized...After being baptized, Jesus came up immediately from the water; and behold, the heavens were opened, and he saw the Spirit of God descending as a dove and lighting on Him, and behold, a voice out of the heavens said, 'This is My beloved Son, in whom I am well-pleased' " (Matt. 3:13, 16–17).

A MESSAGE ABOUT REPENTANCE AND GOD'S KINGDOM

Shortly after Jesus was baptized, the Bible says, "Jesus began to preach and say, 'Repent, for the kingdom of heaven is at hand' " (Matt. 4:17). Elsewhere, it says, "Jesus came... preaching the gospel of God, and saying, 'The time is fulfilled, and the kingdom of God is at hand; repent and believe in the gospel' " (Mark 1:14–15).

Jesus's central message was about repentance and the good news about the kingdom of God: "Jesus was going through all the cities and villages, teaching in their synagogues and proclaiming the gospel of the kingdom, and healing every kind of disease and every kind of sickness" (Matt. 9:35).

Repentance means to change our minds. A complete view of the Scripture suggests that we should think of repentance as a process of changing our mind in ways that improve our behavior. The benefit of true repentance is that it brings the presence of God and His kingdom near to us here (Acts 3:19).

Photo by Humble Lamb on Unsplash

What is the kingdom the Bible talks about? Allow me to use some verses I have already shared.

Jesus taught His disciples to pray to our Father God, "Your kingdom come. / Your will be done, / On earth as it is in heaven" (Matt. 6:10). The kingdom of God and the kingdom of Heaven are the same thing because Jesus said, "Whoever does not receive the kingdom of God like a child will not enter it at all" (Mark 10:15). Speaking of children, Jesus said that the "kingdom of heaven belongs to such as these" (Matt. 19:14).

When the Bible talks about the kingdom of God, we need to think about it as being Heaven because these two things in Scripture are spoken of interchangeably (Matt. 13:11; Mark 4:11). Later it says that the kingdom we are to receive includes the mountain of God, Heaven, and angels (Heb. 12:22–24, 28).

Jesus also explained the holiness and the power of Heaven when He said, "If I cast out demons by the finger of God, then the kingdom of God has come upon you" (Luke 11:20). When God's kingdom comes, Heaven comes upon and around us with the peace, joy, and righteousness of Heaven itself (Rom. 14:17). When God's kingdom comes to us here, the will of God is able to be done on earth as it is in Heaven.

JESUS SHOWED US WHAT GOD THE FATHER IS LIKE

Jesus also came to show us what God in Heaven is like because "He who has seen Me has seen the Father" (John 14:9) and "the only begotten God...has explained Him" (John 1:18). The Father God in Heaven cares about people and feels compassion because Jesus cared deeply about people: "Seeing the people, He felt compassion for them, because they were distressed and dispirited like sheep without a shepherd" (Matt. 9:36). The following verses about Jesus show us more about what the Father is like:

- "You know of Jesus of Nazareth, how God anointed Him with the Holy Spirit and with power, and how He went about doing good and healing all who were oppressed by the devil, for God was with Him" (Acts 10:38).

- "Large crowds followed Him" (Matt. 8:1).

- "All the people were trying to touch Him, for power was coming from Him and healing them all" (Luke 6:19).

- "But Jesus Himself would often slip away to the wilderness and pray" (Luke 5:16).

JESUS DIED

One would think that a person like Jesus wouldn't have any problems. That wasn't true. Jesus died after only about three years of ministry. He was thirty-three when He died.

Jesus died because of the religious leaders of that day. They felt that Jesus was competition, so they had Him nailed to a wooden cross until He bled to death. They were also angry because Jesus "was calling God His own Father, making Himself equal with God" (John 5:18).

Concerning the events surrounding His death, the Bible says,

Jesus cried out again with a loud voice, and yielded up His spirit... and the earth shook and the rocks were split. The tombs were opened, and many bodies of the saints who had fallen asleep were raised; and coming out of the tombs after His resurrection they entered the holy city and appeared to many. Now the centurion, and those who were with him keeping guard over Jesus, when they saw the earthquake and the things that were happening, became very frightened and said, "Truly this was the Son of God!" (Matt. 27:50–54).

Jesus was no ordinary man.

JESUS CAME BACK TO LIFE

They buried Jesus in a cave, and guards put a large rock over the entrance. But that isn't the end of the story because Jesus came back to life. This next section of verses begins by saying that the local ruler wanted to prevent people from tampering with the tomb.

Pilate said to them, "You have a [military] guard; go, make it as secure as you know how." And they went and made the grave secure, and along with the guard they set a seal on the stone.

Now after [three days], as it began to dawn toward the first day of the week, Mary Magdalene and the other Mary came to look at the grave. And behold, a severe earthquake had occurred, for an angel of the Lord descended from Heaven and came and rolled away the stone and sat upon it. And his appearance was like lightning, and his clothing as white as snow. The guards shook for fear of him and became like dead men. The angel said to the women, "Do not be afraid; for I know that you are looking for Jesus who has been crucified. He is not here, for He has risen, just as He said. Come, see the place where He was lying" (Matt. 27:65–28:6).

Some of Jesus's closest followers were in a closed room (John 20:26), talking to each other when Jesus appeared to them. "He said to Thomas, 'Reach here with your finger, and see My hands; and reach here your hand and put it into My side; and do not be unbelieving, but believing.' Thomas answered and said to Him, 'My Lord and my God!' Jesus said to him, 'Because you have seen Me, have you believed? Blessed are they who did not see, and yet believed' " (John 20:27–29).

After Jesus came back to life, Luke writes, "While they were telling these things, He Himself stood in their midst...But they were startled and frightened and thought that they were seeing a spirit. And He said to them, 'Why are you troubled, and why do doubts arise in your hearts? See My hands and My feet, that it is I Myself; touch Me and see, for a spirit does not have flesh and bones as you see that I have.'...While they still could not believe it because of their joy and amazement, He said to them, 'Have you anything here to eat?' They gave Him a piece of a broiled fish; and He took it and ate it before them" (Luke 24:36–39, 41–43).

JESUS CHRIST ON EARTH AND GOD IN HEAVEN

After Jesus rose from the dead, His body was spiritual because He could walk through walls. His body was also physical because they could touch Him and He ate food. You can be confident that Jesus rose from the dead because after appearing to the disciples, He was also seen by more than five hundred people (1 Cor. 15:6). After Jesus came back to life, He even cooked breakfast for several of His friends (John 21:12).

Forty days after being raised from the dead, Acts 2:34 tells us that Jesus "ascended into heaven." We also learn:

> He also presented Himself alive after His suffering, by many convincing proofs, appearing to them over a period of forty days and speaking of the things concerning the kingdom of God...
>
> And after He had said these things, He was lifted up while they were looking on, and a cloud received Him out of their sight (Acts 1:3, 9).

I will discuss the significance of Jesus's death and resurrection later in this book.

GOD IN THREE PERSONS

We must consider what the Bible says about God being three persons because understanding this helps us experience God by "drinking" from Him in everyday life.

Before Jesus went into Heaven, He said, "I ascend to My Father and your Father, and My God and your God' " (John 20:17).

Jesus is also God because one of Jesus's followers said to Him, "My Lord and my God!" (John 20:28).

After Jesus went into Heaven, a man named Stephen saw Him there: "But being full of the Holy Spirit, [Stephen] gazed intently into heaven and saw the glory of God, and Jesus standing at the right hand of God" (Acts 7:55).

But Jesus isn't always standing in Heaven. Sometimes, He sits down. Speaking about Jesus, the Bible says, "He sat down at the right hand of the Majesty on high" (Heb. 1:3) and "I...overcame

and sat down with My Father on His throne" (Rev 3:21). The Bible also explains that "God sits on His holy throne" (Ps. 47:8).

The Bible says the Father in Heaven is God, Jesus is God, and the Holy Spirit is God. Consider why all three statements are factual.

Jesus said, "God is Spirit" (John 4:24). When speaking of Jesus, the Bible also tells us, "Now the Lord is the Spirit" (2 Cor. 3:17). So then, how can three separate and distinct beings be one God?

THREE DISTINCT BEINGS, BUT ONLY ONE GOD

The Bible says, "There is...one Spirit" (Eph. 4:4) and that it is "the Holy Spirit of God" (Eph. 4:30). It goes on to say that the Holy Spirit is "the Spirit of Jesus" (Acts 16:7) and He is also "the Spirit of your Father" (Matt. 10:20).

Jesus explained His oneness with the Father when He said, "You, Father, are in Me and I in You" (John 17:21). The reason for the oneness of God is because of the Holy Spirit. The Father, the Son, and the Holy Spirit are separate and distinct beings. Yet, they are one God because the Father and the Son share the same Spirit (Eph. 4:4). Christians call this the Trinity.

Note here that when I talk about the presence of God, I am talking about the Holy Spirit being close to our physical body. How does that work? We have to talk about Jesus in Heaven.

JESUS IN HEAVEN NOW

With that background, we can now explain why we can drink from God. You need to understand what Jesus is doing in Heaven now to know why you can experience God in practical ways. God doesn't stay in Heaven and leave us alone.

Consider a promise from the Father to Jesus. Before Jesus ascended into Heaven, He said, "I am sending forth the promise of My Father upon you" (Luke 24:49). Then later, it says, "This Jesus God raised up again...Therefore having been exalted to the right hand of God, and having received from the Father the

Photo by Daniel Hodgkins on Unsplash

promise of the Holy Spirit, He has poured forth this which you both see and hear" (Acts 2:32–33).

The promise was that the Father would give the Holy Spirit to Jesus in a way that would allow Jesus to pour the Holy Spirit onto us. We can experience God because His Spirit is continually pouring out from Him. It is helpful to understand from the Bible how this works.

After Jesus ascended into Heaven, it says that the Father God "highly exalted Him" (Phil. 2:9). It also tells us that Jesus has been glorified (Acts 3:13). What do these verses mean?

Jesus was glorified so that He now shines with the Spirit of glory that pours out from Him (John 7:39; 1 Peter 4:14). It is because of the glorification of Jesus that we can drink from God and receive more of the Holy Spirit in an ongoing way (John 7:37–39). The Bible explains of Jesus that He "is the radiance of [the Father's] glory and the exact representation of His nature...He sat down at the right hand of the Majesty on high" (Heb. 1:2–3).

But the radiance and representation are different things.

The character of Jesus shows us what the Father is like. But Jesus is also shining out the light of the Father's glory, much like the sun radiates light (John 7:39; Acts 2:33); "His radiance is like the sunlight" (Hab. 3:4), and He gives to us what pours out from Him (Ps. 84:11). This book explains how you can receive what shines from God.

Jesus explained that the radiance is the Holy Spirit, "whom I will send to you from the Father, that is the Spirit of truth who proceeds from the Father" (John 15:26). And that is why the Holy Spirit is called "the Spirit who is from God" (1 Cor. 2:12) and the "Spirit of glory" (1 Peter 4:14).

HOW DOES IT WORK?

Note again that the Holy Spirit proceeds from the Father (John 15:26). Proceeds means it is still happening. Other Scriptures agree (John 7:39).

Earlier, we saw that Jesus "received from the Father the promise of the Holy Spirit, He has poured forth" (Acts 2:33). In other words, Jesus pours the Holy Spirit onto and into us by what He continually receives from the Father. And Jesus is still the "radiance" of the Father's glory because the Father is still giving His Spirit to Jesus. And the Holy Spirit is still pouring out from all around Jesus.

In Hebrews 1:2–3 above, the word radiance, together with exactly representing the Father, means that Jesus is shining with a heavenly light that is the Holy Spirit pouring out from Him and the Father. But the Holy Spirit that comes to us from around God is also the substance God's love and power. The Holy Spirit comes to us with God's beauty, purity, absolute holiness, goodness, compassion, justice, righteousness, kindness, and healing power.

The important thing here is that Jesus died, was raised, and was glorified so that He could pour the Holy Spirit into and onto us—for salvation as what washes us and makes us acceptable to the Father, and then also for our being able to experience God in an ongoing way after our first contact with Him.

SOMETHING REAL

Many of the descriptions of Heaven are from spiritual visions recorded in the Bible. But they are still an accurate picture of something real.

My wife and I have a beautiful picture of a mountain that my mother-in-law painted. Even though it is a painting, I know the mountain she tried to represent accurately is real. We should not conclude that the writers of the Bible did anything less. The figurative language style does not decrease the validity of the pictures we have of Heaven. The heavenly temple exists, as does the radiance around our Lord.

There was a tabernacle in the Bible that it says was a copy of the heavenly temple (Heb. 8:4–5; 9:24). So the tabernacle was a copy of something real—in spiritual realms.

One of the men in the Bible who saw a vision of Heaven wrote, "As the appearance of the rainbow in the clouds on a rainy day, so was the appearance of the surrounding radiance. Such was the appearance of the likeness of the glory of the Lord" (Ezek. 1:28).

Almost six hundred years later, another man had a similar vision of Heaven. He, too, saw a rainbow around the throne (Rev. 4:3). The Bible also says, "Around God is awesome majesty" (Job 37:22). It talks about Zion (Heaven) being "the perfection of beauty" and out of it, "God has shone forth" (Ps. 50:2). The Scriptures are too consistent for us to consider Heaven any other way.

Why is there a rainbow around the throne? In our world, rainbows happen when sunlight shines through the rain. Heaven is the same. A rainbow is over the throne because the glory that Jesus radiates is similar in some ways to light and water.

God does not want us to forsake that He is a fountain (Jer. 17:13). The Bible calls God "the fountain of living waters" (Jer. 2:13). It says, "You give them to drink.../ For with You is the fountain of life" (Ps. 36:7–9). The Bible explains how God comes to us when it says, "Seek the Lord / Until He comes to rain righteousness on you" (Hos. 10:12). The Spirit of God comes to us like water and light, and He is alive.

The Bible says, "His radiance is like the sunlight; / He has rays flashing from His hand" (Hab. 3:4). It says, "With You is the fountain of life; / In Your light we see light" (Ps. 36:9). Please note that the light that radiates around Jesus is no ordinary light. The Bible explains, "God is Light" (1 John 1:5). So Jesus shines the beauty, greatness, and purity of all God is.

Do you hate the evil in the world today? When we learn to open up to God and believe that we are receiving the presence of His Holy Spirit with us here, God comes to us and washes us clean as He comes. What we are receiving from the radiance around him brings more of His kingdom to earth. By receiving, we do our part in making it easier for the will of God to be done on earth (Matt. 6:10).

TYING IT TOGETHER

Christians should be loving because "the one who does not love does not know God, for God is love" (1 John 4:8). But when we satisfy ourselves with ourselves, it is difficult to feel secure enough to be loving toward people who are unloving toward us.

Earlier we considered the following verse: "O God, You are my God; I shall seek You earnestly; / My soul thirsts for You, my flesh yearns for You, / In a dry and weary land where there is no water. / Thus I have seen You in the sanctuary, / To see Your power and Your glory.../ My soul is satisfied" (Ps. 63:1–2, 5).

When Christians satisfy themselves with God, they feel more secure and confident, and loving others is much less complicated.

Note again that it is by seeing the power and glory of God that one's "soul is satisfied." Seeing in this verse is another way of saying believing that the power and glory of God are shining on us from His radiance. I say this because "we...receive the promise of the Spirit through faith" (Gal. 3:14).

So then, we experience God by believing that the radiance of His Spirit is shining upon us from the fountain of God: "God is

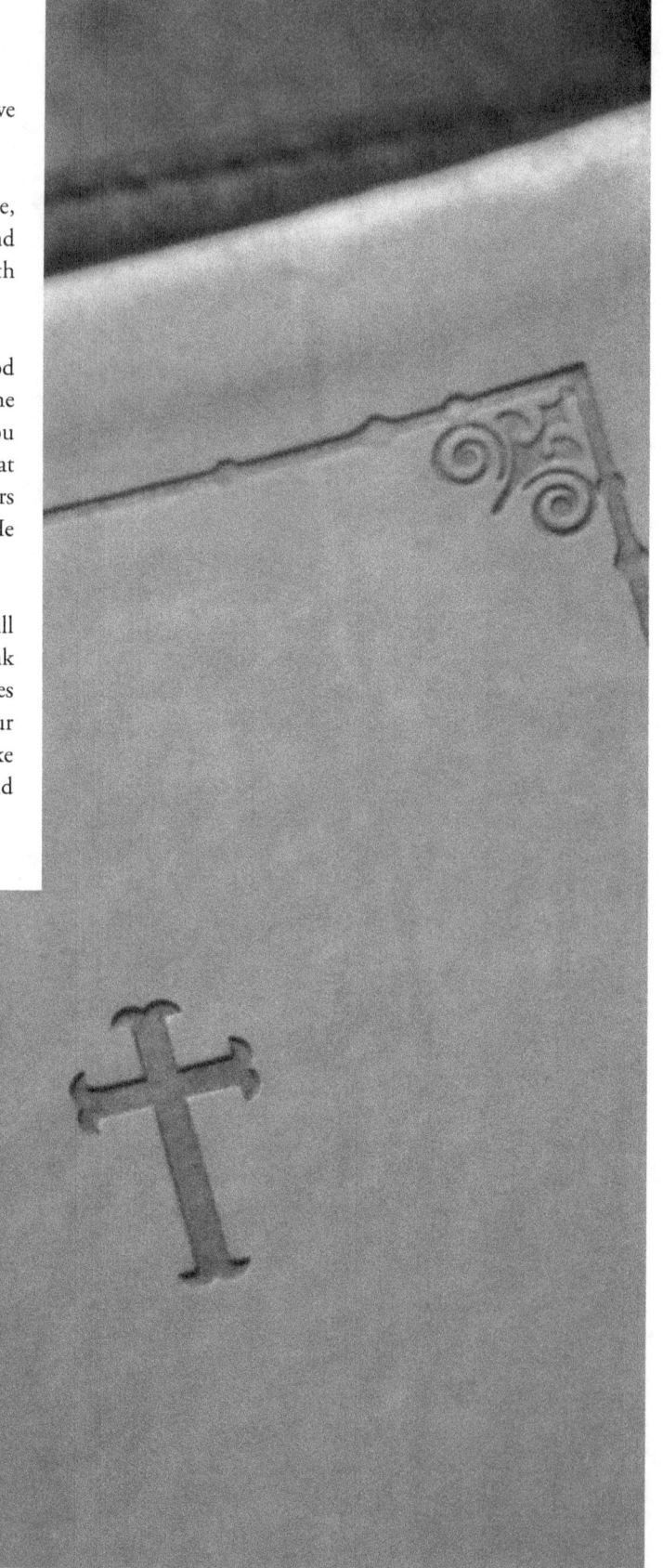

Light...if we walk in the Light as He Himself is in the Light, we have fellowship with one another" (1 John 1:5, 7).

When we do that, we experience the grace of God, His love, and the Holy Spirit: "The grace of the Lord Jesus Christ, and the love of God, and the fellowship of the Holy Spirit, be with you all" (2 Cor. 13:14).

Let me repeat it. The Bible explains why we can drink from God when it says, "You give them to drink.../ For with You is the fountain of life" (Ps. 36:8–9). So the practical reason why you can be confident about experiencing the presence of God is that Jesus pours out the Spirit of the Father like a fountain that roars because of the water gushing through it (Ezek. 43:2). And He never stops.

God wants to do His part: "I will do something new.../ I will even make a roadway.../ And rivers in the desert, / To give drink to My chosen people" (Isa. 43:19–20). Listening to ourselves make joyful declarations of repentance and faith can align our thinking with the Scriptures enough to become more childlike in our faith and our openness so we can receive the presence and kingdom of Heaven more freely.

4

CLEANSING FOR SALVATION AND SELF-ACCEPTANCE

WHERE WE START AND WHERE WE CONTINUE

This chapter considers where to start a life of experiencing God. It also considers the practical side of staying close to Him without shame. The starting point with God requires humility that lets us have faith that the cleansing God offers freely is powerful enough that He can forgive us for our sins and accept us for eternity.

In this chapter, you will see Scriptures showing that God cleanses us from sin, forgives, and saves us when He comes to us by the radiance that shines from Jesus (Titus 3:5–6). The Bible calls this salvation. But salvation is for the inside part of us that lives on for eternity after we die. Salvation does not include our physical humanity because we have to get a new body before going to Heaven after we die (Rom. 8:23; Phil. 3:20–21).

After salvation, God is in us, and He never leaves us (Matt. 28:20; Heb. 13:5). But for us to experience the presence of God intensely as armor twenty-four seven after salvation, we must consider the problems and solutions that come with including our physical body in our relationship with God (Rom. 13:12–14; Ps. 91).

The Bible says, "By those who come near Me I will be treated as holy" (Lev. 10:3). God is perfect and holy beyond our imagination. God is so holy that when the heavens open and God draws near after salvation, it is possible even for Christians to experience shame and fear at the nearness of His holiness (1 John 2:28).

After salvation, how can we accept ourselves enough to draw near to God when we feel spiritually dirty? How can we accept ourselves and the fallenness of our humanity while in a relationship with a perfect and holy God who wants to draw near to us here?

Salvation makes us holy on the inside (1 Cor. 3:16) so that the eternal part of us can go to Heaven after death. But before you die, if you want to draw near to God and don't want to shrink away from Him when the heavens open, you need to abide inside His presence in a way that cleanses your humanity.

The Bible asks, "Who may ascend into the hill of the LORD? / And who may stand in His holy place? / He who has clean hands and a pure heart" (Ps. 24:3–4). Salvation is only the beginning! Because God's holiness is far beyond ours, we need a holiness for our physical body beyond what humans can produce. We need cleansing for our physical body because when we draw near to God, He draws near to us here (James 4:8). For those who have trusted Christ for salvation, God's provision is that He washes our conscience and our body clean and holy as we trust by faith that we are drawing near by entering the holy place where God dwells (Heb. 10:19–22; 12:22–24, 28). We can only stay close to God and keep experiencing His holy presence close to us when our abiding includes faith about the cleansing of God for our physical bodies.

We live in a fallen world. Sometimes, even as Christians, the evil in the air around us can rub off onto our physical humanity. Evil makes us feel shame and want to avoid God. Your job is to humble yourself from thinking you can deal with this alone. Then, you have to make declarations that nurture your faith so you can believe God enough to receive the abundant radiance around Him coming to you here.

Rather than carry around the filth of evil with you, let your heart believe God for a powerful cleansing that washes away the demonic and any shame or hesitancy you feel about allowing God to draw near. Thank God that Jesus died, rose again, and was glorified so that He now shines with the Holy Spirit, providing an ongoing cleansing that includes your physical body after salvation (1 John 1:5, 7).

According to the Scriptures, the ongoing cleansing God provides is necessary for our consciences and our physical bodies so that we can "ascend into the hill of the Lord," where we can easily receive the kingdom of God and comfortably stay in God's presence all the time (Ps. 24:3).

Please don't be confused by this. From God's perspective, we are coming to Him. From our perspective, we must apply our faith to believe God and His kingdom are coming to us here (James 4:8; Matt. 6:10; Mark 10:15). I will explain more later.

So then, to avoid shame and fear in our relationship with a God whose holy presence draws near to us here, we must find the freedom we need to present our body by faith before the radiance of God so that He can wash our humanity and the atmosphere around us (Rom. 6:13; 12:1).

The self-acceptance needed for staying close to God comes to us naturally when we believe enough to enjoy that God's holiness coming to us is washing away the fear, shame, and filth of evil off our physical bodies and out of the atmosphere around us. Direct your heart into enjoying that you can let Heaven come because, by this, you present the evil bothering you before God so He can burn it off you (Isa. 4:4)!

Do you want significance and meaning that has value for eternity? Do you want to punish the demonic for the ways they have hurt you and those you love? By cooperating with God's provision for holiness inside and outside, you can enjoy much greater closeness to God.

You must fight the urge to avoid God when you feel spiritually dirty. Listen to yourself make declarations about God's power to wash you clean. Teach your heart to believe and trust by faith you are drawing near and are presenting your dirt before Him as you focus on believing that God is drawing near to you here. Make declarations that build your faith about the power of the holiness of God's radiance pouring out from Him and onto you here. Then let your heart enjoy with childlike delight that the cleansing of God upon you is washing you all around. By this, God is touching your humanity with His holiness and glory, the atmosphere around you is being cleansed, and you are helping to fill the earth with God's glory (Num. 14:21). As time goes on, your faith will grow, and you will receive God's kingdom and presence for a larger and larger area around you.

For now, though, we have to continue with our discussion so you understand the Scriptures that give a background for you to better apply what I am saying.

THE BEGINNINGS OF SIN AND PRIDE

The Bible explains that after God created the first man and woman, they sinned (Gen. 3:17). Christians call this the fall of man (Gen. 1–3).

That first sin brought humans a horrible level of insecurity before God that had never been there before. Their sin brought an awareness of right and wrong that made all of us after them desperate to ease our sense of insecurity and find reassurance for our fallenness somehow.

Even though we don't think of it this way, finding reassurance eases the insecurity we feel because of the fall. But let me be clear. Wanting reassurance is good! The problem comes when we twist the way we find reassurance and try to find it through rebellion, idolatry, and sinful behaviors. When we sin, we pride ourselves with praise inside for how defiant and controlling we were, and the pride feels reassuring to us.

You have to recognize that more than simply doing sinful things, we all are born with sin inside us, which makes us prone to sinful behaviors.

The Bible calls this proneness toward sin a sinful nature, and this nature is what God changes in us through salvation. After salvation, the world keeps trying to squeeze us into its mold. Growth as a believer then becomes a matter of continuously changing our thinking patterns about what we believe and treasure.

Sin is rebellion against God, and the rebellion we feel is a twisted substitute for God's love and power that reassures our fallenness. The sin of the first people God created resulted in deep feelings of insecurity before God that have been passed down from generation to generation (Rom. 5:19).

Our pride blinds us to how damaging our sin is to us. Whether subtle or out loud, it is self-directed praise that brings pride. Eventually, everything can get so distorted that, at times, sin and pride can seem right to us. But remember again where God says, "I will also put an end to the arrogance of the proud" (Isa. 13:11). Pride and sin are hurtful to us, and God doesn't want that for us. My aim with these books is to help you and me to cooperate with God where we go after humbling our own hearts before God has to take steps that humble us and put an end to our arrogance (Jer. 26:3).

In summary, because of our ancestors' sin thousands of years ago, we have all been born with a nature that is prone to pride and sin. Our nature makes us want to find the reassurance we need in sinful ways instead of God's way. Experiencing a life with God begins with relying on God for salvation. We have to trust Him to put a new spirit in us because that changes our core nature, and we can't do anything to change ourselves on that level. Growth after salvation boils down to learning to entrust ourselves to God as our God instead of other things.

Photo by Jon Tyson on Unsplash

DEAD IN OUR SINS AND A SINFUL NATURE AT OUR CORE

Some of the verses below are frightening. But we must consider what the Bible says about these things to know why we need the payment of Christ for our sins and why we have to trust God for a new nature.

The verses below explain our condition before we trust God and begin experiencing Him.

> You were dead in your trespasses and sins, in which you formerly walked according to the course of this world, according to the prince of the power of the air, of the spirit that is now working in the sons of disobedience. Among them we too all formerly lived in the lusts of our flesh, indulging the desires of the flesh and of the mind, and were by nature children of wrath, even as the rest (Eph. 2:1–3).

It says we were dead in our sins before salvation. That isn't all. It says that we lived according to a spirit of disobedience working in us that is "according to the prince of the power of the air." That's the devil. It even says that because of this sinful spirit, we are "by nature children of wrath." Another place even talks about us being enemies of God (Rom. 5:10). Before salvation, our very nature makes us deserving of wrath. This is central to why we need the Spirit of God to replace the old spirit.

But let me say again here that God is holy, completely pure, and perfectly good. God doesn't want anyone to deserve wrath. God's goodness is so far beyond us that when compared to God, we are not good at all. When it comes to us experiencing God, He is so perfect and good that He cannot ignore our sins. We need cleansing.

The practical problem is that it isn't just that we do bad things. Because of the original sin, we are all born with a sinful spirit in our nature that makes the very core of us unacceptable to God. So we need a new nature.

There are two problems before salvation. One is that we are dead to God because of our sins. Another is that we have a sinful spirit inside us. When we turn to God and trust Him for salvation, both problems get solved.

But what about the good things we do? When our nature has a sinful spirit, even the best things we do aren't good enough for God. The Bible says that "all of us have become like one who is unclean, / And all our righteous deeds are like a filthy garment" (Isa. 64:6).

The Bible also talks about the day when God will judge people by saying, "But for the cowardly and unbelieving and abominable and murderers and immoral persons and sorcerers and idolaters and all liars, their part will be in the lake that burns with fire and brimstone, which is the second death" (Rev. 21:8).

Some people on that list are doing obviously evil things. But the list includes the unbelieving and all liars. Have you ever told a lie or been unbelieving? I know I have.

JESUS DIED AS PAYMENT FOR OUR SINS

Before we have salvation, we need a new spirit in the core of who we are. We also need payment for our sins that is perfect enough for the perfection of God. Without this, our sinfulness would require our being punished, and we would not live through that. The Bible says, "The wages of sin is death" (Rom. 6:23). A perfect payment for our sins and getting a new nature work together. But this is a little complicated, so please stay with me as I explain.

Do you get mad at yourself about the things you do wrong? God designed us with a spiritual sense that punishment is necessary when we do something wrong. Deep down, we know that to be true. And the evidence is in our push to punish ourselves with condemnation and self-inflicted guilt.

But the punishment that is adequate for our sinful nature would kill us. Because God is perfect in every way, death is the legal punishment for sin. While God is a God of holiness and justice, He is also a God of compassion, righteousness, and love!

The Bible tells us, "'As I live!' declares the Lord God, 'I take no pleasure in the death of the wicked, but rather that the wicked turn from his way and live. Turn back, turn back from your evil ways' " (Ezek. 33:11).

Even though punishment is required for our sinfulness, God doesn't want us to be the ones who have to die. God knew that we would never be capable of solving this problem ourselves. So, He sent His Son, Jesus Christ, to solve our problem.

Let me remind you that Jesus lived about two thousand years ago. He lived a perfect life. At thirty-three years old, Jesus willingly gave His perfect life and died as punishment on our behalf.

The Bible says, "God sent Christ Jesus to take the punishment for our sins" (Rom. 3:25 TLB). It explains when it says that "without shedding of blood there is no forgiveness" (Heb. 9:22). Without embracing by confident faith that the punishment Jesus suffered on our behalf was enough for us, God remains far more holy than we can tolerate. But, as soon as we believe Jesus's death was punishment for us personally, something inside us changes.

Before Jesus died, the Bible tells us that people made animal sacrifices for their sins. Why were the sacrifices necessary? Because God is holy beyond our imagination, sin is unacceptable to God and requires punishment. Before Christ's death, the animal sacrifices were an unwanted substitute that was necessary so that the people wouldn't have to be punished to the point of death for their sins (Isa. 1:11).

As you read this, ask yourself if you believe Jesus died as punishment for your sin. Ask yourself if you believe the punishment Jesus took upon Himself was enough to include you. If your behavior suggests that you don't believe His punishment was enough, ask yourself if you are holding back from God because you would rather trust how punishing you are toward yourself.

Punishing ourselves keeps us from being sure about our salvation. How hard you punish yourself can result in a twisted form of self-protection and pride that keeps you from faith in God for your salvation. Remove the obstacles of pride and self-directed punishment by listening to yourself make declarations about the truth of God's goodness and love and the power of the punishment Jesus suffered on your behalf.

In my case, I was so bent on punishing myself that I was completely unable to believe the punishment Jesus suffered was enough to include me. I had to listen to myself making declarations that helped me turn away from self-contempt. My declarations also helped me to trust the power of the cleansing of God and the punishment that Jesus took upon Himself. Getting my heart to hear and believe these truths took work. But I stayed with it because I knew my salvation was at stake, and my self-directed punishment wasn't helping me with purity in my heart.

It might help you to know that I wasn't successful at directly going after faith in the power of Christ's death on my behalf or believing in God for salvation. I first had to use declarations to help my heart turn more fully toward God as my refuge and security.

Photo by Max van den Oetelaar on Unsplash

I first had to feel safe about trusting the punishment of Christ on my behalf.

Even though I know this will sound backward, my heart had to start joyously believing in God Himself as my refuge of security before I was able to believe the punishment that Jesus suffered was enough for me. Self-protection was my security until my declarations cut that off and my faith had freedom to grow enough to start trusting God as my refuge and security. The more I presented myself before God as my refuge, the more He was able to draw near and cleanse me of my self-protection.

Do you struggle to believe the power of Christ's death on your behalf is what saves you? The moment you believe Christ's death on your behalf, the cleansing of God comes to you through the glorification of Jesus (Titus 3:5–6). If believing that isn't easy for you, fight with your disbelief! Turn your heart toward trusting God that He is a better way to feel secure. Wherever you find yourself on the path to believing the power of Christ's death on your behalf, making declarations about its truth will chip away at the hardness in your heart until you can believe it. Just don't let up. Make declarations that cut off other options apart from God. Be kind to yourself, but be firmly determined that your heart will hear and believe the truth.

ONLY A PERFECT SACRIFICE CAN MAKE US ACCEPTABLE TO GOD

The Bible explains, "When you offer a sacrifice...to the Lord, you shall offer it so that you may be accepted" (Lev. 19:5). It says, "You shall sacrifice it so that you may be accepted" (Lev. 22:29). And, "As a soothing aroma I will accept you" (Ezek. 20:41; see also Ezek. 43:27).

Taking the life of the sacrifice was a spiritual and legal substitute that paid the price so that the people wouldn't be the ones to have to die. But before you get the wrong idea about God, let me quote the verse I mentioned before where God says, "I have had enough of burnt offerings.../ I take no pleasure in the blood of bulls, lambs or goats" (Isa. 1:11). So God took it a step further. He made the sacrifice Himself with His own Son, Jesus.

Speaking of Jesus, Scripture says, "Christ also loved you and gave Himself up for us, an offering and a sacrifice to God" (Eph. 5:2). Jesus is "the Lamb of God" (John 1:29). "He Himself is the propitiation [payment] for our sins" (1 John 2:2).

We also know from the Old Testament that the lamb had to be perfect to be an acceptable sacrifice (Ex. 12:5). Only Jesus lived a perfect, sinless life (Heb. 4:15). The Bible says the payment of His blood is far better than the blood of animals (Heb. 9:13–14). Jesus died a cruel and painful death on our behalf so that we wouldn't have to endure the punishment ourselves. He took the punishment to make us acceptable to the Father God.

The Bible calls this "the gospel of God, so that...[we] may become acceptable" (Rom. 15:16). And "Christ also accepted us to the glory of God" (Rom. 15:7).

God is extreme in His holiness. If God were not that holy, He wouldn't be good. So, to our benefit, we align ourselves with God's provision for a relationship with Him in accordance with His holiness.

Our sin is not holy and is, therefore, unacceptable to God. Jesus's death was a legal payment that took the punishment for our sins. He died so that we could be made acceptable to the Father and spend eternity with Him in Heaven after we die: "the wages of sin is death, but the free gift of God is eternal life in Christ Jesus our Lord" (Rom. 6:23).

Our only option is to trust the power of Jesus's payment on our behalf. Where there are obstacles to your believing, those obstacles need to be removed (Isa. 57:14). But there is more.

AT SALVATION, GOD GIVES YOU A NEW NATURE

Let's review. Before being saved, our problem is twofold. We do sinful things. We also have a sinful nature. And both of these problems have to be solved.

The death of Christ on the cross paid the price that brings forgiveness for our sins, but by itself, His death doesn't solve the problem of us being sinners by nature. This is where the radiance of the Father's glory comes in.

God promises, "I will give you a new heart and put a new spirit within you; and I will remove the heart of stone...I will put My Spirit within you" (Ezek. 36:26–27). The way the Spirit of God comes to us for salvation is by the radiance that shines through Jesus onto and into us (Titus 3:5–6; 1 Cor. 3:16). When God puts a new spirit inside you, He gives you a new nature. He provides, and you are receiving onto and into you "the Spirit of God...the Spirit of Christ" (Rom. 8:9).

Note that when the Holy Spirit comes to live inside you, it says that you "become partakers of the divine nature" (2 Peter 1:4). But you don't become divine; it only says you become a partaker of God's divine nature. And those things are very different.

When we trust the power of the death of Christ on our behalf, and then we open up to receive the Spirit of Christ into us, it says of us that "your body is a temple of the Holy Spirit who is in you, whom you have from God" (1 Cor. 6:19).

The Bible explains that God the Father made Jesus "who knew no sin to be sin on our behalf, so that we might become the righteousness of God in Him" (2 Cor. 5:21). When you receive the Holy Spirit from God, you are taking something of God's nature inside you. The Spirit of God coming into you changes your nature at that moment. When you receive the Spirit of Christ into you for the cleansing that brings salvation, it says that you are "a new creature; the old things passed away; behold, new things have come" (2 Cor. 5:17). The moment you trust the power of Christ's death as payment for your sin, you very naturally open up to God inside. Your opening up is similar to how you react when someone smiles at you when you do a good job at something. The moment you open up inside like that, you become acceptable to God because He gives you a new spirit inside that changes your inner nature.

Photo by Ksenia on Unsplash

But please understand this. After salvation, you have a new nature. But even with that, sinful behavior can still make you question your salvation. Try not to do that! The real problem is that your learned thinking patterns need to change as you learn to think in different ways.

After salvation, you don't have two natures fighting each other. After salvation, you only have a new nature. Your core nature doesn't want impurity and sin anymore. You want the holiness of God. Even when you fall back into sin, deep down, you still want God more.

For growth as a believer, your beliefs and affections need to change. What you are open to and pursuing needs to change. Don't be alarmed by this. We all have thought patterns that need to change after salvation. These changes are how we grow in faith and our relationship with God.

So please don't take the behavioral evidence of your thinking patterns as coming from an old nature. The old nature doesn't exist anymore.

If you go after the real problem of changing your thinking patterns, you can correct your behavior and grow as a believer much faster. Your thinking patterns need to change so that you can more easily receive the presence of God and His kingdom instead of receiving from the world, other people, and yourself. Practically doing that is the topic in this book and the others in this series.

TWO COVENANTS, TWO WAYS OF LIVING AFTER SALVATION

Now, let's discuss the two covenants governing our relationship with God.[9] The covenants represent two ways of living to be right with God. At any given moment, all people are living according to one or the other of the covenants.

One is the old covenant, where everything depends on faith in ourselves, faith about how good we are, and the perfection of how well we believe we can perform. The other is the new covenant. Under the new covenant, everything depends on our faith in what God has done and what we believe He is doing now. The old covenant is based on faith in our works. The new covenant is based on faith in God's grace.

The covenant we live under depends on the object of our faith at any given moment. You are not automatically living according to the new covenant because you have salvation.

During Old Testament times, under the old covenant of works, everything about their relationship with God depended on how well they performed the old covenant laws. To find forgiveness for sin and acceptance before God, they had to make animal burnt offerings. It says, "When you offer a sacrifice . . . to the Lord, you shall offer it so that you may be accepted" (Lev. 19:5; see also Lev. 22:29). And, "As a soothing aroma I will accept you" (Ezek. 20:41; see also Ezek. 43:27).

---

[9] Ray Stedman's book *Authentic Christianity* helped me a lot in my understanding of the two covenants. I credit Ray Stedman and John Fischer's album *The New Covenant* for helping me wake up to believing there is more to the Christian life than I had previously understood.

But under the old covenant, they could never be sure they had sacrificed enough. And if you are living according to the old covenant, your faith is in yourself, and you too will be uncertain if you have done enough before God. But a relationship with God based on our performance is never practical. Faith in our works and that we can do everything perfectly is unreasonable.

The topic of identity is directly related. For all practical purposes, identity is something we wear around us. When we find something we feel defines us, there is a sense in which we put it on and wear it. We then hope that others will see it as something that identifies us. As a warning, the Bible explains, "All our righteous deeds are like a filthy garment" (Isa. 64:6). When we try to do something for God, and we put our faith in that as what justifies us, we are coming to God with an identity based on our works. You can't wear an identity that is a filthy garment and expect to experience the presence of God twenty-four seven.

When living in alignment with the old covenant, successful living is impossible because even though good works are important, the goodness and perfection of our works will never measure up to the perfection and goodness of God. Continual failure to measure up to God as the standard is why the old covenant is called the covenant that "they broke" (Jer. 31:32). The old covenant is always broken because our works will never be enough.

Living according to the old covenant is doomed to failure right from the start. The good news is that God didn't let it stop there! "'Behold, days are coming,' declares the LORD, 'when I will make a new covenant...not like the covenant... which they broke...But this is the covenant which I will make...I will put My law within them and on their heart I will write it; and I will be their God, and they shall be My people...for I will forgive their iniquity, and their sin I will remember no more" (Jer. 31:31–34).

Thank God our performance does not determine whether we are acceptable to God because "Jesus has become the guarantee of a better covenant" (Heb. 7:22; see also Heb. 12:24). The good news is that we don't have to live according to the old covenant anymore. Today, we have the privilege of living under the new covenant of grace based on faith in the grace of God and on what we believe He is still giving. God made a better covenant for us based on His grace, what Jesus did for us, and what He is still doing (Heb. 1:3; 7:22).

Now, in one sense, the old covenant has been made obsolete because of the death, resurrection, and glorification of Christ. But that isn't all the Bible says about this: "When He said, 'A new covenant,' He has made the first obsolete. But whatever is becoming obsolete and growing old is ready to disappear" (Heb. 8:13; see also Matt. 5:17).

Why does it say Jesus made the old covenant obsolete and simultaneously that it is becoming obsolete? Even though the old covenant has been made obsolete in one sense, we Christians sometimes go back and try to put faith in ourselves and how well we perform. When we do this, the law takes over, and we are brought back to Christ by the consequences of pain from our sins.

I am not saying our salvation is in question when we are trusting ourselves. I am only saying that even as sheep, we get dirty and need to get washed clean again. The old covenant is becoming obsolete because when we go back to faith in ourselves, we need a tutor that leads us back to Christ (Gal. 3:24). The old covenant is there to remind us again that we fall short apart from God and that we will never be enough apart from Him.

Let me repeat it. We are not automatically living according to the new covenant because we have received Christ for salvation. When we go back to faith in ourselves, the law steps back in and becomes a painful schoolmaster that tutors us back toward Christ. Our salvation is not in question, but we are—in that moment—not living according to faith, and in that sense, we are in sin.

Instead of being forever in bondage to the old covenant, God made a better covenant for us based on His grace, on what Jesus did for us (Heb. 7:22), and on what He is still doing for us (Heb. 1:3; 12:1–2).

WE MUST HAVE FAITH IN GOD FOR OUR SALVATION

Our faith must be in God and what He has done to bring us salvation, not in what we do or might be able to do. When we fit it all together, we are trusting the power of the sinless life of Jesus, the perfect sacrifice of His death as payment for our sins, and the glorification of Jesus through whom the cleansing of God comes to us. All these things work together to bring salvation (Titus 3:5–6).

Consider now more generally the importance of having faith in God for salvation instead of having faith in ourselves. Note the importance of the words believe and faith in these verses:

- "The gospel...is the power of God for salvation to everyone who believes" (Rom. 1:16).

- "Righteousness...comes from God on the basis of faith" (Phil. 3:9).

- "If you confess with your mouth Jesus as Lord, and believe in your heart that God raised Him from the dead, you will be saved; for with the heart a person believes, resulting in righteousness, and with the mouth he confesses, resulting in salvation" (Rom. 10:9–10).

- "Through His name everyone who believes in Him receives forgiveness of sins" (Acts 10:43).

- "For God so loved the world, that He gave His only begotten Son, that whoever believes in Him shall not perish, but have eternal life" (John 3:16).

- "Everyone who beholds the Son and believes in Him will have eternal life" (John 6:40).

- "By grace you have been saved through faith... it is the gift of God" (Eph. 2:8–9).

Are you sure of your salvation? Many have prayed to receive Christ but still have doubts. The Bible is clear. We must believe God for our salvation to be real. We have no choice in the matter!

What about those who want to believe but have doubts? Those who pray to receive Christ for salvation but struggle to believe often do so because they feel they are so bad that God wouldn't want to save them. How do I know? I was one of them. Faith in self-protection is a much bigger idol than most of us realize.

For me to come to a place of trusting God for my salvation, I had to start by being uncomfortably honest with myself. I considered my behavior and the way I seemed to hold back faith from believing in God for salvation. I wondered why I was holding back and made some educated guesses about why that might be. To me, it appeared I felt I had to stop the cycle of sin in my life before I could believe God would love me enough to want to save me. This view was wrong. But at the time, it felt like I deserved more punishment than Jesus had suffered.

> The obstacles to me having faith in God had to be removed (Isa. 57:14).

As I observed my behavior, I noted that I was trying hard to avoid God. Given how much effort I gave to punishing myself with condemnation, I appeared to believe I had to punish myself for my sin before allowing myself to draw nearer to God. Of course, my thinking was completely wrong, and I knew it, but the starting point was to admit that this was how I was thinking. Then I had to change those thinking patterns.

The more I thought about this and asked God to reveal more about the underlying problem, the more I realized I was protecting myself from experiencing faith and hope. I was holding back from God because I didn't feel safe. If I let myself believe God's love for me and then found I was wrong about it for some reason, that would have been worse than never believing in the first place. I was stuck. I needed freedom and set out to repent by changing my thinking.

I focused on making declarations about the love of God. But my heart was hard and unable to hear that as truth. Rather than giving up, I focused first on getting my heart to turn away from condemnation and shame as tools for self-improvement. Here, I had to repent of how I was trying to repent. To accomplish this, I made audible declarations to direct my heart away from believing lies and then told myself the truth that I was determined to get my heart to believe. I also focused on giving my heart reasons to believe from Scripture that I could change by repetitious thanks and praise for the truth.

After a few weeks of making declarations, I could see changes happening. The condemnation and self-contempt died way down, but it still seemed like I was holding back from God.

Next, I made declarations to turn my heart away from earthly and human ways of finding reassurance, security, and protection. I was also making declarations using Scripture to get my heart to believe I could trust God as my security. My repetitious declarations helped soften my heart considerably. Eventually, God used circumstances to convince me of His love for me. But I honestly believe that if I hadn't done the work of softening my heart with the declarations, God wouldn't have been able to get through to me as He did.

We must remove the obstacle of misplaced faith in what we deserve or don't deserve. We must not hold back because we fear that we might make God mad at us for something later. It doesn't benefit us to protect ourselves and hold back from God! If you keep going, your declarations can help you enjoy God in a way that completely replaces the attractiveness of sin. But for this, your joyous declarations must also help you to abide while boldly loving the holiness of God around you as armor that burns off any and all temptation that comes to you from the demonic or witchcraft.

You have some work to do if this section speaks to your situation. You must get your heart to hear and believe God. Repetitious thanks and praise for the truth will help you. Go back through the verses in this chapter and thank God that you don't have to hold back and stay in self-protection.

Thank God that because of your faith, you have the approval of God: "Now faith is... the conviction of things not seen. For by it the men of old gained approval" (Heb. 11:1–2). "And without faith it is impossible to please Him" (Heb. 11:6). Thank God that the verses you read in this book are true for you. Then, keep thanking God for the truth until your heart softens, you humble yourself from self-protection, and you can rest into a place of stronger faith and trust in God.

HOW TO BE MORE CERTAIN

How can you be sure of your salvation? Jesus said that when we receive glory from earthly sources, we find it difficult to believe God for the radiance of His glory upon us (John 5:44). So the most practical answer is to trade more of the earthly glory we feed on so we can delight ourselves more fully in the abundance of what God offers (Isa. 55:1–2). The same is true regarding being certain about our salvation.

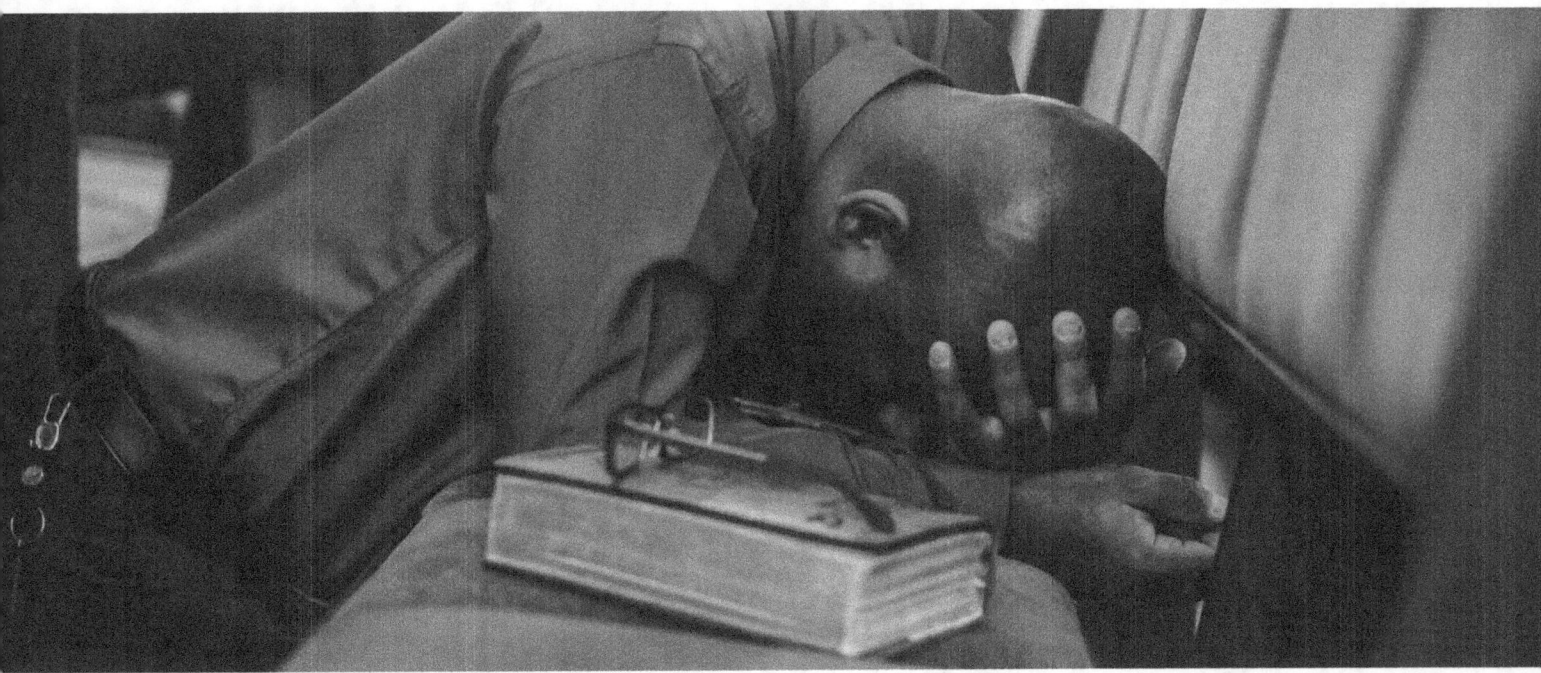

Photo by Samuel Martins on Unsplash

If your heart is hard because of self-protection, you will have to trade the power you feel from how well you punish yourself for the power of the punishment that Jesus took upon Himself on your behalf. You will have to trade in your self-protection for the presence of God as your refuge of security. You will have to trade in your desire to believe the acceptance you feel from people for believing the acceptance you need that comes from God because of salvation.

I did not know for sure any of this would work before I started. All I knew was that I had to repent, and according to the Bible, that meant I had to change my thinking in ways that would help me to rely more fully on God instead of myself. Listening to my declarations of repentance and faith changed my life, but it took time.

When trading in our broken earthly and human sources, we must think of God as He describes Himself in the Bible. He is "the fountain of living waters" (Jer. 2:13). Believing God is a radiant fountain helps us to receive His presence in trade for what we are cashing in when we repent (Isa. 55:1–2).

By salvation, you have God's acceptance (Rom. 15:16). By your faith in Jesus as the guarantee of your salvation, you have His approval (Heb. 11:1–2). By believing God is coming to you when you seek Him, you have God's pleasure (Heb. 11:6). It might be a stretch to see that Scripture this way, but it is a delightful thing when you get your heart to enjoy knowing that you cause God to feel pleasure when your childlike faith depends on Him to reward you with His presence! When I focus on thanking Him for that and steadily trust by faith that I am looking at Him, I can sometimes see Jesus and angels dancing during worship. Repentance by joyous declarations can change your heart-level thinking and greatly improve your dependence on and love for God.

WHEN DOUBTS ARISE

Let me remind you that salvation is only the starting point with God. After that, the devil comes to make Christians question whether God has given them a new nature at salvation. Don't fall for the devil's lies. Your thinking patterns and the old loves of your heart have more changing to do.

When doubts arise, trust you are presenting your doubts—and any demonic being pushing the doubt onto you—before God. Make declarations about the power of God's holiness washing over you. Then, be intentional to enjoy that God is burning away the filth of the doubt and the demonic trying to hurt you (Isa. 4:4; Rom. 16:20).

How far do the changes in our thinking need to go after salvation? Based on honest observations of my behavior, I look for evidence suggesting dullness in my faith and love toward God. When I see something subtle in my behavior, I don't hide from the truth about what I am doing. I make logical assumptions about what might be happening in my heart. Then, I determine I will direct my heart more fully toward God without shame because I am trusting God to wash me of my dullness.

> Without regret or condemning myself, I trust I am presenting my behavior, weaknesses, and heart before the Lord for cleansing (2 Cor. 7:10; 1 John 1:5, 7). I build childlike faith that believes God's holiness is armor around and on me that keeps the demonic away (Rom. 13:12, 14). By keeping my focus on enjoying God in a playfully childlike way, I feel far less shame and far more self-acceptance.

While trusting He is washing me, I use audible declarations to turn and redirect my heart's affections away from pride about my earthly glory. I follow that up with declarations that build my faith about believing the Scriptures that say I can receive from the radiance around God.

I listen to my declarations aimed at changing what I believe about earthly glory and the availability and greatness of God's glory. While I trust that God is washing me, and without making any attempt to change by condemnation, my declarations aim at changing what my behavior suggests I might be erroneously believing and loving.

At the most basic levels, I often remind myself with audible declarations that it is righteousness and purity that I love. I make statements to remind myself that I am miserable with anything less than heart-level purity. Then I trust I am receiving the continuing coming of God upon and around me as what washes and burns away demonic pressure and temptation toward sin (Isa. 4:4).

At times, the clues in my behavior suggest that I have to repent with declarations in which I tell myself again that I don't have to live for the praise of my glory to be OK and feel worthy (Eph. 1:12). I listen while being intentional to believe it when I say that I don't have to feed myself with pride about my human glory because I can turn to God and enjoy praising the radiant glory of God close to me. I fight my disbelief and love of rebellious power by listening to myself while trying to confidently believe it when I say that because of my childlike faith, God is being greatly honored in the heavenly realms, even when nobody here sees

(Eph, 3:10; 6:12). Without condemnation or shame, I repent by joyously declaring to my heart that I can take refuge inside the presence of the Living God instead of having to put on and wear pride from self-directed praise.

But before I get too far ahead of myself with declarations, let me get back to our discussion about why salvation is only the starting point with God.

HOLINESS FOR OUR SPIRIT, SOUL, AND BODY

For holiness to be practical, we must think about it in context with many Scriptures. In one sense, all our past, present, and future sins are forgiven at salvation. But some sins are against our body (1 Cor. 6:18), and God says the blood of Christ cleanses believers when we apply active faith to believe we are walking "in the light" of God's radiance upon us (1 John 1:7). Why is more cleansing needed after salvation? To understand this, we need to consider the Scriptures more fully.

God tells us to consecrate ourselves (2 Chron. 29:31). This means we are to set ourselves apart from evil and to God for holy use. God's part is to sanctify us because "I am the Lord who sanctifies you" (Lev. 20:8; see also Ezek. 37:28). We also know that God sanctifies us when He touches us with His holiness because after the Old Testament altar was made holy, "whatever touches the altar shall be holy" (Ex. 29:37).

The way I see it, entire sanctification is the only thing that makes holiness practical in everyday life. The apostle Paul wrote, "May the God of peace Himself sanctify you entirely; and may your spirit and soul and body be preserved complete, without blame at the coming of our Lord Jesus Christ" (1 Thess. 5:23).

Sanctification brings holiness to us in three ways. Sanctification for our human spirit happens instantaneously the moment we receive the Holy Spirit into us for salvation. Sanctification happens progressively in our soul because of our growth as believers. Sanctification for our body happens in an ongoing way as we learn to "walk in the Light" (1 John 1:7) by faith after salvation (Rom. 13:12, 14).

The Bible says, "As you have received Christ Jesus the Lord, so walk in Him" (Col. 2:6). In other words, because we "received" Christ into us for salvation by faith that we were receiving Him (Eph. 2:8-9; John 1:12), we walk in Him by faith that we are continuing to receive the Holy Spirit onto the outside of us in an ongoing way after salvation. Receiving the cleansing of God onto you is a literal thing because before you received Christ into you for salvation, He first was poured out on the outside of you (Titus 3:5–6).

If we emphasize salvation and none of the other ways God sanctifies us, the ongoing cleansing for our physical body doesn't make sense. But in this case, all we can do for holiness in everyday life is to keep getting back up and trying again when we fail. The practical problem is that temptation comes to us from the devil outside of us, and when we walk in the holiness of God by faith that His cleansing for our body is coming onto us, the holiness we continue to receive for our body sanctifies us in an ongoing way. Thinking of sanctification from these three perspectives will help you make holiness practical.

SELF-ACCEPTANCE BY REMOVING THE VEIL

Moses wanted the presence and glory of God as identity (Ex. 33:15–16). But when Moses came down from the mountain where he had been with God, he kept a veil over his face so that the people wouldn't see the glory of God fading from his face (2 Cor. 3:7).

Later the Bible says, "But we all, with unveiled face, beholding as in a mirror the glory of the Lord, are being transformed into the same image from glory to glory, just as from the Lord, the Spirit" (2 Cor. 3:18). Because of God's grace extended to us now during New Testament times, God's glory on us doesn't have to fade (2 Cor. 3:10). We only have to humble ourselves from pride and be more childlike so we can keep receiving.

To stand before the glory of the Lord and be transformed from glory to glory, we need a level of self-acceptance that is beyond human. In our relationship with God, high levels of self-acceptance come only when we direct our hearts to treasure God as our God and we joyfully unveil our faces to expose our shortcomings and fears before the Lord so that He can purify us. When we joyfully unveil our faces before God, He can shine on us without hindrance, and we are transformed.

How do we recognize we have put a veil over our face? It looks like subtle behaviors manufactured as distractions to avoid God. It feels like fear that scatters us emotionally enough that we appear to want to stay away from Him. Sometimes, the source of the fear is us. Other times, the source of the fear is the demonic, and they are pushing their fear onto us.

We must learn to recognize with honesty that we are holding back, but we cannot let ourselves be condemning about it! We must be patient and trust God for cleansing, but we dare not allow ourselves to stay in that place of being veiled.

God is God. We are only human. We dare not stay in the place where we are trying to depend on ourselves to be our god. Our self-acceptance is not strong enough in that place. Safety and well-being are not found outside the presence of God (Ps. 91). Let me be practical here.

What do I do when my behavior suggests my heart still feels hard even after making declarations aimed at changing my thinking and trying to draw near? By faith, I put the evidence of my holding back before the Lord. I trust Heaven is coming, and as best I can, I expose all the unholy things in or on me to the holiness of God. Then, with thanks and praise toward the

Photo by nader-ayman on Unsplash

holiness and power of God I believe is on me, I rejoice my way into strong faith that the Spirit of God is burning away my fear and whatever it is that is holding me back (Isa. 4:4). By standing before the radiance of the glory of God and letting it shine onto all the reasons for me to hold back, I am "transformed...from glory to glory" (2 Cor. 3:18).

When I go to sleep, I trust that the mountain of God is coming down, going past me, and bringing Heaven all around me here. I trust that Jesus and angels are in the room with me. Then I go to sleep, trusting by faith that I am holding the obstacles that are between me and God before Him. By this, the radiance of God burns them away through the night. When you go to sleep loving God this way, God teaches you His ways during the night, and you wake up refreshed and have a positive outlook (Mic. 4:2; Acts 3:19).

SELF-ACCEPTANCE, COURAGE, AND MANUFACTURED DISTRACTIONS

When our self-acceptance is not high enough, we distract ourselves from God. But simply telling yourself you are worthy is not enough because self-acceptance that is strong enough to let us deserve being near to God is beyond human.

The holiness of God can make you afraid and want to hide. But if you hold humanity and your fear before the Lord so that the glory of God can shine on you, your fear decreases and something of God's worth touches your skin and is transferred to your humanity. When self-acceptance results from God's holiness and worth touching us here, we praise and honor Him while also feeling self-acceptance and confidence that serves us well in every area of life.

When you feel unacceptable and unworthy, this is especially when you need to trust you are drawing near so that God can come and wash you and the atmosphere around you clean. But this takes courage. Self-acceptance before God requires courage because our basis for self-acceptance comes from closeness to God that lets Him wash us clean and burn away our fear. You have to recognize that your lack of self-acceptance results from being human and from demonic pressure toward self-hate. If you avoid trusting that the holiness and worth of God are drawing near, self-acceptance is difficult. If you cooperate enough to love that God is washing your humanity, the demonic element is burned off, and your self-acceptance comes from God.

Our hearts are like deep water that can hide many things (Prov. 20:5). We must be patient because self-acceptance is required when exposing those hidden things. I am aware that I am talking in circles here. But that is how this works! We need the self-acceptance that comes to us because of God. But when self-acceptance is low, we fear drawing near. This is when you must have courage enough to trust that God is drawing near you here.

There are other reasons you might want to stay away from God when your self-acceptance is low. You cannot let the power you feel from rebellion and anger keep you away from God. You must listen to your joyous declarations until you cut those things off and replace them with an openness and love for the powerful purity and overwhelming righteousness of God close to you here.

We all have needs, insecurities, and fears that we must calm by directing our hearts into faith about the power of God's cleansing and His willingness to draw near. Our God is the "God of all comfort" (2 Cor. 1:3). Our need to be comforted is especially high when our self-acceptance is low. When we embrace that we are human and that our God is the God of all comfort, we are presented with an opportunity to be more open to God so we can experience Him being the God who comforts us.

Amid our honesty, we must be accepting of ourselves by declarations that remind us that only God is God and we are human. This does not mean that we can loosen our value of holiness. It means that our humanity and the atmosphere around us need a continual cleansing from God.

We must repent with the understanding that our minds and hearts need transformation, and this will never come to us if we try to improve our behavior by punishing ourselves and holding back! Your declarations must cut off your trust for self-protection and turn your heart toward treasuring the mountain and the kingdom of Heaven as your safe refuge (Isa. 57:13). Listen to yourself make declarations that the most efficient way to grow and change is by transforming your thinking patterns about earthly glory and the availability of God's greater glory.

Be ruthless about not allowing yourself to wallow in earthly and human distractions from God. But at the same time, be patient and self-accepting. Only God is perfect. Only the ongoing cleansing of God upon and inside us burns away evil and brings His perfection to our humanity.

SELF-ACCEPTANCE BY WALKING IN THE LIGHT

The truth is that we are a completely new creation on the inside because of what Christ has done by His blood and death on the cross. We have the righteousness of God inside us because of salvation.

But even with that, the Bible still says to those who are already saved that "God is Light...if we walk in the Light as He Himself is in the Light, we have fellowship with one another, and the blood of Jesus His Son cleanses us from all sin" (1 John 1:5, 7). This verse talks about a continual cleansing that happens to all those who walk by faith that the cleansing light of God is on them, in the same way as God Himself is in the light.

> King David said that his physical body yearns for God (Ps. 63:1). The Bible talks about having "our bodies washed" (Heb. 10:22). It talks about sanctification that makes even our physical body holy (1 Thess. 5:23). And it says, "The body is...for the Lord, and the Lord is for the body" (1 Cor. 6:13). Thank God that you don't have to fight against having Him near. When you learn to expose the imperfections of your humanity to the radiant holiness and power of God, that is when you find the freedom you need for self-acceptance before God.

The Bible explains how to walk in the light where it says, "As you have received Christ Jesus the Lord, so walk in Him" (Col. 2:6). The way we walk in Him is for us to continue receiving Christ after salvation, in the same way as we received Christ for salvation at the start (Titus 3:5–6). By learning to love walking in the light that we believe is coming onto us from God, we are putting on the armor of light that keeps us from sin (Rom. 13:12, 14). The radiance of God upon us is holy, and temptation can't get through God's holiness as armor around us.

If you are trusting the radiance of God is on you and it still seems like the demonic is pushing evil on you, bind the power of the demonic. Then make declarations of praise toward God that strengthen your faith about being able to walk in the light that shines from God and put on His

presence as strong armor. Take refuge in God and punish the devil trying to get at you. Build your faith in ways that help you to be strong because of being playfully childlike in your love for the closeness of God's holiness. Open up to the mountain of God and Heaven above you and trust that as these are coming down onto and around you, God is crushing and burning the demonic trying to hurt you. Determine to enjoy with praise the power of the holiness and peace of God that comes to us when God's heavenly kingdom comes to us by faith.

JUST BELIEVE YOU ARE WORTHY?

Common thinking in the church today is that "you are saved, so just believe you are worthy." The way I see it, you can pump up your faith about who you are in Christ, but without the cleansing of God for your physical body, you might never find the holiness you desire in your heart. The demonic around you must be burned away and crushed by the presence of God and His kingdom. If all you do is believe in yourself, you can go your whole life and never find the sense of worthiness, self-acceptance, and perfection that you need for freely staying in the presence of God all the time.

Who you are in Christ can help you to soak in the presence of God from time to time. But when your worth is based on the greatness of who you are because of God, the motive for receiving God's presence all the time isn't nearly as strong as it would be if you were depending more fully on God being with you as your basis of worth, security, and significance.

When we find our sense of security, confidence, significance, and worth from the kingdom of Heaven and the presence of God drawing close to us, the motive for continually staying open and receiving the kingdom like a child is much higher.

Photo by Ivana Cajina on Unsplash

Let me repeat. A strong sense of worth brings a strong sense of self-acceptance, and nothing works better to motivate receiving like a child than when your security and significance depend on what you continue to receive from the radiance around God.

The importance of Christ inside us is huge, especially for salvation and after we die! Before we die, being inside Him here is just as important. The phrases in Christ, in Him, or in the Lord occur around 130 times in the New Testament. Paul was not sloppy in using these words when he talked about us being in Christ. When Paul talks about us being in Christ, you should embrace it as our literally being inside His presence.

Those who walk in the light by faith in God, who freely gives His radiant glory continually, can live twenty-four seven in the light that God Himself shines onto them and all around them here. Remember that God made the dirt under Moses's feet holy. He can do that for your humanity also! When the light of God shines onto your physical body, your body is washed holy, and the evil in the atmosphere around us cannot get to us.

DON'T BE CONFUSED!

When your self-acceptance comes from the radiance of God around you, it is easy to drop your guard when in church. That is when we should be safe, right? Sadly, being at church is often when I feel the most attacked by the demonic.

Because of walking in the light of God as my armor and resting in Him without reaching, I can go the whole week without feelings of lust. But then, when I go to church, the attacks of lust are often quite heavy and strong.

Is it because I am not doing as well as I think I am? Maybe, and with declarations, I go after changing that. But because my long-term normal is to go without any attacks from

lust, the assumption I make now is that because it seems I should be safe in church, I have dropped my armor enough to feel what others are carrying. This is when I go into attack mode. When made aware of the struggles of others, I will punish the demonic in the room for trying to keep God's people in bondage!

> When things like this happen, don't let yourself be confused. Don't falter on your self-acceptance and hold back from God. In my case, I remember I am human. I just have gotten lazy and lowered my armor. I need to pick it up again quickly.

So I put on more of my armor, and by that, I make the demonic suffer because more of the holiness of God comes. Because God tore the curtain separating Heaven and earth and Jesus is the door (John 10: 7–10), I open up from inside while trusting the gates above me are that curtain, and I can easily swing it open and to the side (Ps. 24:7–8). All I do is open up. Then I trust that God's holy mountain is coming down and bringing Heaven and angels into the room. I then focus my faith on believing Jesus and angels are in the room, and I cling to the Lord by trusting I am holding onto Heaven and the mountain of God under me. By boldly enjoying an abundance of the holiness of God around me, I make every demon in the room pay for the way they are messing with the Christians who don't understand yet how to receive the kingdom like a child and stand before the Lord.

WHAT IF?

Remember again that the glory of something is its value and worth. When God's glory is present, something of His extreme worthiness is with us. Consider what would happen if the glory of God were to show up on earth intensely enough to be visible in various locations.

The effect on people would be overwhelming. Many would come to faith but wouldn't be able to draw near or stay standing in the glory of the Lord (2 Chron. 5:14). Their human basis for worthiness and self-acceptance wouldn't be holy enough to let them near that much of God's holiness.

Salvation is vital, but remember that even true believers can feel shame at Christ's return (1 John 2:28). According to that verse, we must "abide in Him" to avoid shame. But what if the heavens open and we have a strong sense of being before the Lord, at some point before His second coming?

Photo by Caleb Smith on Unsplash

How can we prepare ourselves if the second coming of Jesus literally means He will come back to earth in the glory of the Father (Matt. 16:27; 2 Cor. 3:17)? After His coming like that, some might be able to come to the outer edges of His visible presence until they became accustomed to being in the glory of the Lord. Then they could draw nearer. But what if that were too late? People would need to be already accustomed to staying inside God's glory before He comes so that they can be protected from the onslaught of evil during that time.

The best way to prepare would be for us to direct the loves and beliefs of our hearts away from earthly glory and toward the place of staying in the presence of God before His return.

Jesus tells of inviting people to a wedding feast. But to participate, you must have the right clothes on (Matt. 22:1–14). We are told to put on the Lord Jesus Christ (Rom. 13:14). What if the clothing we need to wear is His presence?

When you learn to walk in the light of God, where you put on and wear the radiant glory of God instead of your own human glory, you are putting on something of the worth of God instead of wearing your own worth. Your self-acceptance is no longer based on anything having to do with you. The basis of your self-acceptance is the value and worth of God. We need enough self-acceptance to let God draw near with His holiness freely, or our self-acceptance will not be enough. We need God with us because when Heaven comes, only God's presence with us has worth equal to the significance and extreme value of God Himself.

What if the presence of God coming to earth visibly in various locations is something like an ark that protects God's people on earth during His last days of wrath? Of course, I am not sure this is what His second coming means, but if that were the case, we would need to have put on the worth of the glory of God around us as clothing before He returns in that way (1 John 2:28). We would need to become accustomed to wearing His presence. Don't you want to be like those with their lamps ready before Jesus comes (Matt. 25:1–13)?

Photo by Akira Hojo on Unsplash

5

IDOLATRY, EMOTIONAL NEEDS, AND GOD

THE IMPORTANCE OF PART TWO

God made an everlasting covenant with us that He would be God to us here (Gen. 17:7; Gal. 3:29). But He doesn't want us to have other gods (Ex. 20:3). Idolatry breaks the everlasting covenant God made so that He is unable to be God to us as He promised (Isa. 24:5; Jer. 11:10). But God tells us to repent of our idols (Ezek. 14:6). We dare not ignore His command or react in hopelessness about it.

For us to repent of idolatry, according to the big picture in the Bible, we have to understand what God considers idols so that we can direct our hearts away from them in the context of also turning toward Him (1 Sam. 7:3; Isa. 57:14).

Photo by Ben White on Unsplash

According to the Scriptures you will see in this chapter, turning from idolatry and toward God means that we have to replace what we get emotionally from sin and idolatry. Since repentance means to change our mind, true repentance changes us from earthly ways of filling our emotional needs and it changes us to depending on the closeness of God as what fills those needs in practical ways. We have to repent in ways that help us to drink from God in ways that let Him come so we can enjoy His presence instead of the sin.

Drinking from God is a radical shift from the current emphasis in the church. But filling our emotional needs with God increases purity and brings God's kingdom to earth more fully. What I say in this section is not meant to erase what we in the church currently understand about experiencing God. I intend to build on what we currently know.

CLEANSING FOR WHAT IS DEEPLY HIDDEN

One benefit of this book is that it will help you experience cleansing for shame in ways that help you bring great honesty and joy to the process of turning your heart away from idols and more fully toward God.

Idolatry is often deeply hidden. Because of that, Christians often ask God to help them stop their idolatry. But to do that, God would have to bring circumstances that would cut idolatry away from us. To me, that process sounds far more painful than what is necessary! Wouldn't you rather repent from your idols with joy before God humbles you?

Part three is important because it helps us to understand heart-level idolatry in the context of our practical need for God. It helps us to understand ourselves and why we do what we do. The more effectively we can repent and joyfully turn away from the hidden obstacles of idolatry, the more easily we can experience God as He has intended from the start of creation. Understanding our practical need for God helps us break out of the cycle, turn, and feast on Him every moment.

This chapter uses Scripture to explain idols as sources we depend on to fill emotional needs. It also explains from Scripture how we can experience God being God to us. It uses Scripture and practical examples to show that we do what we do because of a deep and driving emotional need to make up for our sense of falling short of God's glory. In a later chapter, we will then consider the processes involved when we depend on earthly sources or ourselves and how to reapply them to God in practical ways.

Here, we will consider how we can turn our hearts away from earthly and human sources and toward God with great joy. By this, we can experience God as the one whose presence and kingdom we love close to us and who fights evil when He comes. It also considers the practical spiritual benefits and process involved when depending on God to draw near as our God.

Idolatry has to do with what we try to receive from to fill our emotional needs. Please do not think you should repent of having needs. That would be a grand misunderstanding of what I am saying. It is right that we have needs because God intentionally designed us this way. Making God our God requires us to change how we fill our emotional needs. Emotional needs are powerful motivators for drinking from God instead of from the glory of the world or something about ourselves.

Because we don't always know for sure about the idols in our hearts, joyous repentance looks like childlike gratitude and praise for the many various idols we name as those we don't have to depend on. When we worship God with joy and determination to turn and be more open to Him, we cut off the possibility of idolatry as an option for us. We also are freer to open up and receive Heaven around us here. The repentance I talk about changes our thinking and patterns of dependence, but it looks more like thanksgiving and praise than making yourself feel bad for what you might be doing wrong. The reason our repentance can look like gratitude and praise is because Jesus made payment for our sin, and our role is to turn to Him so we can present our body before Him and He can wash us of idolatry that is, or might be, present.

The more you turn from earthly sources as an option, the more faith and freedom you find for receiving Heaven here like a child and loving God as He desires. The more you do that, the more freedom you have to honor God by enjoying the closeness of God as your God and apart from what He considers idolatry! You can repent of heart-level idolatry by directing your heart into embracing that the more childlike you become in recognizing your emotional needs, the greater your freedom in your dependence on God will be. Joyful repentance concerning how you fill your emotional needs is a practical path for experiencing more of Heaven here. It is also the path toward receiving and then being able to rest in Him so you aren't so pulled on to reach out toward earthly sources.

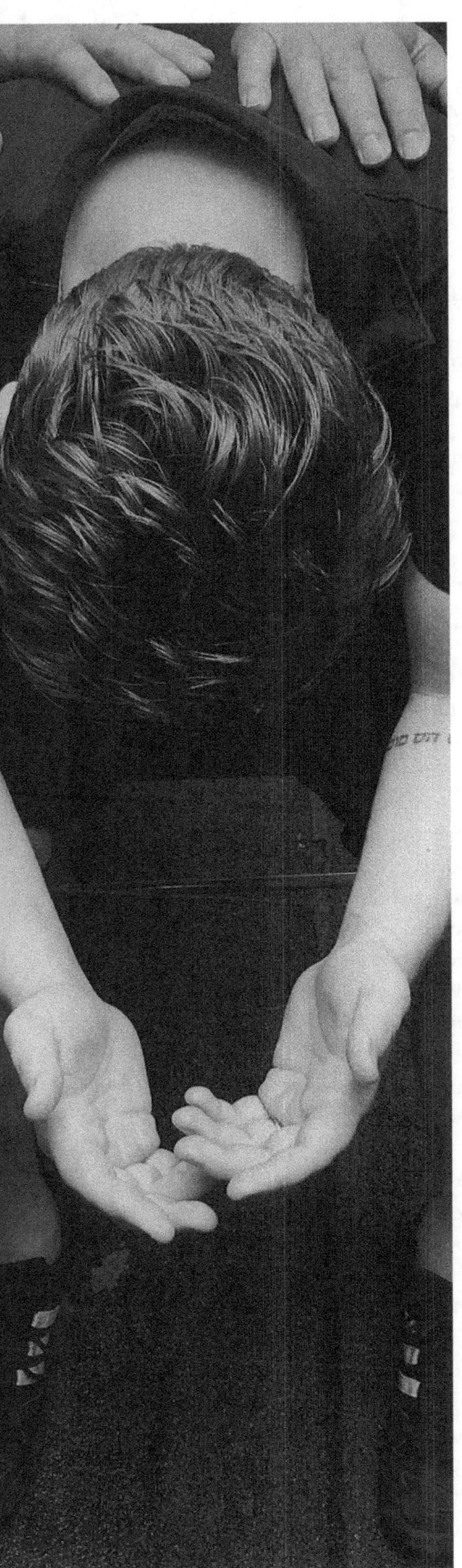

Photo by Jon Tyson on Unsplash

HONESTY ABOUT IDOLATRY REQUIRES ONGOING CLEANSING

I want to help you understand the depth of idolatry in our hearts without making you shut down because of guilt. My goal is to explain why understanding idolatry is a joyous springboard for growth and for worship toward God. These are things you should not be afraid to consider. As you learn more about idolatry, don't hold back from God. Trust you are presenting yourself before the Lord so He can cleanse you in those areas. Then, determine you will take the steps I show you to redirect your thinking and patterns of dependence so you can better turn toward God.

By your declarations, you are cutting off sinful behaviors and idolatry. But because this is such a great opportunity for gratitude and praise toward God as our God instead of the sin, we are going to be as thorough as possible.

The truth about us is that the ways we find glory substitutions for God are various kinds of idolatry hidden deeply in our hearts. We must change from idolatry and sin. But the problem of idolatry is not solved until our repentance brings God's presence and we can abide in Him (Acts 3:19). Repentance is a privilege that greatly honors God. But before we can consider idolatry in our hearts honestly, we also need to be in the habit of presenting our shame and guilt before the Lord for cleansing, or we easily get paralyzed spiritually and can't move forward.

If you are only talking about getting into Heaven, you are covered. The sin that will keep you out of Heaven has already been forgiven because of salvation. But you should not want to stop there because you will miss out on much of what God wants for you.

The need for cleansing after salvation is ongoing. The blood of Christ that cleanses us is the radiant living light of the Spirit that pours out from all around God (1 John 1:5, 7). When we receive Heaven to abide in Him, something of God's righteousness and perfection is transferred to our physical flesh. But the reverse is also true.

Even though we are saved and going to Heaven, we live in a world where evil surrounds us. When we are not abiding with Heaven around us here, evil can touch our physical body; when that happens, we feel dirty. We are still saved and going to Heaven, but in this place, the Bible says, "Those who are in the flesh cannot please God" (Rom. 8:8).

Take heart because there is hope! Receiving the kingdom of Heaven around us lets us walk in the light that touches us and cleanses our physical bodies (Heb. 10:22). When we receive Heaven here with the faith of a child and cling to the Lord to abide in Him, we cleanse ourselves constantly, and God can use us as He desires: "If anyone cleanses himself from these things, he will be a vessel for honor, sanctified, useful to the Master, prepared for every good work" (2 Tim. 2:21).

Don't feel bad about needing to get washed because of newly recognized idolatry. Use the cleansing of God to wash away your shame and fight evil in the atmosphere around you.

I will explain more about the cleansing of God in a future chapter. For now, when God reveals some area of idolatry or sin you haven't seen before, remind your heart with declarations that you don't have to pay the price for your idolatry by punishing yourself. Teach your heart by listening to your repetitious declarations that when God comes to you, He washes your conscience and your physical body holy and clean (James 4:8; Heb. 10:19–22). When we open up to drink from God while trusting that we are walking in the light, we receive from the radiance around Him the blood of Christ that washes us clean (1 John 1:5, 7). But walking in the light is an ongoing process (Col. 2:6). We have to actively believe that the Spirit of God is pouring out from around God and onto us here (Jer. 17:13; Gal. 3:14).

As you read this chapter, remind your heart that the punishment Jesus suffered was more than enough for you. Direct your heart away from holding onto idolatry as a substitution for God. But don't stop there. Immediately present your idolatry before God so He can wash you clean of it. Our thinking patterns need to change, but the freely available cleansing of God is why we can be joyfully honest about idolatry in our hearts and turn to drink from Him with courage and without holding back.

> When we wash our hands, we hold them under a faucet of water. While making declarations of repentance, why not apply faith to enjoying that you are holding your whole body under the radiant cleansing of God's glory that endlessly pours out from Him in abundance?

MAKE GOD'S PRESENCE AND KINGDOM YOUR REFUGE

One category of what God considers other gods is what we seek refuge in: places, people, circumstances, and things. Consider where it says, "And He will say, 'Where are their gods, / The rock in which they sought refuge? /...Let them rise up and help you, / Let them be your hiding place! / See now that I, I am He, / And there is no god besides Me' " (Deut. 32:37–39).

In today's language, a place of refuge is how we feel secure and protected. A good hiding place is what we depend on to ease and soothe our hurts. Think of a hiding place or a refuge as something that surrounds us and is close to us.

In this verse, any time material things, other people, circumstances, or ourselves become our source of security and protection—or when earthly things or people feel like they threaten our security or safety—we have made them more important than God, and they have become idols to us.

Because we fall short of God's glory, we are driven to find a sense of having glory that we can praise. As we find glory, we experience various emotional benefits like reassurance, security, or confidence. God intentionally designed our need for security and protection to be strong. We naturally love what makes us feel secure because that is how God deliberately created us. Because we need protection so desperately, we must direct the attachments and beliefs of our hearts away from earthly sources as our security and into a place of faith and joy about taking refuge in the kingdom of Heaven with us here (Mark 10:15; Ps. 91; Heb. 12:28). Changing this doesn't come naturally; joyous repentance that changes our patterns of dependence is necessary.

God wants to be your entire basis for feeling secure—and you can trust Him to be your security, but we have to apply what the Bible says for this to work. In the words of the Bible, we have to drink from God to experience Him as our refuge. In the verses below, it is not automatic that we take refuge in the Lord just because of salvation. God is a radiant fountain, and there is a direct relationship in Scripture between making God our refuge and drinking from the river and the fountain of God.

"How precious is Your lovingkindness, O God! / And the children of men take refuge in the shadow of Your wings. / They drink their fill of the abundance of Your house; / And You give them to drink of the river of your delights. / For with You is the fountain of life; / In Your light we see light" (Ps. 36:7–9).

Please note that it is when we become childlike that we can open up to God and believe we are receiving from the radiant fountain of God. As we believe we are receiving, God gives us to drink from the radiance around Him, and by this, His Spirit draws near and becomes the refuge around us that we need.

To take refuge in God, we have to drink from Him in ways that let His presence draw near so that He can freely come to us and be a literal place of refuge around us here. According to the verses above, childlike people drink from God's radiant fountain to take refuge and shelter inside what they receive from Him.

But how is this related to the topic of idolatry? Drinking from earthly and human sources to feel secure is idolatry. Opening up to drink from earthly and human sources makes them idols to us.

It is much more natural for us to depend on earthly sources. To make the nearness of God our refuge, we must direct our hearts into a place of treasuring the presence and kingdom of God as what we depend on to be our refuge instead of glory from earthly and human sources. We need God's presence and kingdom around us here because when we find refuge and security by earthly means, they are always close to us—a child's blanket, our personality, our doctrines, the money in our pocket, or hard shells of self-protection.

When turning from earthly and human sources for security, we must cut off drinking from them to feel secure and we must turn to God. We do this with faith enough to drink from Him to feel protected and safe or our repentance is incomplete (Acts 3:19).

We must repent of earthly sources because they are not enough to protect us from our unseen adversary! What we are turning toward is far more effective at protecting us. By repentant declarations, we must teach our hearts to apply our drinking to God instead of trying to drink from earthly and human sources.

According to Psalm 36:7–9 and many other verses, the reason we can drink and receive the presence of God is that our God is a radiant fountain that shines with His Spirit of glory (Jer. 17:13; John 7:37–39). Once you apply confident and childlike faith to actively believing that God is drawing near and you are physically close to the fountain (James 4:8; Heb. 12:28), that is when God cleanses your body and you can lower your guard, open up inside, drink, and receive the presence of God from the radiance around Him (Mark 10:15; Gal. 3:14).

Remember that it was when David looked by faith at the power and glory of God while inside the sanctuary that the thirst of his soul and his body were quenched and satisfied (Ps. 63:1–2, 5). David also said, "I have set the LORD continually before me; / Because He is at my right hand, I will not be shaken. / Therefore my heart is glad and my glory rejoices; / My flesh also will dwell securely" (Ps. 16:8–9). Entering by receiving the sanctuary of Heaven here like a child makes it practical for us to set the Lord continually before us so we can experience Him as our refuge of security here (Mark 10:15; Ps. 91).

We must apply these Scriptures, but because of idols that harden our hearts toward faith, we must teach our hearts to

Photo by Ben White on Unsplash

believe what the Bible says enough for faith to rise in ways that enable us to apply it (1 Sam. 7:3; 2 Peter 1:5).

Childlike people are not proud. Children are free to open up easily and quickly because they do not have hearts that are hard because of self-protection. When our declarations of repentance and faith help us become like children, we can better open up to God and drink from Him twenty-four seven (Ps. 36:7–9).

It is not selfish for us to drink from God! Repent of thinking like that. God defines idolatry in terms of what we depend on for security, so we can be confident that God wants to be a strong refuge around us. Our childlike dependence on the radiance around God greatly exalts and honors Him as God. The closeness of God's presence is also much more deeply loved and praised when we enjoy Him in this way.

Learn to recognize the ways you try to find refuge and hide yourself apart from God. Then, use declarations of thanks and praise for the truth to direct your heart away from that thinking because God wants to draw near to you here and be your refuge in practical ways.

When demons come to attack you, trust that Heaven is coming down and wrapping all around you. Then boast in Heaven's extreme greatness and the holy power of God's presence, crushing and burning evil all around you here. While praising God that His closeness is coming to you as your refuge, intentionally love Him with faith as your strong refuge. Bind the power of demons and witchcraft (Matt. 16:19). Then loose the mountain of God with Heaven and angels and trust by faith that these are all coming down into the situation you are praying about. The demons won't be able to fight back because the peace of God will easily crush the evil as Heaven comes. When Heaven comes, the peace of God comes with it, and God's peace is what does the crushing (Rom. 16:20; 14:17).

We have to repent in ways that change our patterns of dependence and thinking so that we make God our refuge. The Bible says, "As for me, the nearness of God is my good; / I have made the Lord God my refuge" (Ps. 73:28). When you repent in ways that joyfully help you to become more playfully childlike in your faith and dependence on God, you will "have made the Lord, my refuge, / Even the Most High, your dwelling place" (Ps. 91:9). Salvation does not automatically make God your refuge. Making God our refuge is an activity that involves declarations of repentance that remove obstacles and build our faith so we can more freely allow Him to draw near (Isa. 57:14).

God wants to be the one God you need as your place of refuge. The psalmist said, "I have become a marvel to many, / For You are my strong refuge" (Ps. 71:7). The same can be true for you!

Making God our refuge requires the "nearness of God" (Ps. 73:28). But how do we make God our refuge, as it says here in the Bible? David "set the LORD continually before" himself to be safe (Ps. 16:8). When you trust that Heaven comes and God is before you with His radiance on you, His presence becomes a strong refuge around you here.

Years of walking with God can teach you to make God your refuge instead of other things. But for those who don't want to wait that long, you have to direct your heart into depending on God that way. Being specific in your repentance can help you take your Christian practice farther and in much less time.

Making God our refuge requires repetitious repentant declarations that direct our hearts away from the pride that makes us want to deserve God's presence before we allow ourselves to open up to Him and let Him draw near. Our repentance has to joyfully humble us into being more childlike so we can freely open up to God before we feel like we deserve it. We can only drink from God freely when we open up to receive from Him because we believe in His grace to freely draw near so He can accomplish His purposes without us needing to deserve it. Use audible thanks and praise to cut off and direct your heart away from any pressure you feel to perform. Teach your heart to believe you can receive the kingdom of Heaven here so that God's will can be done on earth as it is in Heaven. Receive also because when God's kingdom comes, the mountain of God comes down with Heaven and becomes a safe refuge around us here. For that, childlike freedom in our receiving must become our new normal.

When thinking about the presence of God and His kingdom as your refuge, don't think about the worldly things you are giving up. Think about what you are gaining! God designed you to need a safe place of refuge. He also created you to love your refuge like a child loves their favorite blanket. Reassure your heart with thanks and praise for the truth until your heart believes and you can apply it.

Living as God desires requires that you embrace your childlike need to experience His presence as your hiding place and refuge. Don't think you must be perfect before letting God come to you. When God draws near, He comes with perfection to be the holiness you need, even for your humanity. God wants to be God to your physical body by being your strong refuge here. Embracing God's desire and your practical need for God humbles you into a place of more freely receiving His kingdom and presence like a child.

The presence of God and the kingdom of Heaven drawing near to you as a strong refuge around you is the pathway to consistently living a holy life that honors God. When we open up with freedom and faith to the radiance around God, His presence comes upon us and becomes armor around us that is our refuge.

King David said, "the nearness of God is my good" (Psa. 73:28). Perfection is similar. Embrace that your longing for perfection is met only partially by salvation. After salvation, the perfection we long for is driven by our physical body's yearning for God (Ps. 63:1–2, 5). Rejoice about this truth until your heart hears and believes that God is transferring something of His holiness and perfection to your humanity. God Himself, as a refuge touching your skin all around you, enables holy living and clothes you with the armor and power of God (Rom. 13:12–14; 6:4; Acts 1:8). Jesus told us to "be perfect, as your heavenly Father is perfect" (Matt. 5:48), but we can't do that apart from God's nearness touching our physical humanity. Make declarations that teach your heart to enjoy the reassurance and boldness that comes because of the nearness of God as your strong refuge of perfection.

MAKE GOD'S PRESENCE AND KINGDOM YOUR STRENGTH

Making God our refuge before we make Him our strength in battle is vital because when God becomes our refuge, His presence is a shield that protects us.

Another category of things God considers other gods are the qualities about ourselves, places, material things, circumstances, or other people that give us reasons to feel strong and have confidence. Instead of depending on earthly sources for the confidence and boldness we need, God wants to be the strength we enjoy that benefits us emotionally in these ways. God wants His presence with us to be what makes us strong emotionally, spiritually, and in our character.

The Scriptures strongly rebuke those who trust earthly ways of feeling strong apart from God. The Bible says, "They will be held guilty, / They whose strength is their god" (Hab. 1:11). The good news is that the people who become childlike enough to trust God as their strength will be like a tree planted by an abundant and flowing source of water that flows from God. Depending on God as your strength will only be helpful when you determine that your heart will believe your declara-tions enough to boast about God's greatness while trusting with certainty that God is drawing near (Psa. 18:1; Psa. 68:35).

Thus says the Lord,
"Cursed is the man who trusts in mankind
And makes flesh his strength,
And whose heart turns away from the Lord.
For he will be like a bush in the desert
...But will live in stony wastes in the wilderness
...Blessed is the man who trusts in the Lord
And whose trust is the Lord.
For he will be like a tree planted by the water,
That extends its roots by a stream
And will not fear when the heat comes;
But its leaves will be green,
And it will not be anxious in a year of drought
Nor cease to yield fruit" (Jer. 17:5–8; see also Isa. 12:2–3).

Here, we see again that the people who drink from God make Him their strength. But please note that the drinking in the verses above does not happen just once. A tree keeps on drinking because it needs strength. The same principles we use to make God our refuge apply to making Him our strength.

Remember again where David said that to quench His thirst for God, He entered the sanctuary and looked at the power and glory of God to be satisfied. We have to do the same when experiencing God as our strength. According to the verses above, when you open up to drink from the radiance around God and receive His presence here, He comes close to you, and you can enjoy God as your strength. Don't question whether He is with you or not. Just keep showing gratitude that you are receiving (Heb. 12:28); eventually, faith will grow, your heart will open, and you will receive.

The Bible talks about us being "armed in the presence of the Lord" (Num. 32:32). Listen to yourself giving joyful and boastful praise toward the strength of God and His holy presence close to you because that is what will help you to be strong emotionally, spiritually, in purity, and in your character as a person.

God wants to be our refuge and strength who is a "very present help" in times of trouble (Ps. 46:1). For God to be our refuge and strength, He must be very present with us. Otherwise, when trouble suddenly arises, we might not be drinking from Him in the moment and will have to change that quickly. Our thinking needs to change so we are ready for whatever comes to us. Setting the Lord before him by faith was something David did for protection all the time because God was David's shield, even on the battlefield (Ps. 16:8–9; 28:7).

What is your basis for believing God will draw near to you and stay close like that twenty-four seven? If you wait for pride that makes you think you deserve His presence, you will stay shut down inside, and you won't ever experience the presence of God.

On the other side, don't settle for fear that God is holding back. He wants to be God to you here. God wants to draw near so He can accomplish His will on earth. Your motive for letting the presence of God draw near has to enlarge.

Reassure your heart with declarations about the truth of God in His Word. When you turn away from fear and let yourself believe like a child, God will come. You only have to believe He is coming to you confidently.

Your practice of giving God a continual sacrifice of praise will help your dependence on God to stay sharp so that He can stay close to you here (Heb. 13:15). Think of how a child clings to their blanket and learn to love God by similarly clinging to Him (Jer. 13:11). Giving praise toward the strength of God close to you helps you to identify with Him as your God, and when that happens, you feel significant and courageous because of Him and God can work more freely in the world as He desires.

MAKE GOD'S PRESENCE AND KINGDOM YOUR GLORY

Another idol we must repent from is our dependence on other gods as our glory. Consider that glory is what we fall short of, and when we find glory from worldly sources, we don't feel like we fall short. Because God is so much greater than our pride, our pride is based on a lie. The emotional benefit of pride doesn't last long, and we always have to pump it back up. The practical problem is that receiving glory from the world or other people is uncertain and inconsistent. Glory from the world isn't readily available. Finding glory in ourselves requires that everything has to be perfect or the glory we have doesn't seem like enough.

Declarations of faith that help make God our glory are far better than trying to depend on glory from the world. With God, the Spirit of glory never stops pouring out from Him because our God is always a radiant fountain of glory and grace (1 Peter 4:14; Ps. 84:11).

When God is your glory, His presence and kingdom around you will become your significance and what makes you special. When God is your glory, His presence and kingdom will become your refuge and strength to such a degree that the greatness of His closeness on and around you will also become your identity and worth.

Just as with making God our refuge and strength, in the next passage, we see that God has to be close for it to be practical for us to depend on Him as our identity, worth, and what makes us special. The good news for us is that God draws near to us when we open up and drink from Him.

> "Has a nation changed gods
> When they were not gods?
> But My people have changed their glory
> For that which does not profit.
> Be appalled, O heavens, at this,
> And shudder, be very desolate," declares the Lord.
> "For My people have committed two evils:
> They have forsaken Me,
> The fountain of living waters,
> To hew for themselves cisterns,
> Broken cisterns
> That can hold no water." (Jer. 2:11–13)

Compared to God as our glory, earthly sources don't hold water. Without realizing it, we have traded the glory of God for worldly glory and have forsaken the fountain of living waters. According to the verses above, our misdirected dependence hurts all of Heaven. The result of having forsaken the glorious fountain of living waters is that most Christians today aren't drinking from God and don't even know what they are missing (Jer. 17:13).

By repetition and worldly thinking, our hearts have learned what sources of earthly glory might be dependable and what to avoid. These ways of thinking keep us in bondage to earthly and human sources. Making God our glory is about changing our thinking in ways that help us to cut off earthly glory sources so that we can become more playfully childlike in receiving the Holy Spirit's presence as He comes to us by faith from the fountain of living waters (John 7:39). By repetitious and joyous declarations of faith, our hearts can hear the truth and turn to love depending on something better.

Here also, you can't wait until you have enough human glory to think you deserve God as your glory. That thinking is completely backward! God wants to be our glory because anything else we depend on results in pride and is idolatry. Our repentance must include declarations that change our thinking enough to humble us in ways that help us become more childlike so that we have no option except to depend on God to draw near and be our glory. When our repentant declarations strip earthly and human sources away from us, it becomes much easier to trust that God will draw near and be God to us as He promised (John 5:44).

CLOSING THOUGHTS ABOUT THIS CHAPTER

Given how God defines idolatry in the Scriptures, we need to embrace that when God says He will be our God, He is saying that when we drink from Him, He will come to us so He can be our refuge and we can glory in His greatness instead of the glory we find from idols.

How God defines idolatry demonstrates that God wants to be God to us with practical, emotional benefits. Understanding idolatry is needed for repentance, but it is also helpful because the processes involved when receiving help us to understand how we can improve our receiving from God.[10] God wants us to drink from the radiance around Him so we can easily experience His presence drawing near us here.

Repentance from idols must replace the emotional benefits we are actively trying to receive from the idols with those we find because of enjoying God and receiving Him drawing near. We must repent in keeping with the greater context of what the Bible says about how and why we can drink from God.

Suppose our repentance doesn't take us to stand before the Lord so we can drink from the radiance around Him. In that case, our repentance will be ineffective because our emotional neediness will drive us back to earthly and human sources. If our repentance doesn't help us receive and experience God's presence and kingdom, we won't be cooperating with God in what He wants to accomplish on earth by drawing near.

When you make it your intention to humble your soul from idolatry and take refuge in the Lord as the Bible describes by making declarations of repentance and faith with joy, you gain the **spiritual legal right** to receive and possess the mountain of God and Heaven here (Isa. 57:13; Heb. 12:22–24, 28).

Once your declarations direct your heart into being more open and able to believe the mountain of God and His kingdom are coming down with angels (James 1:17; Heb. 12:22; 28) around you as your armor from temptation (Rom. 13:12–14) and as your strong refuge of protection (Ps. 84:11), you will also understand about spiritual warfare that lets you fight by crushing evil with what you are receiving (Isa. 57:13; Dan. 2:35, 44–45). When we become childlike enough to believe Heaven is coming to us as our refuge, God comes to exercise His justice, righteousness, loving kindness, and truth (Jer. 9:24; Amos 5:24). But if you have trouble believing that at the start, remind yourself that Jesus said we damage our faith for receiving the glory of God by the glory we receive from earthly sources (John 5:44). Therefore, to have the faith needed for doing these things well, you will need to take bold steps to repent by declarations that direct your heart away from your well-hidden idols.

The tabernacle of God is more fully established on earth when we direct our hearts to believe and praise God in ways that help us open up and receive the kingdom of Heaven like a child. The more we do this, the more we help God fill the earth with His glory. Therefore, we must make declarations of repentance and faith that joyously help us turn away from our idols in the context of also directing our hearts toward faith that lets us drink from God instead of receiving from earthly things, other people, circumstances, or ourselves.

---

[10] I will explain more about the process steps later in this book.

6

EMOTIONAL NEEDS HELP GOD FIND TRUE WORSHIPERS

EXPAND YOUR DEFINITION OF GLORY

Understanding the relationship between our thirst for God and our everyday behavior requires that we begin by expanding our understanding of the word glory.

Think of *glory* as the significance and worth of something.

Photo by Jessica Ruscello on Unsplash

Let me repeat that there is a glory God gives and a glory He does not give. The glory God does not give away to anyone is the glory that rightly goes to Him through our worship and praise (Isa. 42:8). The glory that God does give freely is the glory that is the substance of His tangible presence (Ps. 84:11; James 4:8; Ex. 33:18–22). It is right for us to seek and receive the glory that comes from God and not from the world or other people (John 5:44). But we dare not praise ourselves for it or turn His glory into pride.

In this chapter, I will explain that glory is essential to our relationship with God for two reasons: 1) God intentionally designed us to fill our emotional needs by receiving glory from something we can praise, and 2) God wants to be God to us with emotional benefits where the glory that shines from Him keeps us coming back for more (Ps. 36:7–9; Deut. 32:37–39; Jer. 17:5–8; 2:11–13).

Of course, the significance and worth of God's glory is by far the greatest, but the Bible says that earthly things, people, and circumstances also have glory:

- "The glory of kings" (Prov. 25:2)

- "The glory of...pride" (Isa. 13:19)

- The glory of winning a battle (2 Kings 14:10)

- "The glory of...riches" (Est. 5:11)

- "The glory of his house" (Ps. 49:16)

- The glory of a woman's hair (1 Cor. 11:15)

- "The glory of...their strength" (Prov. 20:29)

- "In a multitude of people is a king's glory" (Prov. 14:28)

- "The kingdoms of the world and their glory" (Matt. 4:8)

- People who twist things around, "whose glory is in their shame" (Phil. 3:19)

The glory in these examples is a glory we must earn. The glory we earn from earthly sources brings self-directed praise, which results in pride that makes us feel confident, secure, and worthy. The emotional benefits of earthly glory make it attractive to us. God's glory is greater.

God is seeking true worshipers (John 4:23), so He made earthly sources to have glory that is attractive enough that we have the option of something else to pursue and praise apart from Him. But God's glory is alive, and Jesus earned it for us. Earthly glory is not alive, and the pressure is on us to earn it. When depending on earthly glory we must praise ourselves for what we work to earn. When depending on God we must praise the glory of His nearness and grace that gives it freely. When compared to the truth about God's greater glory, earthly glory is false. The ways we pursue and love the lesser dead glory of earthly sources demonstrate that we may not be the true worshipers that He seeks.

The practical difficulty is that it is easy to see evidence of the glory in earthly things and people around us with our physical eyes. Believing the greatness of God's glory requires a faith that initially feels deeply unnatural.

The faith that satisfies our emotional needs requires a repentance that builds our faith by listening to ourselves make audible declarations that nurture and align our faith with the Scriptures about the power and glory of God drawing close to us by His grace, not by our self-effort or works.

Rather than us having to rely on undependable glory from earthly things, other people, or ourselves, God wants to be the one God whose glory close to us is dependable and certain as what fills us both spiritually and emotionally (Hos. 6:3). Our job is to break up the hard ground in our hearts so that we can receive more freely (Hos. 10:12).

The going forth of God's glory is far greater than earthly glory, is more dependable, and has substance because it has weight (Ezek. 1:28; 2 Cor. 4:17). The good news for us on a practical level is that when we receive God's glory with the freedom of a child who believes they are standing in His radiant shine, God's glory is much more abundantly available to us than what we can ever receive from the world.

Currently, Jesus shines with the radiant Spirit of glory (1 Peter 4:14) that proceeds from the Father and is even now still being given to Jesus freely from the Father (John 15:26; Heb. 1:3). The radiance that shines from God and comes to us like rain is something that never stops (Hos. 6:3). We only have to be open to receiving it and believe He is coming to us in this way (Gal. 3:14). When God draws near to us, it is His Spirit of glory that comes to us here (James 4:8).

It is right for us to receive glory from the radiance around God because God's glory helps us to live uprightly and in newness of life (Rom. 6:4). Jesus asked, "How can you believe, when you receive glory from one another and you do not seek the glory that is from the one and only God?" (John 5:44). Directing our hearts away from idolatry and toward receiving glory from the radiance around God is a hammer that breaks the bondage to earthly sources and idols. God's glory upon and around us helps us to live in greater purity because He becomes a shield around us (Ps. 84:11; Rom. 13:12–14).

The word *glory* occurs in the Bible as a noun, meaning it is a thing (Ex. 24:16). *Glory* appears as an action verb in the phrase *glory in*. When we glory in God, we are putting our confidence in Him and exuberantly enjoying His presence (Phil. 3:3). The

Photo by Tony Eight Media on Unsplash

word glorious also occurs as an adjective that describes the greatness and worth of something (Ps. 145:5).

When thinking about *glory* or *glorious* as a description, we need to think of it as what identifies something as significant and valuable. At the same time, when thinking about *glory* as a noun, we need to consider it a thing that something possesses when it is worthy of praise.

It is challenging to learn this at first, so let me get you thinking about it here. When we receive the Spirit of glory from the radiance around God, we must be careful to keep the praise going toward Him and not let it come back toward ourselves. Otherwise, we are no better than the Old Testament priests who turned His presence into pride (Ezek. 7:20).

EMOTIONAL NEEDS ARE BY GOD'S INTENTIONAL DESIGN

God's intentional design for filling our emotional needs comes from His desire to find true worshipers (John 4:23). Everything about how we satisfy our emotional needs requires worship and praise. How we fill our emotional needs helps separate true worshipers from false ones.

We need glory because, by God's intentional design, only when glory is close to us can we fill our emotional needs. Emotional needs for worth, security, confidence, and identity can only be met well by praise toward the glory of something close to us. God wants to be the one God whose radiant glory satisfies us and keeps us coming back to Him for more (Ps. 63:1–2, 5; 84:11).

SIMILARITIES AND DIFFERENCES

Later in this book, we will consider more details of how we receive glory and what we do with it. But I still need to give you a brief version here.

God's glory has substance and weight and is alive. When earthly glory comes to us, it only brings pride. When God's glory comes to us, His Spirit of glory draws near (1 Peter 4:14). The helpful thing

Photo by Federico Faccipieri on Unsplash

for us is that the processes involved when receiving glory are similar, and we can learn from that.

The most significant difference between earthly glory and God's is that with earthly glory, we have to work at doing something or being something perfectly enough to deserve the glory. With God's glory, we have to believe His grace to draw near because He wants to be God to us here and because of what He wants to accomplish on earth.

When receiving earthly and human glory, we must become worthy before we feel we deserve to open up and receive it. Because God's glory is worth so much more than we could ever earn, it is receiving the glory that shines from God freely with the faith of a child that makes us feel worthy. With God's glory, we have to trust that Jesus earned it and wants to give to us what shines from Him freely. When God's glory is close to us, the significance and value of His glory close to us make us feel worthy even though we didn't earn the glory or deserve to receive it.

To make earthly glory benefit us, we have to praise ourselves. To make God's glory benefit us, we have to praise His nearness around us here. Because of our celebrative, playful, and childlike praise toward God whom we believe has come close, God makes the enemy and the revengeful cease (Ps. 8:2; Matt. 21:16).

I took notes on myself for years before noticing similarities between when I receive earthly glory and God's. The similarities are that we must first open up and believe glory is coming onto and into us (John 7:37–39; Titus 3:5–6). We then have to take ownership of the glory as belonging to us and put it around us for identity and protection.[11] When we put glory around us for identity, we find refuge inside what we have put on.

Earthly glory is an idolatrous substitute for God because when we find refuge inside glory from earthly and human sources, we try to abide in pride about our human glory instead of what we receive from the radiance around God. We are then walking in what is impure and idolatrous. When we take refuge inside glory from the world or the glory of pride (Isa. 13:19), we become easy targets for the demonic to tempt and deceive us.

When we direct our hearts into making God our one God, His glory comes near, and we take ownership of what we are receiving because God being our one God is something that becomes deeply personal. To find emotional benefit and enjoy the glory we are receiving, we have to praise the value and significance of the glory we have received. So everything about how we fill our needs is worship.

---

[11] Glory as our identity and protection is a topic covered in detail later in this book.

Emotional benefits come to us when we believe and intentionally enjoy the nearness of God's power and glory as our refuge of security and strength that makes us confident. When the greatness of God's power and glory is close to us, we feel worthy because of our praise toward His nearness to us as our God. Practical, emotional benefits result when we identify with the glory and power as belonging to us.

Whether from the world or from God, we abide in the glory we receive and put on. For us to depend on God more fully, it is helpful to understand the obstacles of idolatry between us and God so we can make declarations that direct our hearts away from depending on other sources (Isa. 57:14; 1 Sam. 7:3). Below, I will show you diagrams of ways we find substitutes for God.

IN THE IMAGE OF GOD

Human personalities exist because God made us in His image. The Bible says, "God created man in His own image, in the image of God He created him; male and female He created them" (Gen. 1:27). Even though our cultures vary throughout the world, the similarities in our personalities exist because of how God created us.

Although our beliefs and values differ, these four personality styles remain the same.[12] I like to use the names below for the different personality styles.

Task-Oriented	
Analytical Thinker	Driving Doer
Amiable Relator	Expressive Influencer
Relationally Oriented	

Personalities are an outward expression of underlying human emotional needs.

UNDERSTANDING HUMAN NEEDS

People are need-driven. People everywhere need a sense of meaning and impact. We need to feel secure, reassured, and confident to love and be loved. God created us with a need to feel strong and beautiful. But most people call these needs psychological needs or a need for self-esteem. More accurate is to think of them as a need to enjoy having the living substance of God's power, beauty, and love close and resting on us here.

King David's experience of God in Psalm 63 is directly related to categories of ways we try to satisfy ourselves with the greatness of earthly glory and power close to us—apart from God. Human needs that drive our behaviors result from a powerful underlying spiritual need to experience God. It is this way because God designed us this way. Our spiritual need to experience God is more vital and practical than most people realize.

Personalities are outward representations of how we interact with others while meeting our God-given human emotional needs. The diagrams below show that underlying our personality is a way of meeting emotional needs in all areas related to what God is like. As represented in the diagrams on the left, we use all four quadrants in varying degrees, unique to each individual. The reason for this is how God designed each of us.

---

[12] My understanding of this area began many years ago with a class on personality styles. Bob Phillips appears to have used the same source material in his book called *The Delicate Art of Dancing With Porcupines* (available through Christian bookstores at that time). Since then, I have spent many thousands of hours developing these diagrams while trying to think about what is underneath people's personalities. And these diagrams became foundational to developing the tools I will share with you in a later book for directing our hearts toward God.

HOW DID GOD DESIGN US TO NEED POWER AND GLORY CLOSE TO US?

Remember again to think of glory as the significance and worth of something. By the glory we depend on and praise, God learns whether we are true worshipers of what is perfect and good or those whose worship is directed toward the lesser glory of earthly things, other people, or ourselves. By this, God learns which of us will be happy with His extreme goodness, perfection, and holiness in Heaven constantly around us for all of eternity.

This section considers the Scriptures about how God designed us with the needs that drive us toward worship and praise. By God's intentional design, the glory of our humanity falls "short of the glory of God" (Rom. 3:23).

We also know that God designed us with a subtle and vague sense deep inside about the greatness of His glory in two ways. One is where the Bible says, "That which is known about God is evident within them; for God made it evident to them" (Rom. 1:19). The other is that God placed a law in our outer physical body the Bible calls our flesh (Rom. 7:23). The practical purpose of the law in us is to remind us that we fall short of what is known deep inside about God.

So then, it is without choice that the law in us drives us to measure our human glory against what we vaguely know inside about God. When our hearts are bent on filling up our shortfall with earthly and human glory, the comparison makes us feel insecure, insignificant, and lacking worth.

WHAT WE KNOW INSIDE ABOUT GOD

Learning to recognize our desire for God requires carefully considering what we know about the greatness of God (Rom. 1:19). Though it may initially seem cold, sterile, and possibly disrespectful, the abbreviated diagram below will help us discuss our inner spiritual awareness of God's greatness.

God's Pure And Holy Task-Oriented Attributes	
The Wisdom, Knowledge, and Faithfulness of God	The Power, Sovereignty, and Authority of God
The Goodness, Kindness, and Love of God	The Influence, Beauty, and Creativity of God
God's Pure And Holy Relationally Oriented Attributes	

Everything in the diagram above about God has glory in it. To a far lesser degree, the human substitutions represented in the diagrams below also have glory in directly related categories.

Personalities reflect our most natural path to finding glory related to what God is like but generally only in only one or two categories. Just like our bodies need food from different food groups to be healthy, so it is with our spiritual desire and need for God. In other words, it is not just that we want God; we long for closeness to everything true about Him. In time, you will learn to recognize, without condemnation, that you are constantly trying to quench your thirst in ways related to each category of God's attributes.

It is important to organize our idols into diagrams because this helps us with a practical path for deeper repentance. Recognizing these things in yourself should be a reminder to joyously present what you observe before God for cleansing.

The next two diagrams show heart-level idolatrous substitutions for God that are well-hidden and hard to detect in everyday life. Note that we make the things in these diagrams into idols when we find refuge, strength, and glory in them. Later in this book, I will explain how you can use these diagrams as tools for helping you to make declarations that joyously turn you away from human sources and more fully toward God.

GLORY SUBSTITUTIONS WE MAKE

Now, let's consider the related categories of ways we normally try to quench our thirsty desires apart from God. As you look at these diagrams, remember that these things have far less glory than what God offers freely by His radiance. Knowing about heart-level idolatry gives direction about what to trade in when directing your heart into a place of greater delight about the abundance you can receive from the radiance around God (Isa. 55:1–2).

Each quadrant in the diagrams below relates directly to each section in the diagram above, showing what we vaguely know inside about God.

Ways we work to find glory from tasks by faith in our human glory

The significance of what I know; my opinions; what I believe is right; how well I have thought things out; what I justify as right; how well I avoid risk; the wisdom in what I don't do...	What I do; projects I complete; how well I stay in control; my competence and adequacy; how justified I am; my power and authority; respect I get; my being the standard to achieve...
What I Know and Risks I avoid	**What I Do and How Much I Control**
Approval I Sense from Others	**What I Say and How I Appear**
The acceptance and approval I sense from others; people thinking well of me; how much I help others; how well I maintain their approval; how much they need me; my goodness and my kindness...	The impressiveness of what I say and how I appear; who I know; what I acquire; my influence; applause I get; how well I keep people impressed; how I compare to others; how well I keep from getting caught; the pleasure I cause...

Ways we work to find glory from relationships by faith in our human glory

---

Note that working hard, accomplishing goals, and being kind to people are good things. The problem comes when we receive glory from these things and pride ourselves on the sense of security, confidence, or worth we receive from them by self-directed praise. We must find confidence, security, and worth, but God wants to be our source.

That we all are motivated to drink in each of these areas is evidence of our desire for God. Finding reassurance from what we do and our sense of having power is motivated by what we know inside about God's adequacy and His power. We try to quench our thirst with our appearance because of what we know about God's majesty and beauty. We long to find confidence, identity, and value because of our physical attractiveness, but God designed us for something greater.

FEELING SCATTERED?

When you are trying to focus on God, do your thoughts bounce like a ball from one earthly pursuit to another? Do you find this happening to you: "their thoughts alternately accusing or else defending them" (Rom. 2:15)? I call this a *scattered heart* because Luke records Mary saying, "He has scattered those who were proud in the thoughts of their heart" (Luke 1:51).

While the verse above is most likely talking about how God scatters proud people geographically, I think it also applies to our hearts. If we try to quench our thirst with sources that only supply empty earthly glory, we hurt ourselves in the process. One result is a subtle kind of inner panic. That inner panic shows up in scattered bouncing from one earthly possibility of glory to another. When you don't draw near to God and drink, your heart will become scattered because of insecurity and thoughts of wondering whether you are enough.

Am I enough for the task?	
Am I enough to deserve praise inside for what I know?	Am I enough to deserve honor and praise for my power and position?
Am I enough to deserve praise inside for my kindness?	Am I enough to deserve honor and praise for my impressiveness?
Am I enough for the relationship?	

There are some tasks and relationships we may not be enough for. But when our adequacy is of God (2 Cor. 3:5), the human measurement becomes irrelevant because of proximity to the presence of God and His kingdom. When God is our adequacy, He makes us adequate as servant messengers of the new covenant about God's grace and His glory (2 Cor. 3:6–11). The pain from our human inadequacies doesn't hurt as much when we turn away from praising the human glory we gain by works and praise God for His grace that gives His glory freely (Eph. 1:6, 12; Ps. 84:11).

Do you feel scattered? Jesus promised you could find rest for your soul (Matt. 11:28–30). A scattered heart is the result of trying to pride ourselves with glory we earn for our humanity. With God, it isn't about achieving reasons to feel pride. It is about directing our heart to enjoy boasting in the nearness of God (Ps. 34:2).

The practical problem is that pride can make receiving the kingdom of Heaven and staying in the throne room seem impossible. Part of the solution is to understand that one reason for our scatteredness is misplaced delight. If our delight in the Lord isn't strong enough, we will try to quench our thirst elsewhere: "For where your treasure is, there your heart will be also" (Matt. 6:21). In my own life, I use my scatteredness as evidence of my need to increase my delight in God and to reassure myself with His presence. You should too. Trust you are turning toward the Lord and standing in the radiance from the fountain of God. Let Him wash you clean (Heb. 10:22). Hide yourself in the shine of His love upon you. Thank the Lord until you can hear and believe the light of His presence defends you (Ps. 27:1). Doing so will settle your fears and reduce your scatteredness.

Don't let yourself be overwhelmed with grief about the idolatry you see in yourself. Embrace that you are human and need God. These diagrams are tools for repentance and deep change, but when you use them in your declarations, it will look more like joyful gratitude and praise toward God for what you can boldly cut off and don't have to depend on. These diagrams are not for you to use to drill down and figure out what your idols are. Doing that is the job of the Holy Spirit. The purpose of these diagrams is to help you to repent as you use them to help you make declarations with thankfulness about what you don't have to depend on and that you can more fully depend on God.

WAYS WE PROTECT OUR HUMAN GLORY

There are many problems when we try to find the emotional benefits we need from the glory of earthly and human sources.

The sources we depend on are directly related to the quadrants in the diagram about what we know deep inside about God (Rom. 1:19). The diagram below describes ways we react to the insecurity and fear that result when we try to quench our thirst apart from God. When we do that, the pressure is on us to try and protect the level of human glory we pridefully think we have achieved. The problems below result from trying to fill our desires for God with emotional benefits of reassurance and security apart from Him.

Note that even though I have been at this for a long time, I continue to grow in these areas by listening to myself with agreement as I thank God that these are not the ways I need to find glory. I thank God that I can stand before Him and trust the power of His radiance upon me to wash me clean.

Ways we protect our human glory and respond to possible emotional pain

CYNIC: holds back, "the risk is too great"	DICTATOR: gets tougher, busier, demands more
Disguises hopelessness as wisdom; avoids being confrontational even when needed; holds back for safety; avoids admission when wrong; holds to disbelief for self-protection; wants more details before making decisions; safer to stay inside the lines; ignores the problem until it goes away; doesn't want to walk about it; can appear religious while withholding love	Gets tougher; demands more control; works harder to force more results; misuses position and authority; justifies themselves more; condemns more; motivates others by fear and intimidation; "just do it"; fights harder; hardens themselves to what God says and wants; hurts others more; avoids submission; controls and dominates
Fears any potential risk	**Fears loss of control or blocked goals**
Fears disapproval from others	**Fears loss of impressiveness or influence**
Relates more warmly; gives more of self; gives up, "why try?"; blames self; works harder to deserve approval; bitterness for power and self-protection; manipulates sympathy; intentionally submits to tyranny and intimidation to avoid disapproval; passive rebellion; avoids disapproval by justifying what others do wrong; plays submissive to stay safe; finds power by taking offense; self-hate; never says "no"	Laughs to avoid getting uncomfortably deep; avoids being alone; power by withholding relationship; works to prove impressiveness; manipulates with envy; avoids admission of guilt; puts others down; vengeful; blames others; manipulates emotionally; gossips; relational revenge; sarcasm; slander; makes verbal attacks; exaggerates; stays energetic and dominates time of others until they are impressed enough to give applause
FATALIST: holds back, "the risk is too great"	COMEDIAN: stays surface or angry verbal attacks

Self-protection is complicated because of the risk we feel when we might lose glory from earthly sources.

If life doesn't cooperate and we can't glory in what we say or how we appear, then we make ourselves look good by how well we put other people down. If you want approval from people, it may be that you put yourself down. This way, you glory in the power you feel in putting yourself down, and it keeps you from lashing out and making other people mad at you.

If you typically quench your thirst with what you do, then you will likely try to dominate more to maintain control, allowing you to keep accomplishing your goals and plans. Achieving your goals gives you a feeling of success that you can drink from to maintain your pride. But doing this can keep you insensitive and callous and often hurts the people you love the most. Even subtle demands to stay in control keep you trusting yourself and feeling insecure when trying to depend on God as your security.

> One Christian's glory should not be another Christian's pain! Loving others and finding unity in the church is impossible when we are in this state. Because we all fall short of the same God, all God's people must repent in these areas.

Our desperate attempts to protect ourselves result in many problems. The psalmist was right when he said, "It is better to take refuge in the Lord / Than to trust in man" (Ps. 118:8). Protection based on human effort is a tangled and complex web that keeps us in bondage. You can learn to rest from your human ways of self-protection. Listen to yourself making bold declarations that direct your heart into believing God can and will be a better God to you than what you can be to yourself. Fight against holding back with declarations that boldly and joyfully humble you from the pride of self-protection and into loving the fortress of God's calming and holy presence.

GLORY AND SELF-ESTEEM

Emotional health requires that we feel good about ourselves. But there is more than one path to arrive at that end. Think of self-esteem as a label for the process most of us go through to feel good about ourselves.

Since glory is a measurement of worth, self-esteem is directly related to the glory we come to possess throughout our lifetime. We feel worth when we can identify with glory that we believe belongs to us and when we praise that glory close to us. When we feel worthy because of earthly and human glory, the resulting pride damages us spiritually because it decreases our sense of needing God and increases the false belief that we can be a better god to ourselves than He can.

When we try to drink from earthly glory and praise the glory we find, we feel a sense of well-being from self-esteem, but we still feel empty, and our protective shield is only made of the pride we put on around us. Pride is damaging because God resists pride, and pride makes us want to resist God (James 4:6). Pride increases the evil in the world because the demons glory in our pride. They push us toward pride so they can party in our rebellion against God.

Instead of pride from living to the praise of our glory, we need to be intentional to enjoy the confidence, security, and joy-filled significance that comes from living to the praise of God's Spirit of glory that we believe draws close to us here by His grace (Eph. 1:6, 12; 1 Peter 4:14; Gal. 3:14).

God wants to be with us because He is good and wants what is good for us. When we cooperate with God's desire to be God to us, we help Him fill the earth with His glory, and Heaven gets more fully established on earth because of what we receive.

Because God wants to be our glory here (Jer. 2:11–13), He also wants to be the one God whose presence makes us feel worthy. It is right for us to feel worthy because of the glory of God close to us. It is right for us to praise His nearness as the one God who belongs to us personally. The benefits of this path for feeling good about yourself far outweigh the short-term benefits of esteeming yourself.

Don't wait until you feel God's presence! The life we now live is by faith (Gal. 2:20). Before you feel God's presence, you can feel great personal worth because of God; praise the greatness of His presence that you are teaching your heart to believe is drawing close to you here. When you keep praising God's closeness to you, opening up and depending on Him are more natural, and His presence comes easily.

EMOTIONAL BENEFITS OF WHEN WE FIND GLORY

Most people think of the list below as human emotional needs. I see them as emotional needs that get filled when we receive glory from something, and we respond with gratitude and praise toward what we have received. Because of how we fill needs like these, it is better to consider them as benefits that come to us when we find glory from something. The real need is to find glory and respond with gratitude and praise. The items in the list below are the benefits we gain.

Filling emotional needs through enjoying the nearness of God is what He wants for us. Note that the list below is not ordered by importance because the practical benefit needed completely changes from one moment to the next.

When we find glory that we believe comes upon and around us, that we can own as ours, and that we enjoy with gratitude and praise, we fill the emotional needs because we feel:

- reassured
- joyful
- happy
- secure
- protected
- satisfied
- filled
- loved
- approval
- soothed
- comforted
- calmed
- helped
- righteous
- good
- perfect
- attention
- acceptance
- supported
- hopeful
- a sense of belonging
- goodness
- inner peace
- quietness
- healthy
- healed
- financially sound
- provided for
- confident
- bold
- special
- influential
- treasured
- glory
- beautiful
- attractive
- impressive
- courageous
- powerful
- strong
- honored
- dignified
- important
- thrilled
- delighted
- significant
- we have an audience
- applause
- fearlessness
- adequate
- a sense of authority
- able to convince people
- pleasure
- excitement
- newness
- recognized
- great
- validated
- worthy
- valued
- justified
- a sense of meaning
- a sense of identity
- fruitful
- there is a reason for faith

Finding a sense of having glory we can praise relieves boredom and provides a way to escape emotional pain and stress.

These are the emotional benefits that result when we find glory drawing near that we can enjoy with praise. But we know from Scripture that God wants to draw near and be God to us in ways that bring these practical, emotional benefits.

When you boil things down to the heart-level kinds of twisted and human glory in the diagrams above, we all do all these kinds of things listed. Why is that? Our desire for human glory suggests we all want all of God.

Our part is to change our thinking patterns of dependence on earthly and human glory so that our faith can increase to that of a child. Sometimes the glory we must turn away from is the glory we find from how well we hold back and protect ourselves. When your declarations help you cut that off, and you present your self-protection before God for cleansing, God's part is to respond and draw near because we have set our faith to believing that He is coming (Gal. 3:14; Hos. 6:3; 10:12). When God comes, He draws near as a refuge around us and as what cleanses us from the idolatry and sin of our earthly and human dependencies.

Don't let yourself be bogged down in sadness and gloom when you realize you aren't as perfect or righteous as you thought. When you recognize you depend on your own human righteousness and perfection, your attitude needs to be one of joy about repenting from it and making another trade (Isa. 55:1–2). Don't wait to present yourself before the Lord for cleansing and for His presence as your safe refuge. Listen to yourself making declarations that cut off running away and trying to hide yourself in despair and hopelessness. The power you feel from self-hate is not the power you want.

PRACTICAL EVIDENCE OF OUR DESIRE FOR GOD

The diagrams above help us recognize that we naturally enjoy and praise glory related to every aspect of what God is like. We want glory close to us in all these areas because that is how God designed us to want Him.

God enjoys being good to us. He wants us to enjoy that about Him. Could it be that enjoying His goodness is part of what God is looking for when He says He is seeking true worshipers?

God designed us with the capability of enjoying His goodness because of how He wants us to enjoy and praise Him being God to us. Everything about the idolatrous substitutions we make for God is evidence that we want Him. Like King David, we must come to a playful, childlike place in our faith that lets us trust that the sanctuary of God is drawing near so that we can satisfy ourselves with faith that sees the closeness of God's power and glory to us in every aspect of what He is like (Ps. 63:1–2, 5).

Recognizing our practical need and desire for God helps us go deeper in faith about what we can receive. God designed us to experience and enjoy His beauty and majesty close to us. We should not settle for confidence in our own physical appearance. Most of us don't fit into the category of beautiful people. But if you do, what about when you grow old? Reassurance and confidence from how we appear is impractical because it doesn't last. We need to ease our fears and teach our hearts about what to believe so we can let God be the God whose beauty close to us is what we treasure and enjoy as ours.

Photo by Cynthia Magana on Unsplash

I remember being in a crosswalk while a big semitruck was trying to turn. It had to stop for me. Knowing the driver couldn't turn until I got out of the way gave me a twisted sense of power. It didn't have very much glory, but subtly, I was quenching my thirst for God with how well I could stop that truck. Immediately after I realized what I was doing, I confessed it by thanking the Lord that I didn't have to feed myself with the power of how well I stopped the truck. Then, while trusting I was turning to face toward God, I thanked Him that He was washing me clean as I opened up inside to drink from the radiant fountain of His living power and glory drawing near to me.

Even though stopping trucks may seem like a silly example, I believe this is the level at which we often try to find substitutions for closeness to the presence of God. When so much of God's presence is readily available, the last thing we should do is to feed ourselves by earthly means. My point here is that just wanting God instead of earthly glory is not enough to change us. The patterns of thinking and dependence run deep and require intervention before we can change on such deep levels. Our hearts must be directed to believe God enough that we can open up to Him and drink.

Why do we praise ourselves inside for our kindness, how smart we are, how perfectly we did something, how powerful we feel, or the extent of our influence? We praise ourselves because the glory of these things is directly related to the glory of what God is like. All of it relates to measuring up to God in some way. Our hearts have learned that enjoying glory such as this eases our sense of falling short and makes us feel confident, reassured, secure, and worthy. Listen to yourself making declarations that lead your heart into joyfully believing you can change your thinking patterns and dependence to aim toward God and open up to what pours out from all around Him.

Embrace that you feel emotionally needy at times because you sense deep inside that God's attributes have far greater glory and worth than you possess on a human level. According to the verse in Romans 2:15, one minute, our thoughts can be defending us and we are praising ourselves inside for the glory we believe we have achieved in a worldly sense. The next minute, something happens that shows we fall short in some area and we feel insecure and accused by it.

God wants us to enjoy depending on Him instead of earthly and human glory. The big picture of good news in the Bible is that God wants to be God to us rather than us having to depend on the lesser and more uncertain and often damaging glory that comes from ourselves, other people, or earthly things. When your heart learns to receive like a child, everything about God has glory, is good, and is more freely available to you than any glory you could ever get from the world.

GOD'S GLORY IS A SIMPLE TRADE

Of course, it isn't fun to think honestly about our hearts when we recognize that we glorify ourselves with praise because of finding glory from the things in the diagrams above. But the repentance God desires is "without regret" (2 Cor. 7:10). What if we were to repent by changing our minds without the self-inflicted regret that doesn't really change anything and only makes us feel bad?

Jesus promised us an abundant life (John 10:10), and our God is a fountain of life we are to drink from like a child (Ps. 36:7–9). What if we were to make declarations of faith about that and the truth in the verse that follows?

> Ho! Every one who thirsts, come to the waters;
> And you who have no money come, buy and eat.
> Come, buy wine and milk
> Without money and without cost.
> Why do you spend money for what is not bread,
> And your wages for what does not satisfy?
> Listen carefully to Me, and eat what is good,
> And delight yourself in abundance. (Isa. 55:1–2)

Earthly glory is what we work for. God's glory is given freely to us by His grace because of the holiness He wants for us and because of what He wants to accomplish on earth. According to the verse above, we buy an abundance from God by trading the earthly glory we normally try to work for and earn. How would your life change if you were to believe you could trade dependence on earthly glory for what shines from God twenty-four seven? Jesus earned it for you! Jesus lived a sinless life; He died, rose again, ascended into Heaven, and was glorified so that He could freely pour out onto you what brings salvation and what makes you victorious in this life.

What if you were to change your thinking patterns by being delighted about cutting off the ways you receive glory from things like those in the human glory diagrams above and trusting with delight that God is coming freely to you in abundance? If you do your part, God will be true to His Word and come to you.

Just be sure that you don't get bogged down with the idols in the diagrams by trying to determine whether you are living in sin. Doing that is the Holy Spirit's job. Where there is obvious sin, ask for forgiveness while you trust you are standing in the cleansing radiance of God (1 John 1:5, 7). But don't hold back from God when you recognize sin! Boldly trust He is drawing near and washing you with His holiness.

Then use the idolatry listed in the diagrams to joyfully make declarations about the many ways you can turn your heart from works to grace. Changing from works to grace is the essence of what we must focus on for repentance! Thanks and praise about the individual idols we get to turn away from are the tools we use to help us get at changing the root cause. Use the idols listed in the diagrams as tools for repentance that help you aim your joyous declarations at changing from works and pride to God's grace and boasting in His glory that freely draws near if you will open up and believe you are receiving it.

Photo by Ben White on Unsplash

We all are different. But we also are very much the same. One person might specialize in finding glory from how well they impress people, while another specializes in glory from how kind they are and how well they avoid disapproval. Some enjoy the glory of the goals they accomplish. Still others would combine the glory from what they know with glory from some other area. But none of us stop at just one or two categories of glory.

I have tended to specialize in glory from people's approval. Yet even recently, I was told by someone who cares that I sometimes still misuse power in the forcefulness of my speech. I have made a lot of declarations about cutting off my dependence on people's approval. But I still have more work to do in turning my heart away from forcefulness in how I sometimes talk. Do I let myself be discouraged about the growth I have yet to do? For the most part, I do not. I see it as another way I can humble myself from earthly glory and increase my faith for receiving more of the radiance from around God (John 5:44). By repentance that changes my patterns of dependence and thinking, I trade in my human glory, and with that, I get to buy a greater abundance of God's glory given freely to me by His grace (Isa. 55:1–2; Ps. 84:11).

WHY DO WE DO WHAT WE DO?

God designed us as He did to determine whether we will be true worshippers or those who will love and worship a lesser glory than His. Human neediness drives us to worship the glory our hearts learn to treasure. Your heart can learn something new! By listening to your declarations of repentance and faith, you can direct your heart into being more childlike in your faith until your heart treasures the closeness of God instead of the glory of earthly things.

The beauty of this is that our behavior follows what our hearts treasure. So when you treasure receiving the presence of God like a child, your behavior improves and becomes more aligned with what you have come to believe and love.

Evil exists because it gives us a choice to glory in something apart from God. Only by giving us another option can He find those who will be true worshipers. That is all changing in our day because now is the time when God's people need to rise up in their faith and receive what crushes evil. But for this to happen, it must be both effective and practical.

Our hearts must first hear and believe that the presence of God is available, right, and safer than earthly sources. After that, we must learn to open up to God and trust Him to come to us so that we can learn from our experiences that God is a better and more dependable source of glory than what the world offers. So we start with declarations of repentance and those that also build faith in God as our most loved source.

But we dare not be careless about these things. Depending on God and drinking from Him is not purely about filling our emotional needs. God wants that for us. But we must change how we fill our emotional needs so that He can fulfill His good purposes for us and what He wants to do on earth. I will discuss the big picture later. Let me continue here with reasons why we need God's presence with us practically.

We do what we do because finding glory we can praise eases our sense of falling short. But we have a choice. When our hearts come to believe our constant need to have God close to us, we glorify and honor Him with our gratitude for Him drawing near instead of staying in bondage to earthly glory. Let me be more specific.

We need the sovereignty of God close to us because when we lose control, we feel insecure. Having God close may not fix our circumstances immediately, but when we praise the closeness of His sovereignty, our fears decrease and our love for God increases. When we believe the strength and power of God are close and we praise that, we feel powerfully strong, and our confidence is high.

When something happens that makes us feel a lack of power or control, we sometimes try to make up for what we lack by hurtful behaviors. Even when the behavior is twisted and damaging, it can seem worth the pain if the emotional need feels met. You must be honest about heart-level sin and repent with joy to deal with these things decisively. Embrace the truth about your humanity: you will still fall short of God's glory, even when you praise yourself for the power and dominant control you felt in the behavior.

Photo by Jack Sharp on Unsplash

Use the discipline you apply to finding human glory to building faith and confident hope that helps you to receive the kingdom around you, stand before the Lord, and trust by faith that you are looking at Him (2 Chron. 29:11; Ps. 123:2). When you trust the radiance of God is coming into the earthly realm around you, God's kingdom comes, and His will is better able to be done on earth as it is in Heaven (Matt. 6:10, 33).

Jesus became sin for us so that we could receive something of His righteousness onto and into us (2 Cor. 5:21; Titus 3:5–6). The righteousness of God includes His goodness. But when we have not set our hearts on the glory and goodness of God, our falling short takes over, and we praise ourselves when we are good or kind to someone. This eases our sense of falling short, but this doesn't solve the problem of needing to be good compared to God. Only God's goodness near to our humanity and touching our skin can do that (Ex. 29:37). You have to get your heart to hear and believe God's goodness is being imparted to you by believing the radiance of God is coming onto you.

Listen to yourself thanking God that "as for me, the nearness of God is my good; / I have made the Lord God my refuge" (Ps. 73:28). When you trust God to draw near so He can be the one God who is your refuge, His goodness draws near to you here. When you praise God for that, God becomes your God to the point that you feel something of His goodness belongs to you personally.

Consider the unhealthy drive we often feel toward perfection. The Bible says that we are to be perfect as our heavenly Father is perfect (Matt. 5:48). Because of salvation, we already have the righteousness of God in us (2 Cor. 5:21). The righteousness of God also includes His holiness and perfection. When you believe the perfection of God has drawn near and is touching your skin, something of the perfection of God gets transferred to your humanity because that is how things work in spiritual realms (Ex. 29:37). This eases your unrelenting drivenness to achieve perfection. Then, when you praise God for His perfection close to you, the tension to achieve perfection by your efforts decreases.

What if you applied this principle in other areas? Would you feel beautiful yourself if you confidently believed the majesty and beauty of your God was close and you joyously praised Him for the greatness of His beauty touching your physical body here? You would.

The emotional needs we feel because we fall short turn all of us into worshipers of glory from something. Because of God's wisdom in how He designed us, we have no choice except to depend on His grace for the glory and power we need close to us here. Otherwise, our neediness drives us to rely on idols, false gods, and self-directed praise to compensate for our human lack of glory. What is the practical side of directing our hearts to depend on God to draw near so we can fill ourselves emotionally and spiritually by praising His glory close to us? The attractiveness of idolatry and sin falls way off. Our love for God increases. The significance of our spiritual power goes up dramatically.

Because behavior flows from what our hearts believe and love about how we make up for falling short, your repentance must change you from depending on works aimed at earning glory to depending on faith in the grace of God that gives us His radiant glory. Joyous declarations about being able to cut off and turn away from the idols we are, or even might become, dependent on is the key that unlocks greater faith for depending on God like a child who cuddles into His nearness.

THE POWER OF SIN

Sin is the inevitable result of trying to quench our thirst by earthly means that are inadequate to supply what we long for most. The Bible says, "The power of sin is the law" (1 Cor. 15:56). It also talks about "sinful passions...aroused by the law" (Rom. 7:5). The law arouses sinful passions when we ignore the availability of God's Spirit of glory (1 Peter 4:14) and demand to ease our sense of falling short by earthly means. Whenever we view our human flesh as more significant than God's presence drawing close by faith and touching us, the law is right there, reminding us that our humanity's glory falls short of what God is like.

There are two sides to the attractiveness and power of sin. Both result from a sinful reaction to the law in our flesh, where we put faith in self-effort that we must work to achieve glory rather than humble ourselves into receiving it freely from God (Gal. 3:2–3). The first result is that we are "carried away and enticed" by our own lust (James 1:14). The other is temptation. The first comes from inside us because of unmet emotional needs that reveal themselves when the law reminds us that our humanity falls short. The second reason sin has power is because of temptation that comes from outside us because of the demonic. We must solve both problems by applying the solutions God has provided.

Having a law in our outer body that reminds us of our lack forces us to turn to God or to sin. But when we don't draw near to God by enjoying that His glory is drawing near to us as the comfort and reassurance we need, we open ourselves to temptation, and even the twisted power we feel from rebellious sin can soothe us.

The lure of sin is all about a way we can find reassurance, worth, and power apart from God. If it isn't that we are being drawn away to sin because of an in-the-moment emotional need, we are being tempted by the demonic to fill an emotional need apart from God. Most of the time, these two things work together. It is helpful to think of these causes separately to correct our sin problem more effectively.

> While there are two categories of causes for why sin is attractive at times, dealing well with these causes helps us to prevent sin from becoming attractive.

When we feel insecure, finding glory we can call ours is what we depend on to reassure ourselves. But earthly glory is never enough because it only gives us enough to know we want more. We are left empty and desperately wanting. Those are times when even the twisted power we feel in rebellion can feel like it has glory.

The Bible confirms this by saying, "'Behold, the man who would not make God his refuge, / But trusted in the abundance of his riches / And was strong in his evil desire.' / But as for me, I am like a green olive tree in the house of God; / I trust in the lovingkindness of God forever and ever" (Ps. 52:7–8).

> You remove the power of sin when you let yourself receive the presence of God upon and around you as the refuge you depend on and intentionally enjoy as your reassurance and comfort. By hiding yourself in God, the closeness of His power and the worth of His glory help you find the reassurance and soothing you need in a holy and pure way. When you are hidden in the presence of God as armor around you, and you use declarations to bolster your faith about God and His holiness as your strong refuge, temptation can't get through to you (Rom. 13:12–14).

Without quenching the practical emotional side of our thirsty need for God, the pain of unfulfilled desire for God gets the best of us. We then become weak and are tempted to try to fill ourselves with something that might ease the pain, soothe us, and satisfy our craving.

When personal purity results from self-discipline, it is only as deep as your disciplined behavior. But purity from self-discipline does not bring purity to your heart. If you want heart-level purity, you have no choice! You must experience the presence of God lavished upon you as what satisfies your emotional cravings and as the armor you need all around you that prevents temptation. When we lack the armor we need and are weak emotionally, temptation has a much easier time getting to us.

Please trust me in this. When you begin to experience God as the armor you treasure and praise, you can rest in Him without reaching for earthly glory, and it isn't nearly as easy to fall into temptation. When you faithfully remind yourself that it is the closeness of God's holiness and Heaven around you that you love, nothing else is nearly as attractive anymore. When you are being reassured and finding the thrill and pleasure you need purely because of the presence of God, your ability to say no to sin increases dramatically. The push to reassure yourself with sin is much, much lower.

The Bible says, "If riches increase, do not set your heart upon them" (Ps. 62:10). Rather than having a heart set on having to make sin work for us, we need to set our hearts on quenching our thirst with the Spirit of God: "He did evil because he did not set his heart to seek the Lord" (2 Chron. 12:14). When you set your heart on the nearness of God, His presence becomes armor to you, your neediness feels satisfied, God around you fights the demonic tempting you, and sin is much easier to resist.

Sin gets attractive when earthly glory gets old enough that we get bored with it. When your heart believes the abundance of God's glory is always new and always being refreshed as He comes to you, it is easier to thrill yourself about the glory and power of God's kingdom coming in an ongoing way. By this, your boredom greatly decreases.

You can find the strength to say no to temptation by finding reassurance and thrill in a holy and pure way because of God. Listen to yourself as you thank God for the truth until you treasure it; doing so will help you prevent sin (Ps. 119:11). Be like King David who told himself to boast in God (Ps. 34:2). Assertively tell yourself to believe and enjoy that the Bible says you can "put on the armor of light . . . put on the Lord Jesus Christ, and make no provision for the flesh in regard to its lusts" (Rom. 13:12, 14).

Our humanity needs reassurance and protection from the light of God's power and holiness. Humble yourself from pride until you can joyfully embrace that our human glory falls short and that you need God's presence with you here. If, by receiving the presence of God, you put on and enjoy wearing the Holy Spirit with praise, you will be much stronger and won't be "carried away and enticed" by your own lust (James 1:14). Be intentional to forget none of God's benefits by enjoying Him as your reason for courage, reassurance, protection, significance, beauty, and

strength. By this, the close presence of God Himself will be quenching your thirsty desires (Ps. 63:1–2, 5). Only be sure to also enjoy applying faith to believing God's presence around you and that His angels are fighting the demonic and protecting you (Rom. 16:20).

Don't think you have to believe the glory of your humanity before you are good enough to draw near to God. Your justification for drawing near will only be your pride if you do. Your physical body yearns for God (Ps. 63:1–2, 5). Humble yourself into childlike faith by declarations that move you toward filling that yearning, whether you think you are ready or not. Let God draw near and trust Him to cleanse your hands and heart as what justifies you and makes you ready (Ps. 24:3–4; Heb. 10:19–22). You must humble yourself into believing you can receive the presence of God as armor that reassures you and crushes the demonic. Otherwise, the twisted glory of sin will eventually become too strong for you to resist.

The Bible says, "I...affirm together with the Lord, that you walk no longer just as the Gentiles also walk, in the futility of their mind, being darkened in their understanding, excluded from the life of God because of the ignorance that is in them, because of the hardness of their heart; and they, having become callous, have given themselves over to sensuality for the practice of every kind of impurity with greediness" (Eph. 4:17–19). The life of God flows from Him because He is a radiant fountain (Ps. 36:9). If we Christians harden ourselves from believing the radiant glory of God is available to us, then in a practical sense, we too are excluded from the life of God that flows from Him because we will fall back and settle for the twisted glory we find in sin.

Do you want freedom from sin? The Bible tells us, "Through Him everyone who believes is freed from all things, from which you could not be freed through the Law of Moses" (Acts 13:39). The way to find freedom is by believing you are continually receiving so you can walk in the light of God's holiness that shines from Him (Rom. 6:4). Listen to your declarations about playfully receiving God's presence and enjoying Him as you punish the demonic by what you receive into this realm from God (Ps. 27:5–6). Doing that softens the hardness in your heart and builds your childlike faith so you can enjoy loving God with freedom from sin.

The Bible says, "Your word I have treasured in my heart, / That I may not sin against You" (Ps. 119:11). More than knowing the word of God in your head, let your heart believe and treasure God's truth about how you receive His presence instead of the temporary benefits you find from sin. Avoid sin by declarations that get your heart to treasure the truth in God's Word that you draw near to God by trusting Him to draw near to you here.

Don't let yourself think that God doesn't want to draw near to you! He does. Make declarations that help you to believe it! Repent with bold certainty because your repetitious declarations can break down your walls and convince your heart of the truth that you want God more than you want sin. You can have His presence lavished on you abundantly because your God is a radiant fountain you can draw near to, open up to, and freely receive from (Eph. 2:18; 3:12). Make declarations that teach your heart to enjoy and treasure believing it.

RECEIVE AND REST WITHOUT REACHING

When you observe yourself honestly over time, you might notice something inside you that feels like it is reaching out toward sin. In my case, I watched this about myself in the area of lust. It was like I was reaching out from within myself to find glory that way.

The Bible explains this by saying, "If we had.../ extended our hands to a strange god, / Would not God find this out? / For He knows the secrets of the heart" (Ps. 44:20–21). "Like a city that is broken into and without walls / Is a man who has no control over his spirit" (Prov. 25:28). The reason God considers the secrets of the heart is because the hands we extend are from within us. When we reach out toward sin from within ourselves, we become like "a man who has no control over his spirit." When we extend our inner hands to find glory from something earthly, we lower our protection and become "like a city that is broken into and without walls."

Let me say that another way. When we extend the inner hands of our human spirit to find refuge, strength, and glory apart from God, we lower our shield and damage our protection. Temptations can come to us because our walls are broken down and are not protecting us.

Another thing I have noticed about opening up like this is that temptation may not happen immediately. When that is the case, it can be helpful to pause and reflect on the last day or two to recognize when you reached out from within and lowered your walls.

What can we do to keep from extending our hands and lowering our walls of protection? It is all about learning to receive God's presence as a wall of protection around us so we can rest in Him. Listen to yourself making declarations that direct your heart away from reaching toward the twisted glory you desire from earthly sources. Direct your heart into the faith that believes the Scriptures about freely receiving God's presence and kingdom around you as the refuge of protection you need. Then you can rest without reaching by clinging to His closeness to you here.

When we receive Heaven here like a child, the mountain of God and Heaven come down to us with angels from above (Mark 10:15; Heb. 12:22–24, 28; James 1:17). When you believe Heaven has come down, you can cling to the closeness of God and His kingdom.

The Jewish Feast of Tabernacles is a picture of finding refuge in the Lord. It is also called the Feast of Tents or Booths. Think of what it is like to enter a tent when camping or when a child plays tent with a blanket over a card table. When you enter, it can feel like something has come around you that feels safe. Finding refuge in the Lord and resting in Him is like this.

We cling to earthly things because they make us feel reassured and worthy. We cling to God for similar reasons, but remember again that when we take refuge in the Lord as God desires, we possess the mountain of God (Isa. 57:13). To "walk in the Light as He Himself is in the Light" (1 John 1:7), enjoy and thrill yourself that you too are "covering Yourself with light as with a cloak, / Stretching out heaven like a tent curtain" around you here (Ps. 104:2).

If I were reading this in my college years, I would have thought all of this sounded crazy. So please remember again that if what I am saying sounds complicated or unbelievable to you, it will become simple when your faith becomes more childlike after you direct your heart from works that earn earthly glory and toward God and believing His grace for the glory you receive (John 5:44; Mark 10:15).

When you humble yourself into making declarations that teach your heart to believe and you are intentional to confidently trust you are opening the gates above you while believing, you are receiving the mountain of God and Heaven coming down around you as a tent of protection (Ps. 24:7–8; Ps. 27:1–6). Then, while in the house of the Lord (Ps. 92:13), you can trust that roots are growing down into Him through your feet into the top of the mountain. By this, it gets easier to abide before the Lord in the throne room, and we become "oaks of righteousness" (Isa. 61:3). At the time of this writing, I am using thanks and praise to remind myself to trust that leaves are growing for healing (Ezek. 47:12).

This box is important. When the mountain comes, it brings Heaven with it (Ex. 15:17). So when the inner hands of your human spirit hold on firmly to the mountain of God down near the floor around you instead of reaching out of you for earthly glory, something deep inside you relaxes and rests. Even at seventy years old, the inflammation in my body decreases dramatically.

The main advantage to resting in the Lord (Heb. 4:9–10) is that by holding onto the weight of the mountain of God down by the ground around you, it gets much easier to abide and stay focused on being before the Lord with an open Heaven above and around you here. By clinging to the top of the mountain through your feet, you are "planted in the house of the Lord" (Ps. 92:13). You are "walk[ing] in the Light as He Himself is in the Light" (1 John 1:7) and the "perfection of beauty" is all around you (Ps. 50:2). When you "put on the armor of light" (Rom. 13:12) like this, you will be far less likely to reach out toward sin if your inner hands are resting at your sides down near the floor on either side of you (Ps. 44:20–21; Prov. 25:28).[13]

Humble yourself into faith for this because receiving the mountain of God and kingdom of Heaven around you and then resting in the Lord like this is profoundly effective for avoiding sexual sin and lust.

In my case, it works best to trust I am holding onto the top of the mountain and kingdom of Heaven around me where I am resting on my inner hands down by the floor behind me. With practice, I have found I can rest in the Lord this way, even when I am standing or in a group of people. Clinging to the Lord and resting on your hands down by the ground makes it far less likely that you will reach toward a different glory source.

The church today desperately needs greater protection and effectiveness in our fight against evil and in our pursuit of heart-level purity and holiness. Like in Nehemiah, our walls are broken down and need to be rebuilt. To rebuild the walls, our thinking patterns must change from heart-level idolatry to loving and clinging to the Lord. You can train your heart so that you freely receive Heaven here and rest inside without continuing to reach out from within you toward sin or other glory substitutes for God (Ps. 27:5–6). Your motivation for clinging to the Lord stays high when you hold onto Him like a child who loves the kingdom of Heaven around you as your safe refuge and as your basis for significance.

Receiving from God and resting while clinging to Him may be the most important thing I could ever teach for finding ongoing freedom from sin. There is a long story behind how I learned to do this, but it will come in a later book in this series.

IN THE CHURCH

The world is in opposition to a life of faith and loves to promote its idols. Sadly, few in the church today seem to understand the dangers of heart-level idolatry; even fewer know what to do about it. When listening to preaching at church, it is easy for me to get sucked into thinking that the only thing we can do for purity is to keep trying to behave better. I find this thinking deeply damaging and must guard my heart against these views.

Making purity practical requires that I make declarations to realign my thinking with the Scriptures regularly. Trying hard is important, but I often remind myself that the best path to purity requires effort that focuses on what our hearts believe and love about God because everything about our behavior flows from that.

---

[13] For avoiding lust, I cannot emphasize enough the value and importance of resting without reaching like this.

Sometimes, after being around other Christians, I have to use declarations to turn my heart away from pride about God's presence coming to me because of something about who I am. I have to teach my heart by declarations to embrace that God comes to me by His grace. I thank God for salvation, but then I also have to remind myself to abide in a continual cleansing from God so that I am prepared for Christ's coming and will not end up like other Christians who will shrink away in shame when He returns (1 John 2:28; 1:7).

Receiving the kingdom of Heaven like a child is profoundly effective for maintaining holiness and fighting evil. But Christians today need to recognize that the inner muscles of our spirit that easily open up inside us to receive glory from earthly sources must be joyfully redirected and used to our spiritual advantage (Ps. 44:20–21; 24:7–8).

ONGOING DECLARATIONS

As an ongoing practice, I have had to:

1. use repetitious declarations that turn my heart from believing and loving sin, pride, and rebellion toward God as a means of finding any kind of emotional benefit or feeling of power,

2. use declarations that strip everything else away and make me utterly dependent on opening up to God and receiving His presence so that I can fill my emotional needs in a holy and pure way,

3. use declarations that build my faith for using the opening-up muscles inside me to swing open the heavenly gates above me easily (Ps. 24:9–10; Heb. 10:19–22) so that I can rest into confidently believing I am receiving armor that is holy enough to protect me and keep the demonic away or to burn and crush them if they get close (Ps. 27:5–6), and

4. stand before the Lord with angels all around (Rom. 12:1; Heb. 12:22–24, 28) and rest with those same opening-up muscles clinging to the top of the mountain on either side of me near what I believe to be the bottom edges of the tent of God's presence down by the floor around me here.

More explanations come later in this book and then again later in this series. Just know that without directing my heart to joyfully strip away emotional benefits from earthly and human glory, I would not have been able to boldly believe or understand how to do the things I describe in this book. The prevailing paradigm and disregard in the church and the demonic realm fight hard against childlike freedom and faith for doing these things easily.

Persistent, courageous, and joyful declarations of repentance and faith help us break free and boldly trade our human glory sources for God and an abundance of His glory with us here (Isa. 55:1–2).

I don't mean you have to leave your church. Your declarations must help your heart to hear and believe so you can break free of the unspoken pressure to stay controlled and to walk in disbelief. It is not the people you have to fight; it is a spirit of Jezebel at work to control and keep church people in bondage.

Don't wait to feel God's presence. Before you believe God is near to you, teach your heart to find refuge in Him by trusting you are entering inside His presence, that it is like a tent that you believe with confidence is coming down from above onto and all around you here (Ps. 27:1–6; James 1:17). When your heart learns to embrace the availability and the closeness of God as your safe refuge, He will come, and I am confident that if you haven't felt His presence before that time, you will then.

I can't stress enough the value and importance of resting in the Lord by trusting you are clinging to His closeness down low by the floor all around you. Every time you reach from inside toward the world's glory, you lower your armor and are open to temptation (Ps. 44:20–21; Prov. 25:28). The moment you are aware that temptation or evil has come, return to entering again by trusting you are receiving Heaven around you here. Trust that God is washing you as you enter so you can rest inside His kingdom with your physical body before the Lord here (Rom. 12:1). By entering again, you are helping to more fully establish the dwelling place of God on earth (Rev. 21:2–3).

When your heart learns to love receiving and resting inside like that, it is far less likely that you will reach toward lust or sin. When you rest in the Lord, instead of reaching, your inner hands will cling to the lower edges of the tent of God around you, your armor will stay strong, and God will burn up temptation as you make joyous declarations about the power of God's holiness close to you here (Rom. 13:12–14; Isa. 4:4).

By directing your heart into treasuring the availability, righteousness, and purity of God close to you, you can maintain consistent heart-level purity by resting in Him. Then, if evil thoughts do come over you, don't waste time. Trust the cleansing blood of Christ is washing over you as you immediately put the armor of light back on and rest in it again (1 John 1:5, 7; Ps. 104:2).

I have learned by experience that I don't have to settle for impure thoughts or temptation. By teaching my heart to treasure receiving the kingdom of Heaven around me (Mark 10:15), and then by resting in the Lord by clinging to Him with my inner hands, Heaven itself has become my greatest treasure (Matt. 13:44). By this, I can be purposeful to enjoy that witchcraft and the demonic beings that come after me get punished, burned, and crushed every time they try to get to me (Rom. 16:20; 1 John 3:8; Ps. 27:5–6).

A BRIEF STATEMENT ABOUT DRINKING FROM GOD

There is a human side of drinking from God that has emotional benefits to us. There is also a more spiritual side of drinking from God that involves receiving His presence and kingdom. Both are important for purity of heart and practical holy living.

Even though I cover the spiritual side of drinking from God later in this book, I still need to make a brief statement about it here. The difficult thing we have to get our hearts to believe is that when God comes to us, He comes to us purely because we believe He is drawing near by His grace not because of anything we have done to deserve His coming.

Now, let me briefly state the more human side of drinking from God. Because God's presence is not something we can easily see or earn, our hearts need to be taught and led into a place of enjoying and loving God for the emotional benefits that He brings. When you embrace God as your God, your relationship with Him becomes personal. You identify with Him as belonging to you.

When you identify with God as your God and believe like a child that His glory is drawing near, you more naturally feel a sense of personal ownership of the greatness of God's glory that comes close to you here. When you feel ownership of God as your God and enjoy praising the radiant glory you confidently believe is close to you here, you cling with love to His closeness, and the emotional benefits you feel are many. His closeness to you becomes what you identify with and praise as your identity. Our sense of meaning and purpose soars because we enjoy praise and worship toward God with far greater energy and freedom.

IT IS NOT WRONG TO SEEK THE GLORY THAT SHINES FROM GOD

One problem in our thinking is that even though Jesus said we should be seeking the glory that comes from God instead of from the world (John 5:44), many of us Christians believe it is wrong to even consider doing such a thing.

As I have mentioned before, there is a glory God does not give (Isa. 42:8) and a glory He does give (Ps. 84:11). The glory that God gives freely is the glory that is the substance of His tangible presence: "Moses said, 'I pray You, show me Your glory!' And He said, 'I Myself will make all My goodness pass before you . . . and it will come about, while My glory is passing...I have passed by'" (Ex. 33:18,

22). So the glory God gives is the glory that is Himself.

We must have God's glory close to us or the need that drives us toward sin goes unmet. We must direct our hearts into a childlike faith that lets God and His kingdom come because that is how His will can be done on earth as it is in Heaven (Matt. 6:10, 33). Our problem with independence from God is only corrected when we trust God to draw near so that we can satisfy ourselves with Him instead of staying in bondage to earthly and human sources.

YOU CAN LEARN NEW PATTERNS OF DEPENDENCE AND THINKING

Remember that God put a law in our flesh to remind us that the glory of our humanity doesn't measure up to the

> It is not selfish for you to believe God's grace that lets Him freely draw near to you here.

greatness of God's glory (Rom. 7:23; 3:23). Throughout our lives, through thousands of repetitions in our experiences, the result of the law in us becomes written into our hearts as thinking patterns about what to depend on for filling our need for glory with us here (Rom. 2:15).

Our hearts learned to drink from the glory of the world, other people, and ourselves. Our hearts can learn new patterns of thinking! But you will have to teach your heart what to believe and love.

We naturally drink from glory we find in earthly sources because we can see evidence of it with our physical eyes. When starting on this path, it is not natural for us to drink from God, even though that is what God designed us to enjoy doing. When you stay on this path, your momentum builds, and it eventually becomes far more natural to drink from God every moment than from the world's glory!

Based on many Scriptures, it is right for us to believe that God wants to draw near and that He is coming to us here. It is right because God wants purity for us and because of what He wants to accomplish in our world. Seeing with eyes of faith that God's power and glory are drawing close and surrounding us is something we must teach our hearts to believe and love (Ps. 63:1–2, 5). After the patterns become more dominant about drinking from God, you will never want to go back to drinking from the world.

You can learn to depend on God and the radiance that never stops pouring out from all around Him. You only have to intervene with declarations that build your hope and freedom until the glory your heart treasures playfully is redirected. You must teach your heart to more courageously embrace the truth about what is freely available to you in abundance (Isa. 55:1–2). Walking the path of becoming more playfully childlike in your unhindered hope, confidence, and freedom about God and then drawing near so you can stand before Him and abide in His presence is the only way (2 Chron. 29:11; Ex. 15:17; Ps. 91; Mark 10:15).

The beauty of God's design is that we are not in a hopeless place. We can transform our minds in ways that result in new patterns of thinking and dependence on God. More about this topic comes later in this book.

Our hearts learn thinking patterns about what to depend on; you must teach your heart by listening to your joyful declarations that more is available to you than the glory of earthly sources. Be joyously assertive as you keep telling your heart about what you know in your head is right and good for you to believe and love about God drawing near to you so you can stand before Him here and drink from Him instead of the world.

THE BIG PICTURE OF GOOD NEWS IS ABOUT GOD BEING GOD TO US HERE

All of this is tied together. Remember that God's end goal is for Heaven to come to earth so that the tabernacle of God can be among us here (Rev. 21:3). When we turn away from pride and become more childlike in our dependence on God as the one God we drink from, Heaven comes to us so that He can be God to us here instead of us having to depend on what we receive from earthly things. By this, we cooperate with God's grand goal of bringing the kingdom of Heaven to earth.

Remember also that the new thing God wants to do is that He wants to give drink to His people (Isa. 43:18–20). Remember that the gospel is for the "afflicted" and the "needy" who are "seeking water" where "there is none" and that God says He will answer them Himself (Isa. 41:17–18).

Consider now that the gospel is good news. The main benefit of the gospel of salvation has to do with eternity. But the afflicted and needy aren't thinking about eternity. They are thinking about the present. If they aren't thinking about food, water, or shelter, they are thinking about security, being worthy, and being enough.

To be practical, we need to be more specific. We considered the verses about how God defines idolatry. God wants to be our refuge, strength, and glory because these represent the emotional benefits we gain when loving a glory source we can depend on fully.

Photo by Hannah Busing on Unsplash

When people receive glory apart from God, it feels like self-esteem. But glory from the world is inconsistent, and you never know when the source will hurt you. It is an understatement to say that earthly glory is hurtful and doesn't work well enough.

The reason the good news is good news for the afflicted and needy is that beyond the needs of food, water, and shelter, the needy are freely able to drink of the radiant glory around God, and if they are intentional to enjoy the closeness of God to them in this way, they become confident, bold, secure, worthy, and significant, and have a strong sense of identity. When their hearts learn to let the mountain of God come with Heaven and angels, God fights evil on their behalf.

The big-picture gospel is practical and profoundly relevant to everyday living because the main benefits of living the gospel of the kingdom and the glory of Christ have to do with the present (2 Cor. 4:4; Matt. 4:23; 24:14).

Let me repeat that we are not to have other gods before the Lord (Ex. 20:3). According to the Bible, we have to drink from something to receive in a way that adequately fills our emotional needs—and God wants to be the only God we drink from. The beauty of this is that it all fits together perfectly. What blesses us the most is exactly what helps to accomplish God's purposes on earth. When God draws near as our refuge of protection, we receive Heaven here as our shield that bludgeons evil and crushes it under our feet. When we become playfully childlike in our love for God, we fight evil decisively by what draws near as our refuge.

TURNING FROM IDOLATRY AND TOWARD GOD UNCLOGS THE PIPES

We need salvation. But Jesus also told us to abide in Him. On some levels, because of salvation, we already abide in Him (1 John 4:13). But the practical evidence is that we need God's presence and kingdom with us intensely enough twenty-four seven to keep us from being drawn back into idolatry and sin (Rom. 13:12–14; James 1:14).

The Bible says, "We...receive the promise of the Spirit through faith" (Gal. 3:14). So our faith for receiving from the radiance around God is vital because what we believe we are receiving in that moment determines whether we are receiving at all from God. The problem we must correct is that receiving earthly and human glory damages our faith for receiving the radiant glory of God (John 5:44). Even as Christians, our faith can be so damaged by glory from earthly sources that easily receiving from the abundance of glory around God seems unreal and out of consideration.

Doing this is difficult at the start because, without you realizing it, heart-level idolatry can easily be great enough that everything about receiving the kingdom and presence of God seems impractical and utterly unbelievable to us on an everyday level

Even if it is hard to believe that you are receiving enough glory from the world to damage your faith, you should take it by faith that the extent that you receive earthly glory is the extent of the damage done. How many times have you tried to repent and the immediate result did not include the presence of God coming to you as cleansing and armor? When that does not happen, your repentance is not enough and needs to change (Acts 3:19). Repentance that changes our minds about depending on God instead of idolatry unclogs the pipes so that we can receive from God more easily and in simple ways, like a child would.

Without any background understanding, children can be told God will come to them when they open up to Him, like when they open up inside to receive a smile from someone, and God comes. We, as adults, aren't like that because of years of history built up from the glory we have pushed to receive from the world, ourselves, and other people. We need to see Scriptures that explain receiving to our head so that our hearts have something solid as a foundation for our faith. Then, we have to lead our hearts into a place of faith. That is why this book is necessary.

WHY IS IDOLATRY SO DAMAGING?

Earthly and human idols are substitutions for God, and there are demonic beings that push us in those directions. Don't let life get so twisted that you decide embracing evil is better! Think of what it is like to find glory in despair or hopelessness. In a deeply twisted way, embracing despair and hopelessness can feel like security and protection because they make us isolate ourselves.

At the very least, the demons want us to stay away from God, and despair and hopelessness accomplish that goal. At worst, when we fall in love with the protection we feel from hiding ourselves in despair and hopelessness, we are clinging to these things. Like a garbage can lid with handles on the underside, we have extended our hands to hold onto the demons pushing us toward idolatrous substitutions (Ps. 44:20–21).

What do we gain when we get angry and take offense toward someone? It feels like power, but it is a substitution for the sovereignty of God. When we fall in love with that power, without realizing it, our soul clings to the demons behind these idols instead of to the nearness of God (Ps. 63:8; Jer. 13:11).

Note that when we cling to idolatrous substitutions for God, we aren't clinging to something far away from us. We have drawn the idol close to us here. This demonstrates in a personal way how God wants to be God to us and how we were intentionally and specifically designed to depend on His closeness to us here. When we direct our hearts to treasure making God our God and we apply bold faith to the power and holiness of God drawing near to us, He draws near, and with the flick of His finger, He forces the demons off of us and out of the way.

What can we do to change at such a deep level? Don't try to discipline your behavior when the problem is with your heart. True repentance doesn't change you by pushing on your behavior. It pulls your behavior along because you believe and treasure what is a much greater glory.

Listen to yourself make audible declarations with joy where you thank God that you don't have to live in bondage to the power you feel from anger and taking offense at someone. Thank Him with the attitude that your declarations are cutting off your earthly dependencies and that you are gladly turning to open up and drink deeply from God. Thank God with childlike freedom and delight that you don't have to settle for despair and hopelessness when you can have the nearness of God and cling to His holiness upon and all around you here.

Rather than extending your hands to cling to other gods, your heart can learn to cling to God. Let your declarations of joy retrain your thinking and love until it becomes natural for you to believe you are receiving Heaven here and are clinging to the nearness of God in a similar way to how you have been clinging to ungodly substitutions.

WHAT ABOUT SHAME?

We all feel shame when we do things that we know are wrong. But shame can include self-hate, and this makes us tend to avoid situations where we think there is a risk of failure. When the fear of pain from failure gets too high, we fear that failure might cause more shame than we can bear. Here, the goal of the shame isn't to gain more worth but to protect the little amount of worth the person thinks they have.

Self-imposed shame isn't nearly as painful as shame from a legitimate failure, so we try to hold back and avoid even the possibility of failure. In this case, shame becomes a protective mechanism that helps us maintain minimal feelings of security.

When we learn to depend on shame for self-protection, demonic enemies are free to push shame on us almost anytime they desire. I know this sounds twisted, but I lived in this place for many years. My heart had to learn a better way.

When shame becomes a tool for self-protection, what is the emotional need we are trying to meet? Part of it can be reassurance and security. Another part of it can be our longing for perfection and rightness.

When they do something imperfectly, some people react with self-imposed shame that keeps them from ever wanting to try again. Teach your heart to believe the cleansing power of the perfect blood of Christ. Trust you are presenting the failure and the people you hurt before the Lord so that He can pour His presence over them and bring healing. Trust also that the perfection of God is coming into the situation and onto you. What is the basis for believing this?

When considering the topic of shame, we must remember that when the altar was made holy, God said, "Whatever touches the altar shall be holy" (Ex. 29:37). This applies to when Moses felt shame at the burning bush (Ex. 3:6). Moses felt shame, but the presence of God made the dirt holy under the feet of Moses (Ex. 3:5). When God had Moses remove his sandals, the physical feet of Moses touched the holiness of God, and God transferred something of His perfection to Moses through his feet. God washes shame away when we abide with His holy presence touching us inside and outside (1 John 2:28). The holiness of God is powerful for removing shame because whatever He touches is either burned up (Isa. 4:4) or it becomes holy also (Ex. 29:37; Heb. 12:29).

The cleansing of God's holiness washing over you is powerful enough that even when the Heavens open, you won't feel shame because God is washing your physical body as you abide with your humanity in Him (John 15:4).

Self-acceptance comes when your declarations help you value the holy perfection of God close to and touching you as having more glory, worth, and significance to you personally than anything about your imperfections and reasons for shame.

We must remove the obstacles in our thinking and practice that keep us from running to the Lord when we are being attacked or feel dirty from sin. Even if it is the only thing you can do, learn to use the times when you don't feel unworthy or full of shame to direct your thinking and love toward God so that you can more easily run toward Him when life does get more complicated. Your attitude should be to joyfully receive the presence of God and the peace of Heaven to punish the demonic for attacking you (Rom. 16:20; Ps. 27:5–6).

BE DETERMINED TO ENJOY SATISFYING YOURSELF WITH THE NEARNESS OF GOD

I have already used these verses, but let me bring them up again here. King David said that he was thirsty for God. He also said that his physical body yearned for God. But the passage doesn't stop with David staying miserable and thirsty! David says that his soul was satisfied by seeing the power and glory of God in the sanctuary (Ps. 63:1–2, 5). Seeing by faith the power and glory of God in the sanctuary close to us is the result of receiving the sanctuary of Heaven around us and then looking at the Lord before us here. When we enter by receiving Heaven around us and look at God's face, His radiance strengthens, protects, reassures, and makes us confident (2 Chron. 29:11). More is available to you than you may have thought.

Still, though, how often have you read about David being thirsty "in a dry and weary land where there is no water" while not seeing the following verses explaining how David's thirst was satisfied (Ps. 63:1–2, 5)? The reason you have not seen that David's thirst was satisfied is that the glory you receive from earthly sources has damaged your faith for seeing what the Bible says in many Scriptures about freely drinking from God (John 5:44; 2 Cor. 4:4).

This chapter explains the connection in Scripture between idolatry and the emotional benefits we find when glory comes to us here. Later, we will consider how to make the change from well-hidden idolatry to God. Directing our hearts away from idolatry prepares us to drink freely from God with fewer obstacles and distractions.

More explanation is needed, but let me be clear because I don't want you to be miserable.

You cannot just cut off earthly sources without also taking the next step that turns your heart toward God in ways that result in you being able to drink and receive from Him. Don't get stuck in the middle! It works best to make declarations that cut off earthly glory and then quickly follow them up with a declaration that gives your heart reasons to believe you can drink from God.

Even though you may feel uncomfortable with declarations of faith, you must take that step in turning to God at the same time you cut off earthly sources. If you only make declarations of repentance, you might make great strides in your spiritual growth. Still, though, eventually you could easily be enticed to go back to idolatry and hidden sin because self-protection will want to push itself back onto you. You must replace what you are trying to gain emotionally from sin and idolatry with a pure form of an emotional benefit that can come from the closeness of God. You must also find protection because of the mountain of God and Heaven with angels drawing near (Isa. 57:13; Heb. 12:22–24, 28). The sooner you can do that, the better it will be for you.

Remind yourself often that it is holiness and purity that you love. You are miserable with impurity in your heart or a feeling of impurity resting on you. Expose by faith the areas of evil trying to hurt you before the holiness of God and rejoice about the power of God's holiness in you (Isa. 4:4). Thrill your heart about the Spirit of judgment coming to increase the holiness around you.

You cannot be half-hearted in your application of these things. Once you start down this path, you must stay determined to make it work. Your repentance must become both practical and deep enough to result in your ability to depend on God in ways that replace the benefits you gain from sin and idolatry or all of this falls apart and doesn't work. Make your repentance a joyous act of worship with gratitude and praise toward God.

Photo by Botto on Unsplash

7

PROCESS STEPS FOR DRINKING FROM GOD

GLORY AND WORTH BY NEAR-PERFECT SELF-EFFORT OR GLORY AND WORTH BY FAITH IN GOD'S GRACE

I like the definition of *grace* I heard years ago when someone described God's grace as the "givingness" of God. God's grace is in play when He freely gives what is good for us, even when we are unworthy and undeserving to receive the greatness of what He is giving.

Remember again that glory is the worth of something. When we can believe we have glory, we feel worthy. When we feel worthy, we feel self-esteem. But most people don't easily grow up feeling worthy. The most common path to self-esteem is difficult and painful because few of us are born into a situation or with traits that give us reason to believe we automatically deserve glory. Having to achieve glory comes with many failures. These failures are painful. Staying worthy by the world's standards requires a consistent, near-perfect performance that is impractical to maintain.

Because of failure or mistreatment from others, many feel great pain because of their lack of self-esteem. For the sake of those the Bible calls "afflicted and needy" people, we must be practical about this topic (Isa. 41:16–18).

To have faith that you are worthy to receive glory that brings self-esteem, you have to perform perfectly enough to believe you deserve to receive it. With God, it is the opposite. You have to believe Jesus earned the glory that shines from Him for you and for what He wants to accomplish in the world.

The value of God's glory is so great that none of us will ever deserve to receive it. With God's glory, you must humble yourself into believing that Jesus has already performed perfectly and was glorified enough for you to receive the abundant radiance that shines from Him. You must also show gratitude and praise Him for it (Heb. 12:28). Because of Christ's glorification, you can drink from Him the radiance that shines from all around God (Ps. 84:11; Isa. 55:1–2).

With earthly glory, the pressure is on you to achieve enough perfection to be worthy of the earthly glory you receive. Then you can praise yourself in ways that bring pride. With God, the pressure is on Him to draw near so He can perform as your God in a practical way. With earthly and human glory, you have to perform well enough to be god to yourself. With God, you must humble yourself enough to become childlike in your faith that Jesus died on your behalf and that the Father glorified Him so that Jesus can freely give you what the Father keeps pouring into and through Jesus on our behalf. When you can get your heart to trust the grace of God enough to open up and believe you are receiving and being enveloped in the radiant glory of God, you get to praise Him for what you receive and boast in His greatness near to you here (Ps. 34:2; Jer. 9:24).

The question is: will you glorify God with praise and depend on Him to draw near, or will you rely on your human effort to earn glory and worship yourself as your god because of it?

When depending on God as our God, the good news is that we don't have to rely on the glory we earn. We don't have to worry about failure because, with Jesus, the perfect performance is already complete. When we fail, He washes us clean (1 John 1:5, 7). By our response to failure, we can still glorify and honor Him. We only have to believe enough that Jesus earned the glory for us to stay open and keep receiving what shines from Him (John 5:44).

Of course, we have to intervene by listening to declarations that go against the grain of the worldly paradigm around us, but when we direct our hearts away from the world's glory and toward God as our God, everything changes. When we can accept God's glory is coming to us with the unreserved faith of a child, God gives His radiant glory freely (Ps. 84:11). We only have to trust God to draw near and bring Heaven with Him so that He can wash our unworthiness away, cleanse the atmosphere of evil around us, and accomplish His will in our world (Matt. 6:10).

Direct your heart into strong and playful faith about the radiant glory of God coming to you as the abundant life you were promised (John 10:10; Ps. 36:9). The glory that shines from God is far more certain and dependable than any earthly and human glory we could ever earn (Hos. 6:3). We only have to believe with the faith and delight of a child that He is coming to us abundantly as He has promised (Gal. 3:14; Isa. 55:1–2).

INTRODUCTION TO DRINKING FROM GOD

Even after salvation, our humanity still falls short of the glory of God (Rom. 8:10). Because we fall short in every area of what God is like, even earthly glory can feel like it satisfies our lack on some level. Anytime we receive glory from something, we drink from it (Jer. 2:11–13). The good thing about all of this is that we can learn from the process steps we go through when we drink from earthly and human sources. The same process can and should be reapplied to God.

True repentance brings the presence of God (Acts 3:19). If that isn't happening, your repentance hasn't changed your thinking enough yet. Don't get caught in the middle where you have cut off earthly sources and aren't yet drinking from God. Being stuck in the middle between sources is a miserable place. Remember that your declarations of repentance and faith need to become a lifestyle of joyous, audible worship that is filled with gratitude and praise. When that happens, you will find the freedom you need to open up and drink from the radiance around God like a child.

Are you a person who is already familiar with the presence of God? The way I see it, any time the presence of God draws near, we have already applied the process steps of drinking toward God. Even if you already understand about receiving the presence of God, the steps in this chapter can improve your receiving. Experiencing the presence of God doesn't have to be hit or miss. When you apply the process steps to drinking from God, His "going forth" will come to you in ways that are "as certain as the dawn" (Hos. 6:3). You can direct your heart into receiving continually enough to stay in His presence and before the throne twenty-four seven. Improvement is always possible.

The practical key for us is that the inner processes of how we drink and receive from idols are substitutionary steps for the internal processes of how we can drink and receive God's presence. Drinking from earthly and human sources is a natural and ongoing part of everyday living. When reapplying these steps to God, we only need to consider what we are already doing toward earthly and human sources. When we consider the Scriptures as light on the steps we go through when drinking from the world's glory, we can then reapply the steps to our drinking from God in a big-picture way that satisfies our emotional neediness while also bringing the kingdom of Heaven to us here.

Someone has said that you can only improve your repetitious work once you break it down and understand the individual process steps involved. When we break it down into steps, the steps we go through in the process of drinking from God are similar to when we drink from the glory that comes from idols. Don't think you are unfamiliar with the steps involved, though you may need to think about it for a while to recognize them. If you observe yourself over time, you will see that you are doing these things regularly.

Even though we apply these steps to worldly glory, these are also the steps we must use to receive from God and feel like He is satisfying our neediness. To improve our drinking from God, we must be more intentional in applying these steps toward Him. Knowing the steps gives insight that helps us break the process into parts to be more specific about where we can improve.

Don't let this seem complicated. Children apply these steps without thinking about them. You do also. It will only seem complex because I am verbalizing what we do subconsciously. The difficulty for us is that being childlike as adults is challenging. The value of knowing these steps is huge because being specific helps us as adults to more effectively drink from God and keep on drinking from Him.

EIGHT PROCESS STEPS

This section is high among the most important things you will read in this book.

God is our creator, and He designed our need for Him into us because He wants to be what satisfies us (Ps. 63:1–2, 5). The process we go through to drink from earthly things is a reaction to God's intentional design within us. It is just that we are misapplying these steps toward idols and sin.

I broadly state the steps below to include earthly sources, but I do this so you can recognize them and then joyfully turn what you are doing around and aim it toward God.

To apply these things to God, you only need faith that believes the radiance of God at a similar level to the faith you have when receiving acceptance and approval from someone's smile or when feeling worthy because of being inside a new car you own.

❶ First, we have to find a source of glory we believe will be reliable and won't hurt us.

❷ Then we do something that makes us believe we have earned glory and deserve it, we naturally have something that makes us believe we deserve glory, or we believe someone else has earned or deserves glory and they are giving it to us.

❸ We have to open up to it inside and believe the glory of it comes close.

❹ We have to enter what we receive by putting it on around us.

❺ We have to own and love the glory as belonging to us personally.

❻ We must love, honor, and feel gratitude toward the source.

❼ We have to praise the greatness of the glory we have put on.

❽ We have to enjoy the much-needed emotional benefits.

Whether we are drinking from earthly and human sources or God, the process steps involved in drinking from the glory of these things must all be applied or we won't receive full benefit from it.

When drinking from God, we drink by believing God's grace that He is coming to us freely and that as He comes, the resulting gratitude and praise go toward God and the greatness of His glory not toward ourselves. It is all about directing our hearts away from idolatry (1 Sam. 7:3) and into loving the closeness of who God is and Him being our I Am.

Let me remind you again that it is the power and glory of God in the sanctuary close and all around us that satisfies us. God also made us so that our outer physical body yearns for Him. The beauty of God's wisdom in His design is that our emotional needs get met, and we love and praise Him more while receiving Heaven to earth (Rev. 21:3).

According to the Scriptures, drinking from God so we can receive His presence as our shield should benefit us on a practical emotional level. Ignoring our thirsty need for God in everyday Christian living is unwise. We need God's presence close to us here. We also need the emotional benefits of loving and enjoying Him in playfully childlike ways. Forgetting none of His emotional benefits helps us greatly in our worship, loving attachment to God, and purity of our everyday living (Ps. 103:2; Rom. 13:12–14).

Now, consider the steps more closely.

First, we must find a source of glory and power we believe will be reliable and won't hurt us.

We must find a source of glory and power we believe will be reliable. If we don't believe it will be reliable, interests will change, and we will eventually move on until we find something we believe has greater glory.

We also have to believe the source we depend on won't hurt us or we won't be able to open up to it and drink freely. If you fear relying on God in these ways, listen to yourself thanking God for the truth that His glory and power are greater and far safer for you than what you could ever receive from the world. Receiving the presence of God and Heaven around you protects you. Teach your heart to love the closeness of God for all His many benefits.

Second, either we, or someone else close to us, has to earn the glory or deserve it naturally.

Finding a source of glory and power can be good news for us or bad. To find a source of glory, we only have four options. We can depend on ourselves, circumstances, other people, or the closeness of God.

When we depend on ourselves, we have to do something we believe makes us worthy to receive glory. Some people can rely on circumstances, like when they are born with special skills, are strong, or are good-looking. But most of us aren't like that. The other option is that we have to believe someone else has earned or deserves glory and because of their nearness to us, they are giving it to us freely.

Depending on someone else who naturally has glory only works well with God. If we find another person who is popular, strong, or beautiful and they want to be close to us, there is a sense in which they are giving their glory to us freely. But relationships based on human glory seldom work well. If the person leaves us, part of the pain we feel is from the loss of glory we had when they were near. When our glory is from them and they aren't around us for even a short time, the glory we felt fades away.

With God, Jesus earned the glory that shines from Him. When we believe with "full assurance of faith" (Heb. 10:22) that the greatness of His cleansing glory has drawn near enough to wash us and be glory to us here, we can boast in the greatness of His glory and all of life works better (Ps. 34:2; Phil. 3:3).

Photo by Ben White on Unsplash

With earthly and human glory sources, what we do earns the glory that demonstrates our worth. With God, it is becoming childlike enough to depend on Him as a good Father who gives us an abundance of His glory that makes us worthy (Isa. 55:1–2).

The bad news with earthly and human glory is that we have to live life with the constant pressure of needing to perform well enough to successfully deserve receiving glory from our friends, what we do, what we say, how we appear, sports, or what we control. With earthly and human glory, the possibility of failure in our performance is overwhelmingly certain and often results in fear that paralyzes us.

With God, the glory that shines from Him is always dependable and certain (Hos. 6:3). Because of God's grace, we can define success by glorifying God with our love and childlike dependence on Him. We can receive from God by faith and perform at high levels that honor Him instead of ourselves and without fear of failure. When success for us is glorifying God, our performance can be less than perfect, and we can still honor God by how quickly we jump up and return to receiving and loving His closeness like a child (Matt. 18:4).

The good news with God is that we only have to become more childlike in our complete and utter dependence on Him to give His radiance to us freely. With earthly glory, we have to trust that the perfection of our work is enough to earn it. With God's glory, we have to trust that the perfection of the work Jesus did by His death was enough to earn the glory given freely to us by God's radiant grace (Ps. 84:11; Num. 6:22–27).

With human glory, we work to keep achieving and receiving glory to advance the evidence that we are worthy of pride that justifies our existence on the earth. With God and His glory, we only have to keep receiving because that is what advances the evidence of His worthiness and justifies the goodness of what He wants to work on earth.

When it comes to drinking from God, being able to do this step requires that we listen to ourselves making joyous declarations of faith about the truth that we are able to rely on God with certainty about His coming to us and washing us clean (James 4:8; 1 John 1:5, 7).

Listening to declarations of faith helps to transform our minds in ways that align our heart-level thinking with the truth in God's Word (Rom. 12:2). Listening to our declarations of faith breaks up the hardness in our hearts and helps us to believe we can receive the kingdom of Heaven and the presence of God (Hos. 10:12; Gal. 3:14; Mark 10:15).

If you are afraid to open up to God in these ways, listen intently to yourself as you thank Him that He wants to draw near and be your safe refuge. Keep making declarations about God wanting to be your "refuge and strength" and your "very present help" until your fears decrease and you find the freedom you need to allow God's radiant presence to draw near and surround you here (Ps. 46:1).

Photo by Jake Hills on Unsplash

of our ongoing neediness as a child and because He wants to accomplish great things on earth by drawing near to us here (Josh. 3:5). Whether earthly glory or God's, we have to open up inside while believing the glory is actually coming to us and is now close to us here.

Again, note that the faith that pleases God believes He is rewarding us with His presence (Heb. 11:6). Enjoy that your childlike faith about His coming to you makes God feel pleasure! But how much confidence do you need to drink from God and receive His presence here?

You only need to believe God as strongly and freely as when you believe a smile from someone is for you and you open up inside to receive a sense of acceptance from it. Observe your level of faith when opening up to drink from the glory of simple earthly things and people. Then, reapply that same level of unquestioning faith to drinking from God while showing gratitude about His drawing near before He comes and after.

Be patient with yourself on this first step because your heart may be much farther from your head than you realize. When depending on God as your one God and loving Him instead of idols, you have to use declarations to direct your heart into embracing what your head is choosing to believe and love and what you are no longer going to be afraid about (1 Sam. 7:3).

Don't be passive and wait until you naturally respond with greater reliance on God. Assertively lead your heart into a place of depending more fully on God. Give your heart reasons that help you believe God's glory is safer and a far better path to significance than any earthly and human glory you could ever find. Be patient and kind with yourself while transforming your mind, but you dare not be soft or let yourself be indulgent toward idols; "be zealous and repent" (Rev. 3:19).

Third, we have to open up to the source inside and believe the glory of it is close.

We have to direct our hearts to confidently open up to God while believing that God's radiant glory is coming to us because

When directing your heart toward being able to believe you are receiving from God, determine with zeal that your heart will hear the truth of the Scriptures and joyfully make declarations that direct your heart into childlike faith. Take it by faith that the glory you receive from other sources is damaging to your faith for receiving glory from the radiance around God (John 5:44). Listen to your repetitious and joyful declarations that cut off earthly glory so you can trade the lesser glory of those things for an abundance of what you can receive from God (Isa. 55:1–2). Enjoy the greater glory of God coming to you, and direct your heart into being motivated by your ability to receive glory far more intensely than any earthly glory you could ever experience here.

Listen also to yourself making declarations of faith that thank God audibly, over and over, for His coming to you by His grace and His desire to improve our world. Keep listening to yourself give thanks until the truth of it sinks into your heart, and you will find the freedom you need to open up like a child and receive playfully well. If you aren't receiving God's presence and kingdom yet, keep thanking Him that He is coming. Eventually, your heart will hear it and believe the truth. When that happens, He will come.

Sometimes, the demonic or witchcraft try to damage our faith and hold things up. Fight through this kind of opposition in three ways. Make an audible declaration that you are binding the power of the demonic and witchcraft sent to hurt you and your faith for receiving from God (Matt. 16:19). Then make an audible declaration that loosens faith, spiritual skill, and freedom onto yourself so that you can freely receive from God and His radiance. After that, fight through the opposition and increase what you are experiencing by more repetitious and joyful declarations of thanksgiving about God and His kingdom coming to you here abundantly (Isa. 55:1–2; John 10:10; Heb. 12:22–24, 28).

Fourth, we have to enter inside what we are receiving by putting the glory of it on and all around us here.

When we receive glory from the world, we put it on and make what we receive an idolatrous refuge around us. Think about something as simple as the acceptance we feel in a smile. It isn't just that we open up inside to it; we receive it in a way that lets the approval from the smile envelop us all around. The same is true for daydreams about receiving glory from something. We enter into the daydream and put it on all around us here. When daydreams become a hiding place or an escape for us, we depend on them as idolatrous substitutions for the presence of God and the kingdom of Heaven around us.

Putting on the glory we receive is essential on a practical level because when we do that, the glory of it becomes a refuge of protection and identity around us. Think of identity as something we put on and wear, a name tag that completely envelops us. Making God our refuge and shelter makes the closeness of His presence our identity; this helps us with holiness on a practical level.

When identity works as God intended, it is a protective shield around us. The problem is that a smile from someone does almost nothing to protect us. When the strength of our identity comes from us, our identity is attackable by other people, circumstances, and evil.

When the strength of our identity is because of the closeness of God upon and all around us, our identity is unattackable. When the presence of God and the kingdom around you become your identity, the strength of your identity dominates evil while, at the same time, you become more kind and loving toward people around you.

Wanting to put the glory we receive onto and around us directly results from God as our creator. But what we receive and put on around us should come from God. Observe and learn from what you do with the glory you receive from smiles, what you know, daydreams, and your influence and impressiveness. What we do with the glory of these things should be applied to putting on what we receive from God.

Fifth, we have to own and love the glory as belonging to us personally.

Think of when a woman borrows a coat, and someone compliments her on it. Even though the coat looks good on her, she doesn't experience emotional benefit from the compliment because she doesn't own the coat. When she owns the coat and receives praise for it, her love for it increases with that compliment, as does her confidence and sense of well-being. The same is true with God. We must enjoy Him as the God who is close and who belongs to us as our God. If we don't, we are more easily drawn back into receiving from the world and sin.

Owning God as our God involves making Him our God in ways that result in us identifying as one whose God is the Lord and nothing else. It may seem obvious, but in our day, it is essential to be precise. Just because a person identifies as a cat or a person of a different gender does not actually make them become what they identify as. Likewise, we don't become a car when we put on the glory of a new car as our identity. The new car's glory helps define the significance of who we believe we are, but we don't become the car.

The same is true with God. When we own Him as our God, we don't become God. When we identify with Heaven's closeness to us as our identity, we honor God greatly. We also much more clearly define the significance of who we are, but we don't become God ourselves. Like children, ours is a dependent relationship. The more we learn to embrace the profound power and the simplicity of receiving the presence of God and His heavenly kingdom as the identity we wear, the easier it gets for us to enter the throne room by receiving Heaven in significant ways.

When drinking from God in ways that benefit us emotionally and spiritually, we have to own Him as our one God in a way that involves trusting that He is close and all around us here. Part of the answer is in identifying with God as our God to the point of His presence with us becoming the most central thing about us that identifies us as who we are.

It is beyond this book's scope to fully study the word name in the Bible. But the topic fits here because when you study it, many verses suggest that at least part of the meaning is that the name of the Lord is the presence of all that God is.

The Bible says they would call His name Immanuel, which means "God with us" (Matt. 1:23). It explains further that when "you are in our midst, O Lord," that is when "we are called by Your name" (Jer. 14:9). We are called by His name when we own God as our God to the point where we have made God's presence with us the most significant thing that identifies us as an individual. This topic is essential because being "called by [God's] name" is a necessary prerequisite to Him being able to heal our land (2 Chron. 7:14).

The Bible also talks about our name where we are called, "The Lord is our righteousness" (Jer. 33:16). To me, this is a declaration that helps us love the closeness of God's righteousness all around and touching our humanity to the point that we identify with the greatness of His righteousness as literally being our own. No, it is not wrong for us to think of it this way because when the holiness of God touches something, whatever it touches becomes holy also (Ex. 29:37).

How can we identify with God as our one God to the point of owning His presence as what defines who we are?

Make declarations like, "Lord, you are my God! You are my refuge; you are my strength." When you listen to yourself make repetitious declarations like these, your heart will eventually hear and respond by turning toward God, opening up to Him, and loving His closeness for being God to you here.

Teach your heart to enjoy the ongoing cleansing of God for your humanity. When you embrace God as holiness for your humanity, it is a natural next step to also put on and wear His presence for identity (Heb. 10:22; John 15:4).

Sixth, we must love, honor, and feel gratitude toward the glory source we depend on.

It is natural for us to open up inside to the sources in our lives that we love depending on. We naturally love, honor, and feel gratitude toward our glory sources. You can use this to your advantage with God. When your declarations help your heart to hear the truth enough to change your thinking patterns, you will be better able to depend on God to draw near, and your childlike love, honor, and gratitude toward Him will soar.

If we aren't opening up to God in ways that let us receive His kingdom and presence, we aren't free at that moment like a child is free. Don't try to repent by punishing yourself for disbelief because that will only shut you off from entering the kingdom (Matt. 23:13). Showing honor and gratitude for God's radiant glory, even before you receive it, will open you up so you can receive easily.

Rejoice your way into believing the presence of God is coming and washing away the sinfulness of disbelief, and then keep rejoicing about His coming to you until the demonic is burned and crushed. You must direct your heart into gratitude that helps you believe that Heaven has arrived and that more is coming as promised. When you believe the glory of

Photo by Dev Benjamin on Unsplash

the throne room in Heaven has come around you and you love God with praise that the greatness of God's glory is close to you here, your gratitude will soar, and your power in spiritual warfare will increase dramatically.

We need to be honest about what the Word of God says and fit the puzzle pieces together so we can apply it well. When the Bible says that we should show gratitude for receiving the kingdom of Heaven around us here, we should believe we are receiving all of it. When it says to show gratitude for receiving the kingdom, it is talking about receiving to us here "the city of the living God, the heavenly Jerusalem,...myriads of angels...God, the Judge of all... and...Jesus" (Heb. 12:22–24). But what if that is difficult for you and you are not sure you have received all that yet?

Some of your doubt may be from yourself or it may be the result of demonic pressure. Fight the doubt from them with declarations! Then also rejoice as you make declarations that break down the hardness and self-protection in your heart until you can freely believe God's Word and receive like a child (Hos. 10:12).[14] Refrain from putting the pressure on how well you visualize Heaven coming. If you keep the pressure of your faith on believing God's Word, you will be better able to receive freely. Increase your love for God by making declarations where you tell your heart from Scripture why it is safe to believe God will draw near and bring Heaven with Him here. Listen to yourself thanking God for the truth about His greatness close to you until your heart softens enough for you to feel gratitude toward God, which opens you up more fully.

Seventh, we have to praise the greatness of the glory we have put on.

The sixth process step in drinking from God is similar to the fifth, but here, we have to praise the glory we have put on and enjoy Him in ways that honor Him as our God and bring our much-needed emotional benefits.

When we receive glory from ourselves, other people, or earthly things, we believe it belongs to us. But when we praise the glory of it, the praise comes back toward us, and the result is pride. We do feel good about ourselves, and by praise toward the glory of it, we are made to feel confident, worthy, and reassured. But in this, we are worshiping a lie about the greatness of our human glory compared to God. Even though receiving and displaying our human glory around us feels good, we still fall short of God's glory. Our pride eases our sense of falling short and dulls the truth about our profoundly practical, everyday need for God.

The critical point is that we must praise the glory we receive or we will experience little or no benefit. Even on a human level, we must praise the glory we acquire or we will not feel worthy or confident because of it. This principle is vital when trying to drink from God. We must praise the greatness of the glory we receive from around Him, and we must intentionally enjoy the closeness of His glory to us because that makes us feel confident and worthy. Praising the greatness of God's closeness to us also protects us in spiritual realms. We feel significant and influential because of the boastful praise we give toward the only living God who is good and who is worthy of all praise.

We must fit the puzzle pieces of Scripture together to understand and apply it most effectively. Remember that we advance the kingdom of Heaven on earth when we enthrone God with our praises (Ps. 22:3; Rev. 21:3).

Praise toward the greatness of God's glory and His kingdom that we believe has drawn near greatly increases the level of protection we experience and the ability of God's angel army to fight on behalf of Heaven. When you praise the presence of God and His kingdom as a protective tent around you, you align yourself with celebrating the Feast of Tabernacles and Heaven is more fully established on earth (Zech. 14:18–19; Ps. 104:2).

Remember that in one sense, faith is our shield (Eph. 6:16). Yet our faith needs to be faith in something. So it is more accurate to say that our faith in the power and supreme greatness of God's presence surrounding us protects us (Ps. 91).

Do you want more protection? Increase the strength of your faith in and love for the power of God as your shield and defender. The more you enjoy believing it like a child, the more substantial the effectiveness of God's presence will become.

---

[14] As I said before, start with declarations aimed at making the presence of God your safe refuge because your desire for safety will help to break down your walls even when you might be afraid to let God draw near at the start.

Eighth, we have to enjoy the much-needed emotional benefits.

Enjoying the emotional benefits of glory coming to us increases our attachment to the source we are receiving from. If you pause long enough to enjoy God in specific ways related to your neediness, your love for His closeness to you will greatly increase.

In other words, when you feel stressed out, trust Heaven is coming and that the closeness of God is reassuring and comforting you. When you feel insecure or threatened, open up to trust that Heaven is coming and is around you. Then pause to let yourself think of the presence of God and His kingdom as your safe refuge and hiding place.

Sin is attractive to us because of the temporary emotional benefit we gain from it. Make declarations reminding yourself that His beauty and strength close to you are the thrill and reassurance you need. When you are bored, make declarations reminding yourself that the glory of God coming to you is always new and fresh, and never gets old or boring.

There is the more spiritual side of drinking from God and the emotional side of drinking from Him. Both are important as both are needed to help you to find freedom from long-term habits of sin. You need to drink from God spiritually so that His presence and kingdom come to you and protect you in ways that prevent temptation. You also need to drink from God emotionally so that His presence becomes what satisfies and thrills you instead of sin.

The process steps we use to drink from earthly and human sources are the steps we must apply to God. When I started with these things, I always had to keep a short list of the process steps in my pocket. I needed it with me because I often had to go back and read the list of steps to remind myself what they were. I needed to remind myself because I could apply the steps one day and then completely forget what I was doing the next. You may need to keep the list with you also.

Before I finish this chapter, I need to say something about worship leaders and pastors in churches.

A CALL TO COLLECTIVE WORSHIP THAT INCLUDES DECLARATIONS

Far too few of us drink from God as David did by satisfying our souls through entering the heavenly sanctuary and seeing with faith the power and glory of God close to us here (Ps. 63:1–2, 5). The preaching and worship in churches can help with this.

God made an everlasting covenant to be God to us (Gen. 17:7; Gal. 3:29), and for that to be practical, God is doing "something new" by giving drink to His people from the radiance around Him (Isa. 43:18–20).

A worship leader who worships God in song all week can be greatly uplifted by their singing. But for the ordinary person, twenty minutes of singing once a week isn't enough to turn their hearts toward God in ways that sustain them through the week.

Worship and preaching can help people become more unified and childlike in their ability to enter by collectively receiving Heaven here (Mark 10:15; Heb. 10:19–22; 12:22–24, 28). But people need to be taught from the preaching and led by their worship leaders to turn away from earthly and human glory. They need to hear Scriptures repeated often that give them reasons to believe they can enter the throne room with bold faith about the cleansing of God that comes when receiving Heaven here.

If you are a worship leader or pastor, direct your own heart away from loving the human glory and pride you get from your position or from the people in your church (Ezek. 34:10). Make declarations of repentance that turn your heart away from having to beg God to come into your church service. Repent of thinking you must help the people ascend into Heaven to bring Christ down here (Rom. 10:6). Ascending into Heaven in a vision is great, but it is not the same as abiding.

Demonstrate by your worship and preaching that we ascend by directing our hearts to take refuge in the Lord so we can receive Heaven around us here with the freedom of a child (Matt. 19:14). Teach the people with gratitude toward God that they can enjoy drawing near to God by joyously humble and childlike faith that trusts that God is coming here and that He is cleansing their hands and purifying their hearts as He comes (James 4:8).

Rather than trying to feed the people with something about how impressive you are or with how great your church is, lead the people to the place where they can feed on the Lord (Ezek. 34:10–31).

Before the heavens open in your church service and people want to run away and hide (1 John 2:28), teach them to abide by receiving Heaven around their physical bodies here. Include declarations in your times of worship that joyously build love in the people for the holiness of God as we declare to our hearts that it is right for us to believe Heaven is coming to us and that God is washing our humanity of shame and sin as He comes (Heb. 10:19–22).

Any attempts at collectively receiving the kingdom of Heaven for spiritual warfare should be preceded by teaching and preaching that helps the people present their bodies to God (Rom. 12:1–2) so they can take refuge in the Lord by receiving the holy presence of God, His mountain, His kingdom, and angels around them here (Isa. 57:13–14; Heb. 12:22–24, 28). By this, we all can be protected as we go together into attack mode by intentionally receiving the holiness and peace of Heaven that burns and crushes evil together with the mountain of God that crushes demons and witchcraft like a big rock.

Let me tell you something that might be too much information for some people. I normally go all week without awareness of lust around me anywhere I go. Then, many times when I go to worship in churches, I feel sexual lust in the room. I never know who it is coming from, but if leaders in the churches can feel these things, they should not let it go unaddressed.

I am not saying we should try to discern the person who brought the lust into the church. They are in church trying to do the right thing but are in bondage to it, and we should help them fight it! Our attitude in worship should be to punish the devil and his demons for trying to hinder us as believers during the week and in church. People should be able to come to church knowing that their demons will get peeled off them.

Worship leaders need to help the people remind themselves that it is purity and holiness that they love. Impurity and sin make them miserable. Worship leaders need to help the people put on the armor of God's presence so that they are protected from demonic attacks and temptation (Rom. 13:12–14). Help them transform their minds by rejoicing that we can present our bodies to God and that our greatest treasure is the kingdom of Heaven around us here.

Make your worship services terrify demons about bothering your people, especially during your worship services! But please don't use hype as a tool to manipulate God into coming. Joy in our worship is important, but use the joy to soften the people's hearts into more fully embracing the truth about God wanting to be God to us here.

Use your worship services to let the people see a model for repentance and building faith. Worship leaders need to give enough guidance to the people to affirm with words from their mouths what they are joyously turning away from and toward. Don't use songs that beg God to come. Sing songs that build faith by thanking God that He is drawing near. Help the people believe the kingdom is coming down from above and that your whole congregation can stand before the Lord as kingdom priests.

When large numbers of churches hear, believe, and understand how we can drink from the radiance around God instead of glory from the world, unity will increase, demons will be crushed, and Heaven will come in greater ways because we are drinking from God together.

8

PRACTICAL EVIDENCE THAT WE ALL WANT GOD

THE VALUE OF RECOGNIZING YOUR NEED FOR GOD

One of the most important practical steps toward abiding in Christ is to learn to recognize the overwhelming evidence of your desire for God in everyday life. Doing so will help lay a better foundation for learning to welcome the presence of God all the time, no matter where you are or what you are doing, not just on special days of worship.

The practical evidence you see in your everyday life should be a jump-off point to respond by making declarations that redirect your heart's pursuit back toward God, toward opening up, and toward believing that He is coming so you can enjoy Him being with you here.

> God wants to fill the earth with His glory, so He made our desire and love of glory so strong it can sometimes overpower us. Your job is to get your heart to hear and joyfully believe that your wayward behavior proves that you want God desperately and above all else. Then, you will have to believe that because of the Scriptures, God's presence is far more abundantly available than you have believed.

Knowing that your motives, cravings, and behavior all demonstrate an overpowering need for the presence of God, it is much easier to turn to Him and enjoy His presence as what you need. But your declarations will have to stretch your faith so you can believe God for an increasing abundance of what flows from the fountain of life.

The practical evidence strongly suggests that anything less than an abundance of God's presence won't satisfy our thirsty desires and keep us from going back to earthly sources. You must stretch your faith about what God is giving. Listen to yourself as you boldly declare that it is right for you to trust that God can and will supply what is needed to quench your thirst because He has made a covenant agreement to be a better God to you than what you can find from earthly sources (Isa. 55:1–2).

You want God, and God wants to draw near to you. You can find freedom from living in bondage to earthly things and human glory because more of God is always available. Even though you get distracted, your desire for God's presence never decreases, and God never stops wanting to be closer to you. God doesn't get distracted. Ever.

Even though it may be hard to imagine at this point, being able to feed on God is much more readily available than buying something, eating something, accomplishing something, or what you can gain from human relationships.

People need to experience a personal God who is tangibly close to them. It is a need to taste Heaven here and now. Consider the overwhelming evidence of this beautiful truth.

MATERIAL THINGS AS EVIDENCE

Materialism is one of the many examples showing our desire for God. We call our things *possessions*. But is it just more clothes, nicer cars, houses, or toys? Something much deeper is involved.

We can break down the thrill of material things into two parts: getting and having. Part of the fun is in acquiring. Part of it is in possessing something as our own.

But why do we push so hard to get something and almost immediately move on to wanting something else? Part of the reason is that material things don't meet the underlying, more profound need. Glory from material things gets old. God's glory coming to us is always new. As long as we stay open enough to keep receiving, God's glory and power are never boring because what comes to us keeps coming and is always refreshed (Acts 3:19).

God designed us with a need to be constantly receiving. That is how it works with God. Regarding our thirsty need for God, the Bible says, "The water that I will give him will become in him a well of water springing up" (John 4:14). Springing up water requires that we are constantly receiving more.

According to the verses from Isaiah 55, you must trade earthly sources that are inadequate to fill you and you have to "delight yourself in abundance." Listening to yourself make declarations about the abundant presence of God coming to you helps motivate you to stay open and keep receiving from God. When you recognize your misdirected desires, don't shut those desires down. Stay open and redirect your desires toward holiness. Getting and having God can thrill your heart about His being with you here.

OWNERSHIP

Consider that we also enjoy ownership of what has value to us. Whatever we long for, we want to call it ours. Getting and having makes us feel worthy because what we focus on finding has a glory that is valuable to us when we can own it as ours.

Materialism feeds our desire just enough to keep us wanting more. But trying to meet our practical need for God with material things is like giving a thirsty person potato chips but no water. The food is nice, but it doesn't satisfy the need. Materialism gives a satisfaction that is only a fleeting illusion. That is because what drives us is our need for God on a practical level.

We love material things because of the glory we can receive and possess with us here. Related, God wants true worshipers. So God designed us with an attraction to acquire and own material things to give us an appetite for how He wants us to love and enjoy His presence with us. Where our getting and having is directed tells God who and what we value and worship the most.

When I talk about possessing God, I mean we need to learn to have Him in a way that lets us intentionally enjoy His closeness as what satisfies our covetous cravings. Listening to ourselves make audible declarations about the value and worth of God close and touching us helps us to think about God in that way and satisfy those cravings. Doing so, in part, is what it means to make Him our God.

Our love of getting and having must be redirected toward God. The Bible says that "he who takes refuge in Me . . . / will possess My holy mountain" (Isa. 57:13). To take refuge in God is to drink from Him in ways that let you open up and trust you are receiving His presence with you and all around you as your security God (Ps. 36:7-9). When speaking about getting, the Bible talks about people who "receive a kingdom which cannot be shaken, let us show gratitude" (Heb. 12:28). These verses work best when applied together.

It is by God's purposeful design that you have this desire. Your desires to get and to have are evidence of your desire to possess what God offers freely—and to do so in a literal and real way.

WANTING MONEY IS EVIDENCE

Money is certainly helpful, but our need is spiritual.

If you have a lot of money with you, it is easy to trust the money to make you feel secure and significant. The same thing can be true with God. The difference with God is that you don't have to hold back. You can let your desires run free! You only have to direct your heart into the place of enjoying that God is more available and more valuable than the money in your pocket.

The Bible says,
> Every one who thirsts, come to the waters;
> And you who have no money come, buy and eat...
> Without money and without cost.
> Why do you spend money for what is not bread,
> And your wages for what does not satisfy?
> Listen carefully to Me...
> And delight yourself in abundance. (Isa. 55:1–2)

You can experience God but must do it without expecting a limit on what you can receive. According to the verses above, you buy without cost. Think of making declarations of repentance as trading in your worthless earthly glory for being able to "delight yourself" in the abundance that pours out from all around God.

The problem with most people is that when they think about God, they immediately shut down because of hopelessness and fear. Teach your heart by declarations that you don't have to feel those ways about God. When you want more out of life, don't try to stop your longing for more; redirect and satisfy those longings and desires with greater faith and enjoyment in God. When your heart learns to believe you are receiving an abundance of God's presence, you will also need to learn to continually release out of you what God is pouring into you so that you can receive more (Gal. 3:14; Matt. 10:8).

Photo by James Kovin on Unsplash

You have to take this one step at a time. Teach your heart to believe and love that the presence of God and His kingdom have the greatest value. Then, the next time you think about needing more money, don't hesitate to do what you must to improve your situation. But remember that underlying your desire for money and material things is a driving spiritual need to get, have, and enjoy the presence of God in a practical way. We want to get and have God more than anything else because the worth of God as our I Am with us is greater than anything else we could ever acquire.

WANTING CONTROL IS EVIDENCE

Control is important to us. But under the surface, there is something deeper. What do we have when we think we are in control? Security. Control is not the issue. We need to feel secure. Control is just one of the ways we try to feel secure. The Bible says, "God is my strong fortress" (2 Sam. 22:33). The same can be true for you.

Many of us struggle and don't move forward in our relationship with God because we think we have to give up control. Doing so scares us so much that we often fear cooperating with Him.

Don't focus directly on trying to force yourself to give up control. Instead, focus on making God your security. The Bible says, "O Lord, I am oppressed, be my security" (Isa. 38:14). When the closeness of God's presence becomes your security, you will find freedom to move forward in your relationship with Him. You won't hold back.

Control does seem to be reassuring at times. But it is based on a kind of security that isn't real. Is there anything that we can truly control? Not really. Wanting control is only a desperate demand for something that will make us feel secure.

Drawing close to a God who is sovereign, by having Him draw close to us, has far more glory in it than believing lies about us being in control of our surroundings and the people around us.

Don't settle for having to feed on your own sense of being sovereign. When we "cease striving and know that [He is] God," He "will be exalted among the nations" and "in the earth" (Ps. 46:10). While standing before the Lord and receiving the light of His presence, trust that you are also putting on the humility of Christ so you can better enjoy the closeness of His sovereignty with you here.

When you observe yourself pushing for control, try to remember this: control is important to us because we need closeness to a God who is our security. Think about God close to you and be intentional to enjoy His presence with faith about Him being your sovereign security. Direct your heart into faith about the closeness of God's sovereign power crushing evil as His kingdom comes down to you from above.

DEPRESSION CAN BE EVIDENCE

Technically speaking, depression is the result of a chemical reaction inside our brains. Some people have biological problems that mean their bodies are quicker to produce the chemical reactions that cause feelings of depression.

Others experience depression because of horrible losses in their lives. In this section, I am not talking about when someone loses their job or someone dies. I am talking about a completely different kind of depression.

Some people experience depression because of frustration about their seeming loss of ability to live life well. Often, they also feel hopeless about doing anything to correct their lack.

Feelings of loss like these can result in self-hate, and if strong enough, the hatred can bring depression. If the depression continues for months or years at a time, it is possible that an emotional addiction has developed. That was the case with me.

I spent years in self-hate because that brought depression that made me want to stay isolated. The isolation helped me feel safe. Depression became a cave I could hide inside. I felt a complete loss of hope to live with heart-level integrity. If I tried to live with courage, something would happen that would make me feel silly or self-conscious, and I went right back to self-hate and isolation.

Depression is not always the result of biological causes or loss and nothing else. Sometimes there is such a strong pattern of loving the hard shell of depression that we do things intentionally to keep ourselves depressed. The anger and self-hate made me want to hide, but because the hate was coming from me, there was no place to get away. Not being able to get away caused a chemical reaction in my brain that made me feel depressed.

People need security and reassurance desperately. We were designed to depend on the presence of God as our security. It hurts when we don't. It can hurt so much that some develop an addiction to depression in order to try and kill the pain. Depression can be evidence of our need for reassurance and security. When that is true, the real need we are feeling is a need for the closeness of God.

In my case, I was so desperate to maintain the best feeling of security I could hope for that I punished myself with hate to avoid hope. Fear of failure was so strong that I kept myself from hoping for anything better. How did I find the freedom I needed to hope again and turn to God?

I studied the Bible. Then, once I understood about idolatry and repentance, I realized that God wanted to draw near in a way that would make Him my refuge instead of the depression. I had no idea what it would look like to depend on God or how it would work, but I began to listen to myself make repetitious declarations of repentance and faith in order to change my heart-level thinking.

The habit of trying to find refuge in the cave of depression had to be broken. Fears had to be replaced by a belief that closeness to God would be a better way to be safe. I also had to humble myself from self-effort in regard to punishing myself, trusting that the punishment Jesus suffered was more than enough for me.

Listening to declarations of repentance and faith with joy in my tone of voice softened my heart, and my thinking patterns eventually changed. Through thanks and praise for the truth, my heart turned away from self-protection. I began to believe God Himself would draw near so He could be my refuge. My hope and confidence grew when I declared that I did not need to be afraid. Eventually, I believed God would be a better place to hide, and I began to open up more and more to the radiance around Him as my hiding place (Ps. 91).

I assertively declared to the ears of my heart:

- "On God my salvation and my glory rest; /
  The rock of my strength, my refuge is in God" (Ps. 62:7).

- "The Lord is the defense of my life; /
  Whom shall I dread?" (Ps. 27:1).

- "I will say to the LORD, 'My refuge and my fortress, /
  My God, in whom I trust!' " (Ps. 91:2).

- "You are my hiding place and my shield" (Ps. 119:114).

I thanked God repeatedly that "the protection I need is not forcing myself into a cocoon of depression. God is my best hope for a place to hide."

Think about the love you have for the security you find from hiding under the self-protective lid of depression. Now, take that same love, multiply it, and turn it toward enjoying God's closeness and His presence. Think about God being close and love His closeness as protection around you that is greater than depression could ever be.

Habit patterns can be retrained. Be patient with yourself, but be relentless also. Expect some squirming and some insecurity along the way. Teach yourself that it is safer to feel hope. Don't let up in retraining your heart about believing and loving God instead of your earthly and human ways. Direct your heart through declarations into loving God's closeness as your security, and the presence of God with you will increase.

Photo by Ben White on Unsplash

ADDICTIONS AND UNWANTED BEHAVIORS ARE EVIDENCE

Unwanted behaviors and addictions have such a strong hold on us through what we are getting out of them. Behaviors we repeat can become habits that provide us with an emotional benefit that eases the spiritual pain from our unmet need for God. The emotional benefit is what we are addicted to.

Sometimes, we use addictions to try and feel protected somehow. Sometimes, we feed ourselves with the sense of power we feel from being in control. Often, it has to do with reassurance and a desperate attempt to find a way to soothe our hurts in some way. Underlying unwanted behaviors and addictions is a strong emotional benefit that keeps us doing what we don't want to do.

What about the person who has become addicted to injecting themselves with a drug? Or what about the person who likes to breathe in the smoke of a cigarette? Behaviors like these provide an escape from the pain of reality. Addictions can soothe, reassure, or calm us. They can also provide a thrill when life feels boring and dull. The emotional benefit we gain is the underlying reason for the addiction. When the spiritual need and the emotional benefit are being met well because of God, unwanted behaviors and addictions are much easier to correct.

Your addictive tendencies and desires are practical evidence that you long for and need God's presence close to you all the time. Your desire for God never decreases or goes away. It just reveals itself differently at various times. Ask God to help you to recognize better that you want God. The good news is that you can have more than enough of His kingdom and presence to replace the benefits you gain from your addictions. When you stand firm by opening yourself to receive God's radiant presence, He comes, and the demonic element driving your addiction is forced to flee.

WANTING TO HURT OURSELVES IS TWISTED EVIDENCE

Sometimes, our unmet need for God reveals itself in a twisted desire to hurt ourselves. Making ourselves hurt is a complicated mix of wanting perfection, realizing that we aren't perfect, and then turning to feed on a punishing kind of control and power instead. We pride ourselves on the power we feel in how angry we get with ourselves. The truth is that we want power. But God never intended that we feed on a power that hurts ourselves and others.

Try to remember this the next time you find that you are twisting power around and hurting yourself: "It is God and the closeness of His power that I want. Not this twisted and evil power that hurts me!" Listen as you declare to the ears of your heart that Jesus paid the price for your sin: "Jesus suffered on my behalf so that I don't have to punish myself." Then rejoice your way into trusting that the cleansing of God is being poured onto you, that God is touching you with His holiness, and that something of His holy perfection is being transferred to your humanity here.

LUST AND SEXUAL DESIRE ARE EVIDENCE

The emotional benefits of lust and sexual desire are twisted substitutions for what are better found because of closeness to God. What is it about sex that makes it so attractive and driving at times? I'm not talking, of course, about sex between a husband and wife since God told us to be fruitful and multiply (Gen. 1:28). I'm talking about sexual things outside of that relationship. Why are lust and sexual urges so demanding? Is it purely biological? I don't believe so.

Early in my quest, I noticed that my own private struggles with reoccurring sexual sin seemed more related to my emotional state than something biological. Private sexual sin gave me a sense of dominance and control that felt reassuring, powerful, and rebellious. The satisfaction I felt from control and rebellion against God wasn't present when having sex with my spouse.

It was painful to admit, but I had to be honest about myself. My sexual desire seemed to include a driving emotional need for dominance, control, and power over something. But to fulfill that side of my sexual desire with my wife seemed wrong, and I didn't want to hurt her. I was terrified to go through life without learning to fill my underlying needs righteously. Where would my sin lead if I didn't go after God? Would my sin eventually become so twisted that I could hurt someone physically? Thankfully, I never had to find out because God heard my weeping as I prayed for answers to solve this problem.

My need for power and control didn't seem sexual, but I was trying to fill that desire through sexual sin. So, as an experiment, I began thinking about sexual desire as something that was not driven by a biological need as much as a deep and unmet emotional need, together with demonic pressure to rebel against God. The more I listened to myself make declarations that I could wear God's beautiful kingdom and His powerful presence as armor and that the nearness of God's greatness could satisfy me better, the more success and freedom I found! I learned that when temptations or sexual thoughts come, my armor isn't strong enough at that moment. So, I enter by receiving the mountain of God and Heaven coming down around me again. Then, to fight the demonic, I playfully and boldly argue with disbelief they try to push onto me by praising God about His power and holiness, drawing near and coming down all around me here. Doing that lets me enjoy the power and dominance I feel from being able to crush and punish the evil pushing me toward sin. If I had ignored my need for righteous power and dominance over evil, purity, and freedom from sexual sin would never have been possible for me.

The way I see it, drives and desires related to our unfulfilled need for the presence of God contribute far more to our sexual urges than biological causes. Sexual urges are heavily influenced by the spiritual realm of evil. Some of that demonic pressure is in the air around you, and some of it is being carried around by people who don't understand the danger of the demonic side of sexual sin and lust. The good thing for us is that the demonic elements are neutralized when we learn to put on and rest inside the presence of God as a shield and armor around us without reaching out toward what they carry (Rom. 13:12–14).

Photo by Jernej Graj on Unsplash

Let me remind you that God designed us with a deep spiritual awareness of what He is like (Rom. 1:19). And, because of the "law of sin" in us (Rom. 7:23), we are made aware that we "fall short of the glory of God" (Rom. 3:23). The sense we have that we fall short makes us feel insecure inside and creates a need for reassurance.

God wants to be to us what we lack. But when this doesn't happen, our spiritual insecurity drives us to find reassurance from glory in other places (1 Cor. 11:15; Isa. 23:9). We were designed to experience and enjoy God's glory and power close to us and in a pure way.

But when we are not getting enough of that, or we are unprotected from demonic pressure toward sexual sin, we feed ourselves by lust toward the glory and beauty or strength of another person. Afterward, we reassure ourselves with the pride and power we felt from how much glory we fed on from them.

Much of the attraction in sexual sin is because of the rebellion of how wrong it is. When lust and sexual sin make us the predator and others the prey, we dominate them physically or by lust, and we reassure ourselves with how strong we feel. Or we make ourselves the bait and pride ourselves on the twisted and rebellious feelings of power we get when someone is attracted to us beyond their control.

You don't have to feed yourself by hoping to see a lustful look from someone. Yes, at times, it may seem like you want nothing more than to dominate someone sexually. But you don't have to settle for so little. Holiness and purity are available to you. Listen to yourself make joyous declarations that you don't have to love the power you feel when taking sexual or lustful advantage of another person. Make declarations that God's power drawing near is more beautiful, strong, and thrilling than the twisted rebellion there is in sexual sin.

You can teach yourself to love the closeness of the holiness of God until His closeness touches you and helps you with holiness. You only have to direct what your heart will depend on. Unless you intervene and change what your heart treasures, you can easily have all your hope for glory set on lust and sexual desire or on waiting for someone to reassure you by looking at you with desire. Enjoying the closeness of God's beauty and strength is pure and far more deeply satisfying than the power we can feel through rebellious sin.

Yes, letting yourself enjoy being wanted by God without holding back is different from sexual desire. It is entirely different to thrill yourself with closeness to God because when His kingdom comes, "the perfection of beauty" is all around you here (Ps. 50:2). It is different, but it also feels pure and good. A nonsexual thrill and pleasure can be yours if you keep reminding yourself to enjoy the extreme greatness of God's power and beauty close to you more than what you could get from sensual sources.

Though you may not believe it yet, finding the reassurance you need by experiencing God can be more satisfying than sex. Lust and sexual sin are among those things that become glory that reassures us. The greatness of God close to you can reassure you more and in a pure way.

The key to learning to turn your heart to God in this area is that you have to learn to tabernacle yourself inside the kingdom of Heaven and its beauty around you to such an extent that you can rest inside enjoying the closeness of God without needing to reach out in lust and sexual desire (Ps. 44:20–21). You have to learn to enjoy the power and glory of God close to you as what reassures and thrills you instead of reaching out toward the dominance you find from sexual sin (Ps. 63:1–2, 5). Repetitious declarations of repentance and faith can change your thinking and your patterns of pursuit so that you find freedom from the natural urges and the demonic pressure pushing you in this area.

> Christian leaders who fall to sexual sin have yet to become childlike enough to playfully love the closeness of God as what reassures them; eases their boredom; and makes them feel loved, beautiful, and strong. They have yet to learn to put on the armor of light by receiving Heaven around them so they can rest in the Lord without reaching with their inner hands toward the "strange god" of sexual sin (Ps. 44:20–21). They need to humble themselves until they become playfully childlike enough to receive and rest with the mountain of God under them and the kingdom of Heaven around them here. By holding onto the weight of the mountain under them, they can control their human spirit and won't lower their walls of protection (Prov. 25:28).

> They must teach themselves to enjoy playfully receiving Heaven here as a means of punishing the demonic the moment evil dares to tempt or arouse them to sin sexually. They have yet to learn they can't hold back when it comes to receiving the holiness of God and trusting that God is washing every part of their physical body, burning, crushing, and peeling off the demonic that are trying to push them toward sin.

When the kingdom of God comes, the finger of God is all that is needed for deliverance (Luke 11:20). Teach your heart to treasure that you can receive Heaven here and stand before the Lord as a kingdom priest (2 Chron. 29:11). Instead of finding reassurance in sexual sin and dominance, make joyful declarations that help you humble yourself into being more childlike in your enjoyment of God's purity and the beauty of His holiness close to you here.

Getting close and feeding on God's presence feels pure and holy. It is refreshing, calming, full of pleasure, thrilling, reassuring, and deeply satisfying. But is it enough? It is and more. Tell your heart that "the beauty and strength of God are greater than any earthly glory that I could ever see, feel, taste, hear, or want." Keep telling yourself that until your heart hears, believes, and treasures His closeness enough for you to easily open up, receive, and rest inside God's kingdom and presence.

Learning to enjoy God in this way is far more practical and relevant to everyday living than most have ever considered. Your heart can learn to believe and enjoy that the thrill you feel from the purity of God's power and beauty close to you is more enjoyable than what you could ever get from lust and sexual sin.

OVEREATING IS EVIDENCE

Don't equate being overweight with overeating. Some people diet by starving themselves so much that their metabolism changes, and it becomes almost impossible to lose weight. Others overeat without being overweight. Being overweight isn't what I am talking about here.

Food fills our stomachs and eases the pain we feel from hunger, but it can also be reassuring and comforting to us. We have to eat to live. But God is the God of all comfort (2 Cor. 1:3). When food becomes our comfort, food has become a substitution for God's presence as our twenty-four seven comfort. You can't have both.

Sadly, many overeat because of hopelessness about being able to experience God more deeply. The food deadens the pain from their unmet need. Others overeat for pleasure. Many also try to find refuge and protection in the excess weight that they wear around them. We hide under increasingly thicker layers rather than face the painful truth that we are not finding the acceptance and approval we desperately need.

The Bible says, "It is good for the heart to be strengthened by grace, not by foods, through which those who were so occupied were not benefited" (Heb. 13:9). Listen to yourself make declarations that change your patterns of thinking and dependence until your heart turns toward God and you find the faith and freedom you need to let yourself feed on receiving and enjoying the presence of God and His kingdom. We need to eat, but the truth about us is that God's presence can comfort us better than the soothing we feel from physical food.

WANTING BEAUTY IS EVIDENCE

Why is appearance held in such high honor in our society? Beauty has glory in it that is attractive to us because we want God and the perfection of His beautiful kingdom close and all around us (Ps. 50:2), and He created us with a hunger for beauty that we cannot ignore. But it can only be fully met by the closeness of God Himself.

Remember when we considered that all people have an inner awareness of what God is like? Part of that awareness includes a deep inner sense of the greatness of God's beauty. Rather than getting close to God and thrilling ourselves with His beauty close to us as our beauty, we try to achieve beauty for ourselves and settle for self-directed worship instead of praise toward God.

Photo by Jurien Huggins on Unsplash

But age is catching up to all of us, for "all flesh is like grass, / And all its glory like the flower of grass. / The grass withers, / And the flower falls off" (1 Peter 1:24). Someday, you will wake up and realize your body doesn't look attractive anymore. How confident and secure will you feel if your human beauty had been your basis for being confident and secure in relationships?

If you are physically attractive, teach your heart by thanks and praise for the truth until you learn to enjoy God's beauty more than your own. If you wish you were more beautiful, teach your heart to identify with God as your God so much that you believe His beauty is reflected onto you because of His proximity to you here. Praise God for His radiant beauty, which you teach yourself to believe is coming close and touching you here (Hos. 10:12). Build your faith and love for God by boasting about the greatness of His beauty around you when you are abiding inside His presence here.

Success should not be defined by how well we impress others with our appearance. Depending on God has practical benefits that are also more significant spiritually.

Think about what it feels like to love the emotional benefits that you feel from earthly addictions, unwanted behaviors, sexual things, and food-related strongholds. Then think about God being close and loving His closeness in similar pure and holy ways. Make declarations that remind you that God has the beauty and strength you love being close to.

Draw nearer to God by trusting He is drawing near you here. Make declarations about the greatness of God's love, strength, and beauty close to you even before you feel His presence with you. Make declarations that help you disown your physical beauty as the thing you want to increase. Remind yourself that other people are not the standard your heart longs to measure up to. God's beauty is the real standard.

Use declarations of thanks and praise for the truth so that you cut off comparing yourself to others. Humble yourself by teaching your heart to embrace the beauty of God as greater than yours. Then, make declarations that teach your heart to believe God is drawing near to you with abundant beauty so you can love and enjoy the glory of His beauty all around and touching you here.

Remind yourself until you believe and enjoy that to "walk in the Light as He Himself is in the Light" (1 John 1:7), you must make declarations that help your heart to hear and believe you can and should enjoy that God wants you, like Him, to be "covering Yourself with light as with a cloak, / Stretching out heaven like a tent curtain" around you here (Ps. 104:2). It is right that you turn your heart from idolatry and humble yourself into depending on Heaven to come down around you as your "perfection of beauty" (Ps. 50:2). Don't ignore your need for beauty! "Glory in Christ Jesus and put no confidence in the flesh" (Phil 3:3)!

137

Photo by Mayur Gala on Unsplash

NEEDING LOVE IS EVIDENCE

Our need for love is evidence of our need for God. The love of God can touch your human need for love more fully than you may now realize. The Bible says, "The Lord loves His people" (2 Chron. 2:11) and "The Lord takes pleasure in His people" (Ps. 149:4). Listen to yourself making declarations until your heart believes it is safe for you to believe God loves you in this way.

One way God expresses His love is in His desire to be close to us. Jesus told us to "abide in Me...abide in My love" (John 15:7, 9). The Bible also talks about the love of God resting on people: "Let Your lovingkindness, O LORD, be upon us, / According as we have hoped in You" (Ps. 33:22). When God's unfailing love rests upon us, we enjoy by faith that God has drawn near, and we love Him because of His nearness. God's love is holy and pure, and He can love us best when His presence is close.

When you're in love with another person, you enjoy when they hold you with their arms around you. It can be the same way with God because the Bible says, "The eternal God is a dwelling place, / And underneath are the everlasting arms" (Deut. 33:27). It also says, "How often I wanted to gather your children together, the way a hen gathers her chicks under her wings, and you were unwilling" (Matt. 23:37). God wants to draw you right up close and hold you. It is not automatic for us to experience God loving us this way. We have to believe and treasure the truth of what the Bible says about God's love.

You don't have to wait fifty years for God to teach you these things through a lifetime of experiences. It takes much less time if you direct your heart into faith by joyous and repetitious declarations that God is good, He wants to be close to you, and He is holding you inside the substance of His love, as the Bible teaches.

God can hold you because God's love has substance. We are told to "keep yourselves in the love of God" (Jude 1:21). The Bible isn't saying here that you should make sure God keeps loving you. With people, that might be true but not with God! Instead, we are to keep ourselves inside the substance of His love. Jesus said it this way: "Abide in My love" (John 15:9). That means we should live lives of strong faith that let us stay inside His love.

God not only defines love, but the love of God is God Himself: "God is love" (1 John 4:8). God's love comes to us because His love pours out from the radiance around Him. It is realistic for you to find the love you long for inside the closeness of God. We only have to believe we are receiving what He is pouring out (Gal. 3:14).

Experiencing the love of God requires that you become childlike enough to believe the Bible. Then growth takes over, and you become more faithful in your faith until you can keep believing confidently. When the presence of God and His kingdom become the security and what you treasure above all else, the motivation to stay faithful in loving Him with faith increases and becomes consistently practical.

King David said, "My soul clings to You" (Ps. 63:8). Consider a child who holds onto a teddy bear even while they sleep. As soon as you can believe God is near, trust you are clinging to Him (Josh. 23:8; Deut. 13:4).

Your heart has to learn it is safe for you to drop your guardedness so you can confidently trust God is drawing near so that He can hold you. Jesus told us, "'Permit the children to come to Me; do not hinder them; for the kingdom of God belongs to such as these. Truly I say to you, whoever does not receive the kingdom of God like a child will not enter it at all.'

And He took them in His arms and began blessing them, laying His hands on them" (Mark 10:14–16).

God is not a predator with secret intentions to hurt people. Are you afraid to believe His goodness? As much as you can, assert the truth into your heart with joy in your voice, even when your heart wants to hold back and resist it as truth. Thank God for that truth about His perfect and loving goodness until your heart softens enough for you to believe it. Joyously, thank Him that your need for love isn't greater than His ability to supply.

If you don't believe in the love someone has for you, then you can't enjoy it. The same thing is true with God. To enjoy God's love enough to have your love-need met, you have to let yourself believe that you are close to God and that His love is all around you here intensely: "The one who abides in love abides in God, and God abides in him" (1 John 4:16). Keep telling your heart that the only safe thing you can do is enjoy the love from God so you can abide in Him (Ps. 91).

Stop fighting and submit to believing that it is the best thing for you if you trust Him. Keep thanking the Lord until your heart becomes soft enough to hear and believe that "great is your love toward me" (Ps. 86:13 NIV).

WANTING STRENGTH AND POWER ARE EVIDENCE

We feed on pride from glory directly related to what God is like. But we also feed on pride from the glory that is the opposite. God is kind. God is also a God of great power. If we twist things around, sometimes we feed on the misuse of power—even on how we hurt someone. At times, it may be open and confronting. Other times, it is subtle and deeply hidden.

Photo by Jason Hogan on Unsplash

Why do people do bad things like murder, rape, theft, and abuse? I believe these behaviors are evidence of how far down we can go if we don't quench our thirst with the presence of a God who is both powerful and good.

God designed us to experience and enjoy Him as our God, not the twisted and evil power we feel from hurting other people or from sin that hurts us. God is strong. He is also good (Ps. 73:1). Our God is "the Rock! His work is perfect, / For all His ways are just; / A God of faithfulness and without injustice, / Righteous and upright is He" (Deut. 32:4). It is safe for you to trust that God's strength and power will also be strong in His uprightness, righteousness, and goodness toward you.

How great is our need to enjoy the strength and power of God? I remember a time when I had to laugh at myself. I was in the bathroom just after having taken a shower. I glanced at myself in the mirror. I was not anything special to look at, especially with my shirt off. But my biceps looked much bigger than normal. In my head, I knew that my upper arm was pushed down, and my muscles had only jellied out against my side. Even so, I went, "Hmm." I thought it looked good. It didn't matter that it wasn't muscle. I knew it wasn't the truth, but I was still impressed. That was silly.

Why do we do things like this? We are so needy for the power and presence of God that when we haven't been drinking from Him, we will even try to fill the void with prideful lies about our strength and how impressive we look. The substitutions we make are often both silly and sad. The Bible says of God, "He does not delight in the strength of the horse; / He does not take pleasure in the legs of a man" (Ps. 147:10).

In contrast, King David said, "I love You, O Lord, my strength" (Ps. 18:1). We can and should do the same. Praise and love toward God increase the significance of our spiritual protection and power (Ps. 27:6; 2 Chron. 20:21–22; Jer. 9:24).

Don't settle for powerlessness. Praise the closeness of God. When you receive Heaven here, God comes to stand before you as He did with Moses (Ex. 17:5–6). This way, you can present your body to God and stand before Him like Elijah and Elisha (Rom. 12:1; 1 Kings 18:15; 2 Kings 3:14). Standing before the Lord and thrilling yourself with the closeness of the strength and holiness of God is far better than having to depend on yourself as god. You will feel more significant and confident. Purity becomes practical. Demons are afraid of you. Still, though, you will need to be careful.

Praise is a natural response to glory. But praising and boasting in ourselves is much more natural than in God. When God is near, and you believe in the greatness of His glory close to you, it gets more natural to praise God. But you must consciously keep the boastful praise going toward Him without it returning to you. The Old Testament priests were prone to turn the beauty of their priestly garments and the ornaments of the temple into pride (Ezek. 7:20). It is easy for us to do the same with the glory of God's presence. It takes time, but you can learn to consciously keep the inner praise flowing toward the closeness of God's beauty and strength instead of yours. Otherwise, your boasting will turn into religious pride and weaken you spiritually.

WANTING TO BE GOOD IS EVIDENCE

Why do we pride ourselves on how kind or good we are? We pride ourselves in all areas related to what God is like because we want to measure up. Yet we will never be like God.

Of course, we should be kind and good. But rather than pat ourselves on the back when we are kind to people, we need to trust God to draw near so we can make the closeness of God our good. King David said, "But as for me, the nearness of God is my good; / I have made the Lord God my refuge" (Ps. 73:28). Did you see that? It is the nearness of God that was David's good. When your heart comes to trust God as your safe refuge, you open up inside, God draws near, and it is much more natural to praise Him instead of yourself. When God comes as your refuge, He surrounds you with His goodness, and when you identify with Him as your God, you feel good yourself because of praise toward His goodness near and touching your physical body all around.

The Bible also says, "Many are saying, 'Who will show us any good?' / Lift up the light of Your countenance upon us, O Lord!" (Ps. 4:6). When the radiance of God shines from His face onto you, God is actively being good toward you. Direct your heart away from pride in your goodness. Listen to yourself making joyful declarations that help you believe the shine of God's face is on you and that His good presence is coming to you. Then, erupt in praise toward His goodness while trusting that God is also being good to those who are in the wake of what He is pouring out onto you.

You don't have to find the energy you need by trying to thrill yourself with how good or powerful you are. The Bible says, "Delight yourself in the Lord" (Ps. 37:4). When you do that, God will draw near and fulfill your heart's desire by bringing the goodness and power you long for.

BLESS YOURSELF IN GOD

Is it wrong that we feel good about ourselves? No, God wants that for us. When we drink from earthly things and relationships, natural chemicals (endorphins) are released in our brain, and we feel a brief surge of energy and pleasure. When you feel a sense of well-being, it is because of the way God designed you. He wants us to enjoy quenching our thirsty desire to find glory from something.

Imagine being a child in first grade again. The teacher just asked a question, and you knew the answer. You felt excited. Your hand waved wildly as you said, "I know, I know!" When you answered the question right, you felt important. You felt confident. You felt good about yourself. That feeling of well-being came from drinking onto and into you a feeling of satisfaction from the glory in the answer. Let your heart hear this: God designed you to feel pleasure when you drink from the glory of something.

The practical problem is that knowing the right answer seldom has enough glory in it for us to feel good about ourselves and stay confident all our lives. Knowing the correct answer cannot protect us from the unseen evil realm. It is different with God.

We feel blessed when we drink from God's glory because His blessing shines from His face (Num. 6:22–27). We are told to glory in Christ and put no confidence in the flesh (Phil. 3:3). It is right that you bless yourself in the Lord because "the nations will bless themselves in Him, / And in Him they will glory" (Jer. 4:2).

We need confidence. We need security. Desperately. Someday, rather than esteeming themselves, entire nations will bless themselves in God. Rather than the sense of pleasure resulting when we drink from earthly things, we will drink the living and Holy Spirit of God that comes to us from the radiance around Him (John 7:39). We will bless ourselves in Him because our greatest thrill will be the presence and kingdom of God.

When you learn to drink from God with freedom, you won't shut yourself down inside when you catch yourself drinking from earthly sources. Instead, you will stay open and immediately repent by directing your heart back toward loving the cleansing of God upon you (1 John 1:7, 9). Rather than closing up because of drinking from human sources, you will turn to God, present your filthiness before Him, and treasure His holiness washing over you while you stay open and drink from Him. Repentance will let you immediately turn to God for cleansing and a strong renewing of His presence and kingdom all around you.

Set your thirsty desire free, and don't hold back! Trust God to come to you so He can wash you and so that God can do His will on earth as it is in Heaven. The better we get at receiving Heaven here, the more we help to establish the tabernacle of God on earth (Rev. 21:3).

9

GOD'S PRESENCE AS OUR IDENTITY SHIELD

IDENTITY AND ABIDING

In this chapter, we consider the Scriptures and the practical reasons why it is right for us to depend on God to draw near so it can be practical for us to rely on His presence as our identity and protection in everyday life.

Photo by Luca Baggio on Unsplash

Think of identity as the accumulation of glory we receive over our lives that, in time, comes to define who we are. Directly related is where the Bible says, "This is the name by which she will be called: the Lord is our righteousness" (Jer. 33:16). When our identity becomes "the Lord is our righteousness," God's righteousness is the name we know ourselves by. The benefits of directing the thinking in our hearts toward living this way are profoundly practical.

When we receive Christ for salvation, we become the righteousness of God in Christ, and something of the worth of God comes to live inside us (2 Cor. 5:21).[15] Receiving the righteousness of Christ into us makes the eternal inside part of us worthy of keeping in Heaven for eternity with God (Matt. 13:47–51). Receiving the righteousness of Christ onto us is also important. The Bible also tells us to "break up" the fallow ground in our hearts until the Lord comes to "rain righteousness on you" (Hos. 10:12; see also Luke 8:15). Receiving the presence of God and His kingdom around and upon us after salvation solves the practical problem of worth and identity for our outer humanity.

Most people would say that to improve our identity, we must recognize the intrinsic value and glory of us as people or as believers. While it is true that people have value and the worth of who we are as believers is great, this is not what the Bible teaches about what we should depend on for identity. Please stay with me as I explain.

In the Bible, identity for us has far more to do with the presence of God with us all around the outside of us than Christ inside us. Since identity is something we put on and wear around us, identity is what we abide inside. To make our abiding in Christ practical, we must think of identity as involving us being in Christ in the sense of His presence coming and staying around us here.

It is helpful to think of abiding in this way because, by God's intentional design, it is natural that we put on and wear our identity. By this, the natural motivation to experience the benefits of having a strong identity becomes motivation to abide in Christ.

Yes, you can fight God's intentional design and try to think of identity as something you believe about who you are inside. But what you believe about who you are does little to put armor on the outside of you where you need it. What we put on around us should be Jesus Himself (Rom. 13:12–14). When we receive and wear the presence of God's name around us as our identity, we are called by His name and God Himself becomes our refuge and protection. By this, our everyday application of the Scriptures fits God's natural design.

GLORY, PRAISE, IDENTITY, PRIDE, AND SPIRITUAL WARFARE

Since identity is something we wear, the glory we receive and put on in this life is directly related to what eventually comes to identify us as who we are. When speaking on a human level, the glory we receive, put on, and accumulate throughout our lives identifies and defines us as who we are. But wearing glory for identity only benefits us with confidence when we praise the glory enough to support our faith about how great it is. Only when we believe the greatness of the glory we wear does it provide us with a

---

[15] The idea of the righteousness of God having worth isn't original to me. I first heard it when Ray Stedman talked about it many years ago.

Photo by Matt Botsford on Unsplash

strong sense of identity, confidence, and worth. But because praise inside can be subtle, we must be careful to keep the inner flow of praise moving toward God and not coming back toward us.

When the strength of our identity is from praise toward our human glory, the result is pride. While we do feel bolder and more confident, pride tends to make us feel more independent from God, weakening us spiritually. An identity based on pride is spiritually weak because of the direct relationship between identity as something we wear and protection as something we depend on as armor.

When identity is strong, it functions well as a shield. But consider where the Bible talks about our shield of faith that protects us during spiritual warfare against the demonic (Eph. 6:16). When the literal shield we wear is based on faith in the glory of how significant we are, our protection against the demonic is only as thick as how strongly we boast in our greatness. When difficult times come and the object of our faith is ourselves, our basis for remaining strong is seldom enough. When our faith is built up by boasting in the strength and holiness of God drawing close and all around us, God responds to our boasting in Him. He fights on our behalf, and our shield against the demonic is far more effective.

Pride doesn't crush or burn the demonic when they get close enough to attack us. Who you are in Christ doesn't crush evil under your feet. Only the presence of God and His kingdom have the power to do that! A shield of faith based on who you are in Christ does little when compared to the weight of God's mountain and the peace of Heaven coming to burn and crush the demonic (Rom. 16:20; Isa. 4:4). Hide who you are in Christ behind the more powerful glory of God and kingdom of Heaven around you as your shield (Ps. 84:11).

Photo by 卡晨 *on Unsplash*

you have in Christ, your shield of faith is based on who you are. The authority of God Himself as armor around you is much stronger than any armor you put on because of faith in your authority or in the greatness of who you are.

If you want to avoid backlash from the demonic after spiritual warfare, you have to put on the armor that is the presence of the Lord Jesus Himself. Listen to yourself making declarations that build your faith about the power of God's presence coming upon and around you as what burns up the demonic. When you believe that with the freedom of a child, Heaven comes and God's will is done in ways that crush the demonic under your feet.

Of course, we Christians have authority because of Christ in us. Our words are powerful swords against the demonic. But because the battle against evil is all around us, the need for twenty-four-hour protection is vital. It is difficult to wield a sword while you sleep. You need a protective shield based on faith in God.

It is good to pray the blood of Christ over your home, yourself, and your family. But why not walk by faith in the light that is the blood of Christ that you believe is continually shining from God and onto you here (1 John 1:5, 7)? When you make it your habit to stay open and continuously drink from the radiance of God that you believe is before you here, the blood of Christ is washing over you and everything around you constantly.

Elijah and Elisha described themselves as standing before the Lord (in most translations) because doing that was central to their identity (1 Kings 18:15; 2 Kings 3:14). Their spiritual authority resulted from standing in the radiance of God upon them. If you are doing spiritual warfare based on the authority

The protection promised in Psalm 91 happens only when we build our faith in God as the strong refuge in whom we abide. The identity we wear and experiencing God as our shield are directly related.

The Bible talks about how we wear pride like a necklace (Ps. 73:6), and identity from the world's glory is like that. Don't settle for abiding in pride around you when you can have an identity shield that is the presence of Jesus Himself (Rom. 13:12–14). Even wanting to receive glory from earthly and human sources damages our faith in receiving the glory of God easily and in a childlike way (John 5:44; Mark 10:15). Glory from earthly sources makes it hard even to consider receiving the kingdom of Heaven and the glory of God freely. Your bold declarations of repentance that turn your heart and cut off earthly glory sources pave the way for greater faith.

For any of what I write to be practical, our repentance has to change our mind enough to humble us from earthly sources before faith is present to believe that we can realistically receive Heaven here like a child.

Let me repeat here that Jesus earned God's glory for us through His sinless life, death on the cross, resurrection, and glorification. It is because of the glorification of Jesus that we can drink from the radiant fountain of God (John 7:37, 39; Ps. 36:7–9). Jesus earned the glory for us, and as we praise God for the greatness of His glory drawing close to us here, we honor Him, and we feel worthy and washed clean by association with Him as our God who is near.

When depending on God, our identity is more potent than is otherwise possible. We feel worthy and have a strong identity because of two things. One has to do with the boastful thanksgiving and praise we give toward the greatness of God's glory, drawing close enough to put it on and wear it around us. The other concerns how we associate ourselves with Him as our God. With God, the strength of our identity is the result of how well we have identified with His presence and embraced Him as what defines us instead of other things.

The tassels on the Old Testament priestly garments were physical symbols of the presence of God with them. But the Bible says the priests turned the ornaments of their garments into pride (Ezek. 7:20). Guard your heart from self-directed praise and pride about the presence of God! But don't hold back in your praise and childlike enjoyment of God's closeness to you here. When you recognize praise going toward yourself, don't ignore it, and don't shut down out of guilt. The praise is already flowing, so redirect it toward God and enjoy that you are honoring Him because you are turning to embrace Him as your God instead of yourself. Embrace the truth that your faith is causing Him to feel pleasure (Heb. 11:6).

The glory we put on as ours is directly related to what we depend on for identity because glory is what identifies and defines us as someone significant and valuable. When we make the closeness of Heaven our glory, we make the presence of God our identity and our worth. But please note that gratitude and boastful praise because of God and His kingdom near us will maintain our confidence and faith in God's closeness as our identity.

> Make declarations of gratitude and praise that support and build your faith about God drawing near even when nobody else around you seems to care about such things.

Please make no mistake about it. The emotional benefits I speak of are not purely human because the benefits spill over heavily into the spiritual realm. The benefits to us and God are directly connected. When we praise God—whose living glory we depend on as our security, confidence, and worthiness—we believe God is drawing near in an ever-increasing way. We are made powerfully strong in spiritual realms as a result. In spiritual warfare, our boasting in God, whom we believe is continuing to come to us with His kingdom and angels, builds the strength of our shield of faith that protects us decisively better than who we are in Christ. Staying open and continuing to receive also completely reverses the backlash we experience from the demonic because our warfare is ongoing. The kingdom of Heaven advances when God delivers us from evil, and the demons get punished when we receive the kingdom of Heaven upon and around us here.

> When you make God your refuge, what you receive around you as your refuge does the fighting. When you become playfully childlike and praise God as your refuge, your protection and the effectiveness of the angels in battle increases. Direct your heart into having fun with that.

Our boasting in the greatness of God's closeness shuts down the demonic and witchcraft sent against us. You become the one causing them to feel backlash. When you playfully boast about the power and holiness of God close to you, what you receive becomes a dangerously massive hammer to demonic enemies that crushes them under your feet.

But none of this becomes practical until you direct your heart away from earthly sources and make it your habit to praise the closeness of God. Thank God that the kingdom of Heaven is coming to you and is all around you here. Trust by faith that you are looking at the face of the Father. If you are terrified by that, the terror you feel may be what a demon is feeling, and you feel it because they wrongly have their claws sunk into your flesh. Don't crumple with guilt or fear about that. When God's kingdom comes, you only need a flick of the finger of God to get them off you (Luke 11:20). Build your faith with bold declarations, then pray that God delivers you from evil (Matt. 6:13).

Confess bitterness and any unforgiveness you may have toward someone, then do your best to consciously believe that your eyes are looking at Jesus and the face of your Father before you here (2 Chron. 7:14; Ps. 123:2; John 14:6; Matt. 18:10; Heb. 12:2). Doing that will go far to loosen any grip the demonic has on you.

HOLINESS, PROTECTION, AND FIGHTING EVIL

If your prayers aren't helping, seek someone to help you with deliverance. It can be challenging to recognize the underlying basis for the attack. Look for help with deliverance in charismatic churches. Be sure you don't shut down spiritually. Get the help and keep thanking God that the kingdom of Heaven is around you and that because more is coming, the kingdom of Heaven is advancing and is crushing other kingdoms of evil on earth (Dan. 2:35, 44–45; Matt. 21:42–44). Thank God that Jesus is on the right-hand side of the Father (Acts 7:55) and that Jesus is walking with you here (2 Cor. 6:16).

Don't let yourself think that you have to be repetitious to get God to hear and respond to you. Repetition in your thanks and praise breaks up your heart's hardness. You must keep up with the repetition in your declarations until your faith becomes more playfully childlike and you can confidently believe that God is coming to rain His righteousness on you here (Hos. 6:3; 10:12). Even though the repetition is a form of worship, the practical thing about it is that it helps us to strengthen our faith. Repetition is for our benefit, not God's.

GOD AS OUR I AM

Again, even though identity is something we wear outside and around us, identity is not us. When Moses was unsure about himself and the call of God on His life, he said, in essence, "I am not enough for the task. Get somebody else." But God solved his identity crisis by saying, "Certainly I will be with you" (Ex. 3:12). Then God said He wanted to be introduced to the people as "I AM" (Ex. 3:14).

Note that God did not say to Moses, "Believe who I say you are!" God said, "I will be with you. And by My being with you, I will be your I Am." Who you are in Christ is helpful. But that is still about who you are. Having the presence of God as your I Am is much more.

God as your I Am is how God wants you to know Him. God as your I Am is how He wants us to introduce Him to the world (Ex. 3:13–14). Our job is to introduce Christ to the world, not ourselves.

The glory of God is connected with identity because Moses said to God, "Is it not by Your going with us, so that we, I and Your people, may be distinguished from all the other people . . .?" (Ex. 33:16). Two verses later, Moses asked God, "Show me Your glory" (Ex. 33:18). The presence of the glory of God can be your identity also because "the Lord gives grace and glory" (Ps. 84:11). Joyfully reassure your heart with bold declarations about the truth that you don't have to stay in bondage to earthly and human glory!

Drinking from God and enjoying the many benefits of His presence work far more consistently than when you try to depend on earthly sources for what you need. But you cannot be your own I am and expect to experience God as your I Am.

The beliefs and loves of your heart need to be directed toward God so that the ways you usually try to receive and drink from earthly glory get reapplied to God. Drinking from God isn't any more complicated and doesn't require more faith than when you receive glory from earthly sources and believe that you have glory on a human level. The tricky part is that you have to learn to receive by faith in the grace of God to draw near instead of faith in your ability to earn glory from the world. Keep making joyous declarations until you become childlike enough to open up freely and receive what shines from God. What does it look like in everyday life?

STANDING BEFORE THE LORD AS OUR IDENTITY

Let me repeat that Moses depended on God as his identity, which distinguished him and the Israelites from others (Ex. 33:15–16). When we stand before the Lord with our physical body, the practical result is that the presence of God and His kingdom become the identity we put on and wear around us.

Standing before the Lord is directly related to presenting our body to God as an acceptable service of worship (Rom. 12:1). Jesus is the lamb of God that makes the inside of us acceptable for eternity when His radiance comes to wash us clean. The cleansing of God for our humanity washes our bodies and makes the outer part of us holy also.

Let me now quote the verses where Elijah and Elisha introduced themselves as standing before the Lord: "Elijah said, 'As the Lord of hosts lives, before whom I stand' " (1 Kings 18:15). And, "Elisha said, 'As the Lord of hosts lives, before whom I stand, were it not that I regard the presence of Jehoshaphat the king of Judah, I would not look at you nor see you' " (2 Kings 3:14). By introducing themselves as standing before the Lord, we know what they considered the most significant thing about their identity. It should not seem strange to us that we can stand before the Lord because "the Lord said to Moses, '...Behold, I will stand before you there on the rock at Horeb' " (Ex. 17:5–6). We can stand before the Lord and present our body to God because we can receive the kingdom of Heaven here with the faith of a child.

> When we listen to and believe our repetitious declarations of thanks and praise that direct our hearts away from earthly glory, our declarations of faith can then increase the capacity of our freedom and faith to that of a child (John 5:44; Rom. 12:2; 10:9–10; Matt. 18:3). When that happens, it is much easier to believe you can enter before the Lord by receiving the kingdom of Heaven around you here so you can stand before the Lord as a priest (Heb. 10:19–22; 12:22–24, 28; 2 Chron. 29:11). By this, the presence of God and the kingdom of Heaven around you become what you boastfully wear for identity and protection and as what fights evil.

The two witnesses in the book of Revelation are those who stand before the Lord (Rev. 11:4). What they will be giving a testimony about will have to do with the significance of what it means to stand before the Lord. In a similar way, it should not be strange to us that we can walk with God like Elijah and Enoch because to us "God said, / 'I will dwell in them and walk among them; / And I will be their God, and they shall be My people' " (2 Cor. 6:16). By salvation, Jesus lives in us. By directing our hearts to be more childlike, we can more easily believe we can enter by receiving Heaven here. By this, Jesus can walk among us, and the proximity of His living and strong radiance upon and around us becomes our identity.

Related is where Jesus commanded us to abide with Him in us and us in Him. I find 19 verses about Christ in us but well over 250 about us being in Him, in Christ, or in the Lord. Salvation is about Christ in us, but it does not guarantee that we are in Him in a literal sense. We have to drink like a child from God to take refuge in Him (Ps. 36:7–9). We also have to drink from the radiance around God to abide inside His literal presence (Jer. 2:11–13).

When you trust by faith that you are presenting your body to God (Rom. 12:1) by believing that Jesus is walking with you here, you can boast with praise toward God about an identity based on the holiness and power of God's presence with you here. By this, you greatly honor God, you love Him more, His presence becomes your refuge of protection, and your sense of identity and confidence are strengthened. After that, your spiritual significance increases because you add to your faith that the radiance of the Father is coming down onto you and everyone around you like rain (Acts 2:17; Hos. 6:3; 10:12).

JESUS IS HIS NAME, BUT HIS NAME IS ALSO JESUS HIMSELF

We have two verses in the Bible telling us that His name is Jesus. First, "His name was then called Jesus, the name given by the angel before He was conceived in the womb" (Luke 2:21). And it says Joseph "called His name Jesus" (Matt. 1:25). So Jesus is His name in the same sense that we know the name of a friend. But when it comes to the name of the Lord, the Scriptures make it clear that there is a lot more to it than this, and we have to fit the pieces of the puzzle together before we can see the big picture.

Clear thinking about the name of the Lord is paramount because "this is His commandment, that we believe in the name of His Son Jesus Christ" (1 John 3:23). Note also where it says, "As many as received Him, to them He gave the right to become children of God, even to those who believe in His name" (John 1:12). Believing that Jesus was the human name of our Lord while on earth doesn't necessarily seem connected to receiving Christ in the rest of the Bible. But when we consider the Scriptures as a whole, the John 1:12 verse takes on a much fuller meaning.

Jesus is His name because of the two verses we have in the Bible, and salvation is simple. But because the Bible emphasizes that the name of the Lord is the presence of God Himself, it makes sense to say that when we believe in His name, we receive Christ for salvation because we literally receive the presence of His Spirit coming to us (Titus 3:5–6).

THE NAME OF THE LORD AS THE PRESENCE OF GOD HIMSELF

There are more than a dozen Hebrew names for God in the Old Testament. There are several dozen more verses that connect the name of our Lord to His presence. Jesus is His name, but His name is also the presence of Jesus Himself.

The Lord's name, glory, and presence are directly related. "Moses said, 'I pray You, show me Your glory!' And He said, 'I Myself will make all My goodness pass before you, and will proclaim the name of the Lord before you...and it will come about, while My glory is passing by, that...I have passed by' " (Ex. 33:18–19, 22). When God proclaims His name to people, His glory and God Himself have come near. When the name of the Lord draws near us and we identify with Him as our God, we praise His name close to us and being called by His name becomes practical and personally meaningful.

The name of the Lord is directly related to the blessing of God coming to us when the glory of God shines onto us from His face. Note especially what this priestly blessing says about the name of the Lord: "'The Lord bless you, and keep you; / The Lord make His face shine on you, / And be gracious to you; / The Lord lift up His countenance on you, / And give you peace.' / So they shall invoke My name on the sons of Israel, and I then will bless them" (Num. 6:24–27).

When the name of the Lord is invoked onto people, His presence comes to them through the shine that comes from God's face. According to this passage, the name of the Lord, the blessing of God, and His peace all come to us through the substance of God's brightness pouring out from God's face. Living by faith includes an active faith that believes the radiance of God is coming onto us and into our world. We need the Word of God as our foundation because this topic is vitally important.

Twenty-two times in Scripture, the name of the Lord is said to dwell or stay in a physical location. Here are some examples:

- "The place in which the Lord your God will choose for His name to dwell" (Deut. 12:11).

- "You shall eat in the presence of the Lord your God, at the place where He chooses to establish His name" (Deut. 14:23).

- "The place which the Lord your God chooses to put His name" (Deut. 12:21).

When we consider the Scriptures as a whole, the greatest emphasis is that God is there when His name is present.

Regarding the presence of God and Jesus Himself, it says, "Now the Lord is the Spirit" (2 Cor. 3:17). So, while we have to believe that Jesus is His name, when we consider the Bible as a whole, we also have to believe that His name is literally the presence of Jesus Himself.

When Jesus is present, His name is with us: "For where two or three have gathered together in My name, I am there in their midst" (Matt. 18:20).

Jesus is His name, but His name is also the presence of God, which includes the essence of everything about who Jesus is. When we are in His name, we are wrapped in the presence of the Living God, whose presence with us includes everything about who He is.

The connection between the name of the Lord and God's presence is made clear when it says, "You are in our midst, O Lord, / And we are called by Your name" (Jer. 14:9). Related is where it says, "Make Your name known to Your adversaries, / That the nations may tremble at Your presence!" (Isa. 64:2), and "The Lord descended in the cloud and stood there with him as he called upon the name of the Lord" (Ex. 34:5). It is prophecy where it says, "They shall call His name Immanuel, which...means, 'God with us' " (Matt. 1:23). When you understand that His name is His presence, that is when you call His name "God with us."

We are to "glory in His holy name; / Let the heart of those who seek the Lord be glad" (1 Chron. 16:10). When like a child, we glory in the presence of Christ Jesus whom we believe is with us, we are glad because we are praising His name with us here. We might even "praise His name with dancing" (Ps. 149:3). "Save us, O Lord our God, / And gather us from among the nations, / To give thanks to Your holy name / And glory in Your praise" (Ps. 106:47).

Speaking of the priests, the Bible says: "They shall invoke My name on the sons of Israel, and I then will bless them" (Num. 6:27). Of those who have received God's presence, it says, "We give thanks to You, O God, we give thanks, / For Your name is near" (Ps. 75:1). Then later it says, "Surely the righteous will give thanks to Your name; / The upright will dwell in Your presence" (Ps. 140:13).

IDENTITY AND BEING CALLED BY HIS NAME

We need God to heal our land, but the conditions must be met: "[If] My people who are called by My name humble themselves and pray and seek My face and turn from their wicked ways, then I will hear from heaven, will forgive their sin and will heal their land" (2 Chron. 7:14). We have to be a people who are "called by His name." According to the Scriptures, being called by His name and praying in Jesus's name differ greatly.

Certainly, the logic flows that we are called by His name because of salvation. But according to the Scriptures on this topic cover to cover in the Bible, salvation is only the beginning of where it becomes possible for us to be called by His name.

When you study the word *name* in the Bible, you find there are very few times when the word *name* is used, as when we pray, "For Your name's sake" or "In Jesus's name." But there are many times when it is clear that the word name is talking about the presence of God. Why is this important?

The name our parents gave us is what identifies us as individuals. But being called by God's name has to do with being known as those who live in the presence of God, as we saw in Jeremiah 14:9.[16]

The main message of the Bible about our being called by His name has to do with us being inside His name in the sense of being in His presence, where our identity is the presence of God's name with us here. Because identity is something we wear around us, being called by the name of the Lord is profoundly practical for everyday living.

---

[16] I have had worship leaders tell me they can feel God's presence when I dance, but in everyday life, I have yet to have someone tell me anything like that. Obviously, I still have room to grow in this area.

Photo by William Farlow on Unsplash

The verses that connect the name of the Lord to His presence make it suitable for us to think of the closeness of God as what defines us as believers and as what gives us an identity that we put on and wear. When the presence of God Himself becomes the identity we put on and wear, and we praise His name close to us, the strength of our identity becomes powerful in spiritual realms. We become bold, secure, confident, and more loving than is possible any other way.

When God Himself is close to us as the identity we praise, we feel worthy and strong to the extent that we can be kind even when others are unkind. Their lack of kindness isn't nearly as painful because nothing others do or say can reduce the significance or worth of our identity.

Remember again that there are twenty-two times in Scripture where God looks for a place where He can put His name so His name can dwell there. We are called by His name when we have become a place for His name to dwell.

God's name is the name that belongs to Him because it is His name. Yet, when you take ownership of God as your God, your experience of God escalates to the point of becoming something deeply personal, God Himself becomes your I Am, and being called by His name becomes realistic for you.

The Bible tells us that "the name of the Lord comes from a remote place" (Isa. 30:27). Jesus was obedient unto death, ascended into Heaven, and was glorified by the Father when He was given the "Spirit of glory" (1 Peter 4:14). That Spirit even now still proceeds from the Father (John 15:26) and from His Son Jesus (Heb. 1:3). In other words, we are called by His name dwelling with us here because when the Father glorified Jesus, the Father gave Jesus a name (Phil. 2:9) that in essence is the living Spirit of glory that now pours out from all around Him (John 7:37–39). By the death and subsequent glorification of Christ, we are now able to be a people whose identity is that of His presence with us. The name of the Lord is His Spirit that pours out from all around Him, and denying His name is to deny the benefits of Him being a radiant fountain (Jer. 17:13).

Let me say again that we receive Him when we believe in His name as the Scriptures teach (John 1:12). Thank the Lord until your heart hears and enjoys believing that Jesus is His name, and the presence of His name is the presence of Jesus Himself.

FOR THE SAKE OF HIS NAME

Note also that God does what He does because He wants His name honored. The Bible says, "He saved them for the sake of His name" (Ps. 106:8), and "your sins have been forgiven you for His name's sake" (1 John 2:12). After salvation, God leads us on the "paths of righteousness / For His name's sake" (Ps. 23:3).

God says, "I acted for the sake of My name, that it should not be profaned in the sight of the nations" (Ezek. 20:9). In other words, God honors His name for the sake of people knowing the truth about what He is like and His greatness. People tend to have so many misguided ideas about what God is like that He must represent Himself well or they keep misunderstanding Him.

So then, it is reasonable to say that it would be for the sake of His name, or for the sake of those called by His name, that God would heal our land (2 Chron. 7:14). It is also reasonable for us to believe the grace of God for His drawing near abundantly not because we earn His presence, but for the sake of what honors His name and what accomplishes His will and purposes on earth.

We honor and glorify God the most when we open up to Him and expect to receive an abundance of His glory because of our childlike faith that He is coming to us here. We all need to do this as individuals, but when multitudes of believers apply bold faith to receiving Heaven here, that is when God will accomplish His will on earth, and His name will be glorified and praised more than ever before.

If we are pushing to make a kingdom and name for ourselves, then being called by His name isn't realistic because our heart-level preoccupation is with exalting and honoring ourselves and our name. If we intend to make a name for ourselves, we are trying to receive glory that we can turn into pride. It is not possible to be trying to be called by your name and glorify God at the same time.

The verses on this topic stretch us, but we must ask, Can God heal our land if we, His people, are called by our name instead of His? We must be careful to make His name famous not ours.

Remember again that God does what He does to honor His name so that people think of Him accurately. Therefore, because God is perfectly good, being able to receive an abundance of God's presence must be simple enough for a child to do or we wouldn't be able to be called by His name in a practical way.

SPIRITUAL AND PHYSICAL SAFETY

There are strong promises in Scripture about physical and spiritual protection. But I see that our security is based conditionally on the childlikeness of our freedom and faith that lets us receive the tabernacle of Heaven, stand before the Lord in the tent of His presence, abide in His presence, and praise Him for His greatness near to us here (Mark 10:15; Ps. 91; 27:1–6; Matt. 21:16).

My experience is that these Scriptures are true. Directing my heart away from idolatry and toward believing God has been decisively powerful for deliverance and protection (1 Sam. 7:3). But experientially, I don't know how far we can take this for entrusting our physical safety from evil people to God. I only know that the promise of physical safety involves a confident faith about setting the Lord continually before us here (Ps. 16:8–9). So any time my physical or spiritual safety seems threatened, the things I am writing in this book are what I do my best to apply.

Some Christians believe their protection depends on how well they fight the demonic with the authority in their words. I, too, am confident that my words have authority. But I have never understood how to make declarations that protect me while I sleep. For me, it is easier to receive Heaven here and cling to God's presence for protection like a child. When you become childlike and playfully fall in love with the kingdom of God and His presence around you as your security, you cling to God's presence even while you sleep.

In olden times of war, rocks and swords were weapons. Warriors also used their shields to bludgeon enemies. In the Scriptures, God wants to be our rock, shield (2 Sam. 22:3; Ps. 84:11), and our sword (Eph. 6:17). More than using my words as a sword in one-on-one combat, it fits my personality and the Scriptures to depend on God as a shield of powerful holiness and a rock of overwhelming peace that bludgeons and crushes demonic enemies in a wide area. I fight evil by playfully loving the closeness of God and maintaining my faith about receiving Heaven around me here. I use my words to bind the power of the demonic and witchcraft (Matt. 16:19). Then I loose the weight of the mountain of God and the crushing peace of Heaven with angels into this realm. I started just by applying this around myself, but God has been teaching me to apply this to other people and much larger areas. By this, the kingdom of Heaven became my most treasured way of fighting evil and doing my part to help advance God's purposes on earth (Rom. 16:20; Matt. 6:10).

Whatever your preference—a sword, a big rock, or both—our focus should be on receiving Heaven here so we can stand before the Lord with our physical body and abide in Him so we can drink of His living radiance and experience Him as a shield around us.

Ultimately, the bride of Christ will make herself ready (Rev. 19:7), the goodness and power of Heaven will come as the wedding dress we put on (Rev. 19:8), and God will tabernacle Himself among us here on earth (Rev. 21:3). The more of God's people that ready themselves by receiving Heaven here, the more our protection will increase and the more we will put on the wedding gown of His presence. We will all be more in love with God and more effective in battle when we prepare ourselves by joyfully aligning with the new thing God is doing in our day (Isa. 43:18–20).

PRAISE HIS NAME WHILE GOD IS INCREASINGLY DRAWING NEAR

The Bible says, "We give thanks to You, O God.../ For Your name is near" (Ps. 75:1). I also count sixty-five other verses about praising His name.

> Since the name of the Lord has to do with His presence, praising the name of the Lord involves praising God, whom we believe is and has drawn near to us here.

Remember again that God comes to us like rain and that every good and perfect gift from God comes to us from above (Hos. 6:3; James 1:17). But in our world, it rains, then stops, then rains again later. It is not this way with God.

The sun doesn't stop giving its light, and our God is like the sun who gives His radiant glory as a shield around us. We dare not ignore that our God is a radiant fountain that never stops giving (Jer. 17:13). We are to drink from God and keep on being filled (Eph. 5:18) because He never stops gushing His presence onto those who are open and have active faith for receiving (John 7:37–39; 4:14). The more we praise the greatness of God's name and the more we believe He is drawing near, the more of His presence we buy because of delight in the abundance of what God is giving freely (Isa. 55:1–2).

By connecting the translation of a quote in the New Testament with the way that same verse is translated in the Old Testament, we can conclude that when we praise the nearness of the name of the Lord with childlike faith and joy, our praise has strength that makes the enemy and the revengeful cease (Matt. 21:16; Ps. 8:2). The more we praise the greatness of the name of the Lord close to us, the more our childlike dependence on God increases, the more Heaven fills the earth, the stronger our protection becomes, and the more effectively God can fight evil on our behalf.

When we praise the strength of God's holy name upon and around us with the faith and joyful freedom of a child, God's win is increasingly decisive. Given that we are to keep walking in Him by continuing to receive (Col. 2:6), we should think of God as coming to us ever-increasingly and continuously.

We are to praise His name, and we are to give thanks to His name because of His being near (Ps. 75:1). But to make this protection effective, we use our words to build our faith when we "say to the LORD, 'My refuge and my fortress, / My God, in whom I trust!' " (Ps. 91:2). Speak to God, but listen to yourself and determine to let your heart believe the words you are saying! Related is that "the righteous will give thanks to Your name; / The upright will dwell in Your presence" (Ps. 140:13). Don't just give thanks from your mouth; give thanks from your heart. When we give thanks about His nearness, living upright becomes practical.

Photo by Marie Dehayes on Unsplash

Giving thanks for the presence of God's name helps to keep us safe because in Psalm 91, the people who abide in the presence of God are kept safe. Praising the name of the Lord like a child also brings strength. These verses are connected:

- "Because he has loved Me, therefore I will deliver him; /
  I will set him securely on high, because he has known My name" (Ps. 91:14)

- "The name of the Lord is a strong tower; /
  The righteous runs into it and is safe" (Prov. 18:10)

- "A humble and lowly people, / And they will take refuge
  in the name of the Lord" (Zeph. 3:12)

Receiving God's presence and praising His name close to us help us to abide in God's presence as our safe refuge.

BOASTFULLY PRAISING HIS NAME

People with the most confidence and the strongest identity boast in their name's greatness and the earthly glory they possess. We don't have to be like that. The Bible says we can boast in God. "Some boast in chariots and some in horses, / But we will boast in the name of the LORD, our God" (Ps. 20:7). "In God we have boasted all day long, / And we will give thanks to Your name forever" (Ps. 44:8). "My soul will make its boast in the Lord; / The humble will hear it and rejoice" (Ps. 34:2).

Photo by Nathan Dumlao on Unsplash

We must direct our dependence away from human glory, which we boastfully praise because of our works; to glory in God, we boastfully praise with childlike and joyful faith in God's grace for drawing near in great abundance. The more we boastfully praise the name of the Lord, instead of earthly and human glory, the more of an abundance of God's presence we experience.

To praise the name of the Lord, we must trust His name has drawn near (Jer. 14:9), and we still have to resist the demonic fear put on us to keep us from boasting in His name. But our boastful praise does not manipulate God into coming to us. Our boastful praise toward God humbles us from faith in ourselves and helps build faith in God, which helps us to open up better and receive from God more easily (John 5:44).

Declarations of thanks about the nearness of His name should be said in God's hearing, but our declarations need to aim mostly at the ears of our own heart so that our fears decrease and our childlike love and faith toward God can increase. We should never beg God to come to us! It is all about trading what we get from earthly sources in order to increase our delight about the abundance that God is giving freely (Isa. 55:1–2). It is all about becoming more childlike as we take refuge in Him by possessing His holy mountain (Isa. 57:13–14; Mark 10:14–15). Boastful praise increases our spiritual strength when we become like children who enjoy receiving the gift of God's kingdom and presence like we enjoy receiving gifts at Christmastime (Matt. 21:16; Ps. 8:2).

We must think clearly about the name of the Lord drawing near because "through You we will push back our adversaries; / Through Your name we will trample down those who rise up against us. / For I will not trust in my bow, / Nor will my sword save me. / But You have saved us from our adversaries, / And You have put to shame those who hate us. / In God we have boasted all day long, / And we will give thanks to Your name forever" (Ps. 44:5–8). That passage fits with where I earlier connected the verses in the Old and New Testaments saying that by boasting in and giving thanks for the nearness of the name of our Lord, our enemies get trampled down and God makes the revengeful cease (Matt. 21:16; Ps. 8:2).

It is fitting that you boast in the Lord. But God doesn't have an emotional need for us to boast in Him. Our praise advances the kingdom of God and benefits us emotionally and with a more impenetrable safety shield. Subtle forms of inner boasting and self-directed praise give us energy and a positive outlook to face the day's difficulties. In the same way, when we boast by praise in the greatness of God's closeness to us here also, we find a sense of physical energy and confidence. We mount up with wings as eagles (Isa. 40:31).

The greater our boasting and praise toward the greatness of God's presence as clothing around us, the more we will be worshiping the Lord in "holy array" and ascribing glory due to His name (1 Chron. 16:29). The more boastfully we praise the greatness of God close to us and all around, the greater our protection. The more of God we put on and wear, the more He fights against our enemies.

When praising the name of the Lord, you can rightly believe you are receiving Christ upon and around you as protection from temptation (Rom. 13:14). But when protection isn't there, fight evil and temptation by assertively making declarations that build your faith and playful enjoyment that Jesus is walking with you (2 Cor. 6:16) and that the power of His holiness and strength protecting you are crushing and burning demonic enemies around you. When praising the name of the Lord, you can rightly believe you are doing your part to fill the earth with the living glory that shines from God.

RESISTANCE TO PRAISING THE NEARNESS OF GOD'S NAME

Praising our name is natural for us; praising God's name is not. We feel pride when we honor our name, but protection because of our name doesn't help us at all. God becomes our protection when we take refuge inside the presence of His holy name. How can it be more natural to praise the name of the Lord who we believe is drawing close to us here? We must come to the place of identifying with Him as our God so much that we naturally think of His presence as what identifies us, even when others around us don't think of us that way.

When the presence of God's name becomes our identity, we honor God with praise toward the closeness of His name in a much more natural way. Let me remind you of where the Bible says, "We give thanks to You, O God . . . / For Your name is near" (Ps. 75:1). The more we honor God by praising the nearness of His holy name, the stronger our faith becomes. The more we identify with Him as our God, the more Heaven comes and the easier it gets for God's will to be done on earth as it is in Heaven (Matt. 6:10).

How do we put on the Lord Jesus Christ to more easily praise His name as our identity? We do that when by faith we receive the kingdom of Heaven here like a child. Like a child, we should "enter His gates with thanksgiving / And His courts with praise.

/ Give thanks to Him; bless His name" (Ps. 100:4). The better we are at receiving Heaven here with freedom in our faith and boldness in our praise toward the greatness of God's holy name around us, the better we will abide in Christ and the stronger our identity will be because we are called by His holy name (2 Chron. 7:14).

We must come to the place of praising His name with greater passion and demand than we give to praising our names. Even I have a lot of room to grow here. But how can we do that?

You and I both need to repent in ways that change our thinking more deeply. After having directed our hearts toward relying on God to draw near so we can identify with His presence as what identifies us, we must then recognize that the resistance to praising His name is not coming from us.

> The resistant pressure to avoid praising the closeness of God's name is from the demonic. After coming to the place of making God's presence your refuge, the resistance to praising His nearness is put on you by the demonic; it is not from you or God at all. The demonic resists us when we are praising the name of the Lord because the holiness, love, unhinged peace, and power of God come into this realm, crushing and destroying evil.[17]

Recently, in worship, I noticed myself getting caught up in thinking that people were watching me dance before the Lord, and I could feel pride starting to come on me. I have done a lot to listen to myself make declarations cutting off pride about the presence of God and fear of other people's opinions. So yes, I did try to get my focus back on God, but it worked far better to think about what was happening as a demonic attack and then expose the whole thing before God.

I found the freedom I needed when I bound their power to attack me (Matt. 16:19) and made boastful declarations of thanksgiving that Heaven was dropping down hard, crushing the demonic, and that the holiness of God was washing me and burning away the attack of pride against me. Immediately, I was able to dance with childlike freedom again.

---

[17] Entering by receiving the mountain of God and Heaven here has gotten fairly easy for me. Purity is consistently good. But after that, more than anything else I am aware of, I struggle with praising His name after I receive and am before Him. Demonic pressure to avoid ongoing praise has been horrible. I also think maybe that I am holding back for some reason. If you think to pray for me, please pray that I would be more faithful to praise His nearness continually. More repentance is needed!

AN IDENTITY SHIELD THAT CRUSHES THE DEMONIC

Protection from self-esteem does nothing to protect us from the demonic. The only thing self-esteem does is bring pride that dulls us to the truth about what is happening in unseen realms. You might feel self-esteem enough to say no to temptation for a time. You may also feel strong enough to yell at the devil and tell him to leave. But you will eventually get worn down, temptation and some form of demonic backlash will come, and you will fall.

In contrast, Jesus commanded us to abide in Him (John 15:5) and to abide in His love (John 15:9). Of course, you can believe that you are a blood-bought child of God and that God loves you. Doing that does help to improve your behavior on many levels. You might, on occasion, also be able to feel the tangible presence of God. Believing who you are in Christ does give you authority in spiritual realms and can help you have courage when making declarations for fighting evil.

The practical problem for me has been that believing I am loved and a child of God has not been enough to decisively keep the demonic and temptation away on a regular and practical ongoing basis. I have had to be intentional about filling my desires by loving God as armor around me instead of what I could get from sin.

Who we are in Christ is helpful, but if you glory in that, there is nothing about wearing that as your identity that will decisively crush Satan under your feet. Only God can do that by the coming of His kingdom and His peace (Dan. 2:35, 44–45; Heb. 12:22–24, 28; Rom. 16:20). Directing our hearts into trusting the presence of God drawing near to us is greater than who you are in Christ.

No matter how hard I tried, I could not make declarations that built my faith about who I am in Christ enough to be protected from the demonic while I slept. I had to take my shield of identity further than anything about who I am to crush the demonic decisively and keep them away.

The Bible talks about our "shield of faith" protecting us (Eph. 6:16). But we must hold a shield between us and something else that is trying or might try to harm us. Our shield of faith is not a shield made of faith alone. Faith must have something we believe is protecting us. In that sense, it is not the faith that shields us, but rather, it is what our faith believes is around us that shields us. When the object of your faith is who you are in Christ, you might be living the gospel of salvation. But are you living the gospel of the glory of Christ (2 Cor. 4:4) and the gospel of the kingdom (Matt. 24:14)? We must be careful to include the glory of Christ and the kingdom of God in our daily application of the gospel (Jer. 2:11–13). When we consider how God defines idolatry with the related verses saying that He wants us to drink from Him instead of the idols, it follows that forsaking the incredible truth about God as a fountain is the same as turning away from Him (Jer. 17:13). Because God is a radiant fountain, it is practical for us to trust He will come to us so we can depend on Him as our identity and shield (Ps. 84:11).

If faith in my identity has anything to do with me, even when it has to do with who I am in Christ, I can't be consistent enough in the boldness of my faith to shield me because my faith is in who I am. If I am actually inside the presence of Christ Himself, where that is the crucial thing, I believe that only then am I protected consistently and practically. Only then am I wearing a shield that will fight evil on my behalf while I am asleep. Make celebrative declarations of faith until you enter the throne room by receiving the tabernacle of Heaven around you with a child's faith, built up by joy about receiving (Ps. 27:1–6; Rev. 21:3).

When the object of my faith has even a little bit to do with me, eventually, I get discouraged enough that I fall apart. If you are anything like me in this, functioning in a healthy way as a believer requires that the object of your faith is more significant than anything about yourself. Who we are in Christ gives us great authority. But who we are in Christ does not have the power to bludgeon the demonic and crush them under our feet. Only God Himself can do that, and He does it when we receive the kingdom of Heaven here with His peace and the weight of His mountain. Our application of the Bible must be aligned with what it says.

Of course, you can stand firm and make the demons flee (James 4:7–8). You can also use your authority in Christ and demand that they leave (Mark 16:17). I do these things, but I also want to punish demons for the damage they try to do to you and me. I do not tolerate backlash from the demonic. I want them to feel the backlash for messing with me. You can do the same.

The word of God is like a hammer that shatters rock (Jer. 23:29). The only other things I see in Scripture that crush Satan are the peace of God and the kingdom of Heaven as it expands in the earthly realm (Rom. 16:20; Dan. 2:35, 44–45). Related to something that crushes the demonic are the Scriptures that talk about the "weight of glory" (2 Cor. 4:17) and that "every perfect gift is from above, coming down from the Father of lights" (James 1:17). Still another place it talks about the fire of God burning His enemies and the "spirit of judgment and . . . of burning" washing away the filth of what is evil (Isa. 4:4; see also Ps. 97:3). If you want to cause demons to be terrified, then your application of Scripture needs to include what the Bible says hurts them the most.

Repent by directing your heart into loving that you can't earn God's presence and that all you can do is open up like a child and receive His coming to you so He can be your God. Repent by transforming your mind so that you believe the grace of God enough to trust Him to give you an abundance of His presence freely. Jesus wants us to receive the kingdom in a way that peels the evil off us and out of the atmosphere around us and then crushes it.

Much of the fruit resulting from the kingdom of Heaven coming to earth is that the devil gets crushed under our feet. We must believe God is actively crushing evil by His kingdom coming because God gives His kingdom to the people who believe enough to produce the fruit of it (Matt. 21:42–44).

BEING A TESTIMONY TO THE GREATNESS OF HIS NAME

Being clothed with power from on high helps us effectively testify about Jesus (Acts 1:8). We must become a testimony to the greatness of His name—not our name.

When we open up and receive the presence of God, He clothes us with power in ways that strengthen our identity. But God says to us that "'there was no strange god among you; / So you are My witnesses,' declares the Lord" (Isa. 43:12). Therefore, being the most effective witness possible requires repentance that helps us to turn away from idolatry and then also turns us toward God so that He can clothe us with His presence and power.

But this kind of repentance must be an act of worship by declarations of thanksgiving and praise. If not, condemnation will take over and our repentance will shut us down before God instead of setting us free. Thanksgiving and praise help us to turn away from idolatry and sin, and turn more fully toward God.

The more we joyously turn away from trying to wear glory from earthly sources and the more childlike we become at receiving the glory that shines from God and praising His closeness to us, the stronger our faith will be in the presence of God as our identity, the better we have become at abiding in Christ, the more we will stay pure in our behavior, and the more power we will have for giving a clear testimony about Jesus (Mark 10:15; Ps. 84:11; Rom. 13:12, 14).

After the resurrection, ascension, and glorification of Jesus, Peter based his identity on the confidence he had in the power of the presence of Jesus on and around him here. Of course, it was Jesus who healed the man, but it was also Peter's confidence about the greatness of what he had put on as his identity that healed the person when Peter's shadow passed by (Acts 5:15). I want that, and I am sure you also do. We both need to praise the power of His closeness to us to see more of His power displayed.

Some of the insights I am sharing now about boasting in the Lord and praising His closeness feel like they are brand new to me. In my own growth toward God, I am trying to remember that praise toward the identity we wear makes God's power able to be seen as a strong testimony. My boasting in God is increasing, but I should do more (Ps. 100:4). Thinking about this makes me wonder, where will boasting in God take me? What will be the fruit of it? The adventure continues!

IDOLATRY IS THEIR GOAL; OUR IDENTITY AND EMOTIONS ARE THEIR TARGET

The goal of the demonic is to push us into idolatry and sin because these are twisted substitutions we can depend on and praise instead of depending on God. Toward that end, they target our identity and emotional needs to try to push us into making idolatrous substitutions. If our hearts aren't turned to depend on God, we become vulnerable to the attack, and we end up in deeper bondage to idolatrous sources. We must align our thinking and practice with God's provision for abiding that is strong enough to protect our emotions and identity. When the kingdom of Heaven becomes our hiding place and refuge, our emotions are protected behind a strong shield. What we put on for identity is directly related. Think of your identity as the accumulation of glory you find in life that you put on and wear outside around you as what you believe defines who you are.

Because identity is something we wear outside us, identity is where we abide, and identity is the target the demonic shoots at to keep us living beneath what is freely available to us. They use other people, circumstances, failures, and anything else they can find to harm us in ways that threaten the value, worth, security, and confidence we have about our identity. When the demonic is successful, we feel emotionally insecure, unworthy, imperfect, and whatever else they can stir up. By this, we become easy prey for temptation.

When demons target our identity, they are trying to hurt us emotionally. When they are effective, and we don't run toward God, we run toward idolatry and sin or sinful reactions. When we aren't depending on God to draw near as what soothes and protects us spiritually, we run to our idols because the emotional benefits we gain from them are the best we know at the time.

Behavior is need driven and learned. When a behavior feels like our best hope for filling a need, we repeat the behavior, and thinking patterns that support the behavior become engrained. Behaviors and reactions get repeated because of the emotional benefit we gain.

When you don't get your needs met by God, you can feel vulnerable emotionally, and in that state, you can do things out of self-protection that hurt people. It is right that you need reassurance and want to feel secure, but when you try to meet those needs by controlling your environment or other people, people and relationships get hurt. When you see yourself

Photo by Amir Arefi on Unsplash

pushing to stay in control, recognize you are trying to find a sense of security and to maintain your sense of worth by what you control. If accomplishing your goals is glory to you, then controlling the circumstances and people around you can be a damaging source of worth. You must meet that need healthily because of the closeness of God.

When God draws near, you must recognize that something of His sovereign power has come close to you. Your faith increases when you identify with God as your God and praise the closeness of His sovereign power. You feel a sense of calm reassurance that is more deeply comforting than any amount of control you can force onto something or someone yourself.

Even though people around me don't know it, I am often intent on receiving the kingdom of Heaven on their behalf. Because I am so often trying to take ground and crush demonic enemies trying to hurt people, I must abide and stay before the Lord or the attack on my emotions can get unbearable. Heavy discouragement can come over me quickly, but when I recognize my emotions getting pushed around, it is easy to boldly build my faith about God being greater and enter again and stand before the Lord. The peace of God comes quickly, and the attack goes quiet.

OPEN UP LIKE A FLOWER TO THE SUN

For clarity, let me now say the same thing I have been saying but in a different way. It is essential to talk about opening up to God as clearly as possible because when opening becomes central to how you receive Heaven here and rest in Him, it gets much easier to receive for a larger physical area around you. By opening and resting before the Lord, you can love people around you by presenting them before God so that the radiance and love of God is over them and surrounding them, even when there is a large number of people.

There is great insight in the old Christian hymn "Joyful, Joyful, We Adore Thee." One line in the song says that "hearts unfold like flowers before Thee." I believe this song talks about a natural response to God that we have when we believe God is drawing near to us and that it is safe for us to open up and receive.

Beyond a response of feeling safe about opening up, the truth is that it is far safer for us to open up to Him than trying to open up to other things. Our hearts need to hear and believe that with joy. Opening up to God protects us because when we trust He draws near to us, His radiant glory becomes a shield around us.

Photo by Edward Kucherenko on Unsplash

The Bible says that the Lord God is a "sun and shield" and that He "gives grace and glory" (Ps. 84:11). Since it says God gives grace and glory like the sun gives light, it seems fitting that we should open up to God like a flower. In my experience, learning to unfold before God like a flower is a vitally important skill Christians can benefit from.

Remember again that when I talk about opening up to God, I am talking about opening up in the same way we open up to a compliment or the feeling that we did an excellent job on something. Opening up is simple because it is something we do all the time toward earthly things. We only need freedom to apply our opening to God instead of earthly sources.

When we open up to the Lord, we rely totally on His grace to draw near. All we are doing is opening up. God is the one who is moving, not us. Opening up to God is a restful way of applying what we usually do toward earthly sources to try and receive by works (John 5:44).

Trust you are opening yourself up inside before Him without thinking you have to go up to Heaven and bring Jesus down (Rom. 10:6). Practice this with God by trusting you are before the Lord as best as you are currently able.

To receive here while opening up to God, we must receive from the radiance around Him for our humanity while remembering that our humanity is here in the earthly realm. If we go back into a works mode while trying to receive, it is easy to reach again and try to press ourselves out into Heaven. But doing that contradicts the childlike faith that trusts God's grace to draw near. Because of Romans 10:6 above, we know that trying to reach out from the inside to ascend is not based on faith.

I often practice opening up to God because this is the main building block that helps us to more effectively receive the presence of God and Heaven around us here. It is also what I do when praying.

When you are opening up to God to receive, it is helpful to remind your faith that "God is light" and that we are to walk in that light (1 John 1:5, 7). When we walk in the light that shines from God, the radiance of His Spirit of glory is shining onto us in a way that causes the presence of God to come into contact with our physical bodies and cleanses us (John 7:37–39; 1 Peter 4:14).

When receiving, expect God to touch your humanity. On a related note, when receiving God's presence for physical healing, you must trust He is coming to touch the area where the physical healing is needed because that is the place you need God to come in contact with and literally touch.

Also related is where the Bible talks about putting on the armor of light. Doing this requires that we receive the mountain of God and Heaven in a way that lets us put on what we are receiving around our physical body here as Heaven comes down (Rom. 13:12, 14).

When I felt the Lord was asking me to receive Heaven from above rather than taking a step forward, it was a very natural thing for me to apply my opening up upward rather than in front of me, as a flower opens up to the sunlight. Doing this brought a whole new dimension to my understanding of how to enter before the Lord.

Let me say again that when receiving the mountain of God and Heaven coming down from above, the inner activity of opening up like a flower is very similar to what we might do to put on a shirt or a coat that is open and falling down onto us from above.

When we open up to earthly things, it feels like there are hands inside us that extend out and reach to receive glory from earthly things and other people (Ps. 44:20–21). With God, we are not reaching to receive; we are resting into receiving. In the flower analogy, the hands inside us are like the petals of a flower. The petals of a flower do not leave the flower or reach way out into the heavens to receive! We can't let ourselves think of opening up that way either. We open up to receive; we don't reach or press in.

To clarify further, I want to add that your faith grows when you repent by directing your heart from earthly sources and to God as your God. Then, when you use the opening-up muscles inside you to open up to God above you as a child would (instead of opening up in front of you to earthly sources), your opening up easily pushes back the second heaven, and it moves out of the way to let the weight of God's glory with the mountain of God and Heaven come through to you. By this, the mountain of God comes down upon you and goes past you until you are standing on the mountain with the third heaven around you here. When you teach yourself to rely on the presence of God and His kingdom as your refuge of protection, you can stay open before the Lord. By staying open with those inner hands resting like a flower before the Lord, Heaven is around you and Heaven keeps the second heaven back because Heaven has come here and extends all the way up above you.

Photo by Tim Foster on Unsplash

MORE PRACTICAL THINGS ABOUT ENTERING BY RECEIVING

When I go to bed at night, if I have done any amount of reaching out or pressing in to receive, I wake up discouraged, sad, and hopeless. When I go to bed, and I enter by receiving Heaven into the room, and I focus on loving the mountain of God and Heaven coming down around me as protection, I wake up in the morning feeling hopeful and courageous. The difference is remarkable.

I am sure this sounds strange to some people, but in the early days of my life, I was afraid to hope for anything better than a hard shell of discouragement, hopelessness, and despair. Sadly, those things had become the best kind of safety I could hope for.

Now, because I have done so much with joyous declarations to cut off and direct my heart away from those things, if at any time I notice myself starting to feel discouraged or hopeless at all, I figure my armor has gone soft and the demonic is pushing those things onto me. In that case, I don't waste any time trying to punish myself for letting that happen! I receive again and trust that the kingdom of Heaven is peeling the demonic off me and is crushing any witchcraft sent against me in those areas.

When I am in a group of people, the same thing can happen, but in this case, I am picking up the spiritual baggage they are carrying. I don't waste time trying to figure who it is coming from or if it is me. The real problem is that the demonic is trying to push those things onto me, so I enter by receiving the mountain and the kingdom of Heaven again. I also bind the power of the demonic and witchcraft to push those things on the others in the room and loose the mountain of God, with Heaven and angels, into the room in order to receive on their behalf (Matt.16:19; Heb. 12:22-24, 28).

USE A DOORJAMB TO REMEMBER

It is a natural thing when we open up to earthly glory. But in the early days of my journey, when I intentionally tried to open up to God, I sometimes forgot how to do it. It made sense to figure out how to remind myself what it felt like inside to open up. I found that if I went to an open doorway in the house and pressed my hands against the doorjamb, it helped me to remember. Let me explain.

Stand in a narrower than usual open doorway because that is easier. Raise your hands about chest high, think about what it feels like in your chest to put the backs of your hands against the doorjamb, and press out with your hands for about five or ten seconds. Now, lower your hands to your sides and feel in your chest again what it was like when you were pushing against the doorjamb with the backs of your hands. The sensation in your chest feels the same inside as what it is like when we intentionally open up to God.

When your heart can trust that you are before the Lord, open up inside to Him. It is helpful to practice this while sitting in a chair. Trust you are looking at God and that His radiant glory is in front of you here and is washing over you, making you and everything in the room clean. Then, stretch yourself open while believing God is coming to you here. Practice opening up to God by stretching yourself open while trusting that His radiant holiness is all around you and is protecting you as you open up.

When it feels like there is a separation between you and Heaven, you have to fight to get back to receiving again! Let me say again that when I find these things difficult, I go back to reassuring my heart with the truth of the Scriptures about our access and about how we can receive abundantly with faith like a child (Eph. 2:18; 3:12; Gal. 3:14; Isa. 55:1–2; Mark 10:15).

In my experience, the most essential building blocks for abiding in Christ are learning to stay open before God and using your opening up as a spiritual activity to help you put on God's presence and kingdom that you are receiving with the faith and freedom of a child.

We open up to receive from earthly glory sources, then shut back down inside. When you keep practicing this with God, you eventually learn to believe His presence and kingdom are freely drawing near so that He can be the one God who is your refuge, as He desires, and you eventually stay open this way.

Reassure your heart with the truth that when you make God your refuge, He comes to you so that He can keep evil away from you and complete the crushing He desires! Reassure your heart with the truth that when you make God your refuge, the mountain of God comes with Heaven and the angels of God, and you possess His holy mountain. Once you entrust yourself to confidently believe the presence of God is your strong refuge, you will be able to stay open before God more and more throughout the day.

LEARN TO RELEASE

When it comes to the Spirit of God that pours out from Him, freely you have been given, so freely give (Matt. 10:8). When you teach yourself to stand open before the Lord, you will have to also teach yourself to release what God is pouring onto you and through you.

To learn this, sit down in a comfortable chair. Then while open before the radiance of God, think about releasing what He is freely giving through your hands. Once you get a feel for that, then one at a time, add releasing through your arms, then your chest, and legs. Don't expect this to happen quickly, but it is important to learn especially if the presence of God is making you uncomfortably warm.

Once you are able to release with your whole body, get up from the chair and go wash dishes or do some other activity you can do while continuing to think about releasing. Eventually, you will be able to stay open before the Lord, and releasing what He pours through you will be easy.

REFORMATION-LEVEL CHANGE

By salvation, we become part of God's family, but it is not automatic that we are called by His name because of salvation. Being called by the name of the Lord is a topic that is much more a thing of the heart than most of us realize.

It is far too natural for us to receive glory from earthly sources and then try to call ourselves by our names. We must all repent and turn from the wicked ways in our thinking before we can freely receive God's presence and kingdom enough to be called by His name (2 Chron. 7:14). We are to live to the praise of God's glory, not our own (Eph. 1:12). But doing that has to go deep without even a hint of regret in our repentance (2 Cor. 7:10). Your heart needs to be joyfully turned away from even wanting to live for the end goal of being able to praise your name.

We can't push to make a name for ourselves and be called by His name simultaneously. Great reformation-level change needs to happen here. We must repent away from the glory that comes to us through our self-effort and works. We also must repent toward the glory that comes freely to us through our faith in the grace of God and His desire to come to us abundantly. This series of books is to help you apply both of these things in everyday life. But the repentance needed must be worship with declarations of thanksgiving and praise about what we don't have to depend on and that we can depend on God to draw near and be God to us here.

Then, by praising the nearness of God's name, instead of our names, we become a people who are called by His name. God knows those called by His name, even when others don't see it. When we are called by His name, God's presence with us becomes what we think of as our identity, and then boasting in His name becomes much more natural for us. As we apply the Scriptures in alignment with how God designed us as people, we become those who naturally open the gates above us and bring Heaven to earth so we can stand before the Lord as priests and glory in seeking His face (Ps. 24:6–8; Heb. 12:22–24, 28; 2 Chron. 29:11; Phil. 3:3).

Everything works together for the ultimate end of good when we align ourselves with the purposes of God (Rom. 8:28). God is honored, righteousness reigns over evil, and practical and emotional human needs get met. By our application of the Scriptures, we prove that the will of God is "good and acceptable" (Rom. 12:2).

10

THE PRICE WE PAY

VEILS OF PRIDE

This chapter preaches a lot. As you read, remind yourself that repentance can't happen by condemnation and guilt. Your heart must come to believe and love something different before your behavior can improve. Read and try to be honest about idolatry and twisted thinking in your heart, but then, without waiting, present yourself before the Lord so He can wash you clean inside and outside.

Don't let condemnation and shame be what motivate you to change. Remember as you read this chapter that you don't have to live like this because more of God's presence and kingdom is available to you than what you have believed. Remind yourself that more glory is available than what you have been living on. Read this chapter while keeping yourself in the presence of Christ (2 Cor. 3:17) so you can gain insight without the condemnation that often comes with it (Rom. 8:1).

The Bible speaks of "Moses, who used to put a veil over his face so that the sons of Israel might not look intently at the end of what was fading away" (2 Cor. 3:13). When Moses was on the mountain with God, his face was shining. But the Bible says that he covered his face after he came down from the mountain because the glory started to fade away.

Chasing the world's glory is like living according to the old covenant based on faith in our works. We work to achieve earthly glory, but after we do, it quickly fades away. When living according to the old covenant, we work hard to achieve a sense of glory and worth, but when something happens that makes it fade, we feel inadequate all over again. Just like Moses, we cover up our sense of lack. We hide behind metaphorical veils that keep our shortcomings from being exposed to ourselves, others, and God.

The Bible says, "But their minds were hardened; for until this very day at the reading of the old covenant the same veil remains unlifted...whenever Moses is read, a veil lies over their heart" (2 Cor. 3:14–15). Figuratively, the law in us is like a constant reading of the old covenant. Every time something happens that reveals our inadequacies, the law is right there, reminding us that we are not God and that our humanness does not measure up. Rather than embracing that we fall short and that we need God's presence touching our humanity, we veil our inadequacies and hide from God. We push ourselves to achieve more glory for our flesh or bury our sense of lack and live in denial.

Turning to God requires us to humble ourselves and remove the veils. We must run to God to admit the truth about our hearts with a ruthless kind of delight. We must expose our shortcomings to the radiant holiness that shines from God and trust God to wash us clean and make up for our spiritual lack.

The Bible says, "Whenever a person turns to the Lord, the veil is taken away" (2 Cor. 3:16). Turning to the Lord can feel like death—but it remains only as long as your deep-down intention is to hide your inadequacies from God. Learning to delight in the cross requires that we can't keep running from the truth about the sins of our humanity. We are not enough. We all fall short. The good news is that God wants to be our God. We don't have to depend on the glory and worth we earn for ourselves. Turning to God and the glory that shines from Him requires a completely different underlying pursuit for how we feel good about ourselves, interact with others, and relate to God.

The Bible says, "'I will fill the soul of the priests with abundance, / And My people will be satisfied with My goodness,' declares the LORD" (Jer. 31:14). Rejoice your way into believing the goodness of God will fill you and be poured out around you. Disbelief that God can or will come intensely enough to satisfy and protect you is doubt in the goodness of God. Humble yourself into believing the truth that you can take refuge in Him. Your only option is a life that is focused on two things—dying to earthly sources with joy and building a strong faith and love toward God that lets you drink from the radiance around Him with praise.

It is time to turn our hearts from constantly trying to ease the pain caused by the truth about falling short. Get your heart to hear and joyously believe that God will fill you as He promises in His Word. Humble yourself by listening as you thank God audibly that He can and will draw near and quench your thirst for Him. Let your heart believe that God wants to fill up your lack.

TRAPPED AND FULL OF PAIN

God made us spiritually aware of His glory, but we have reacted wrongly to the law that reminds us that the glory of our humanness is inadequate compared to God. God wants to draw near to us, but we are trapped in a prison of disbelief and need intervention.

> Who is...
> ...so blind as the servant of the Lord?
> You have seen many things, but you do not observe them;
> Your ears are open, but none hears.
> The Lord was pleased for His righteousness' sake

> To make the law great and glorious.
> But this is a people plundered and despoiled;
> All of them are trapped in caves,
> Or are hidden away in prisons;
> They have become a prey with none to deliver them,
> And a spoil, with none to say, "Give them back!"
> Who among you will give ear to this?
> Who will give heed and listen hereafter? (Isa. 42:19–23)

God wanted to make the law great and glorious, but we have reacted with a lifelong habit of drinking from how well we keep people impressed, maintain their approval, and achieve our goals. Working hard and people being impressed are good things. But those things can't be what we depend on as our worthiness or what comforts us. Our natural tendency with God is to think we have to earn and work for His approval. This thinking is wrong, and you need to repent by changing your thinking patterns and what you depend on for worth.

Believing that God is inside us for salvation brings His acceptance and approval (Rom. 15:16; Heb. 11:1–2). After salvation for inside us, God's presence upon and around us is significance and worthiness for our humanity. But sadly, it is hard for us to believe God will draw near freely and abundantly (Ps. 84:11; Isa. 55:1–2). It is so deeply ingrained in us to live by faith in ourselves and what we earn that we don't hardly realize we are approaching God the same way (Gal. 3:3, 5).

The church today wants God's presence, but many of us are secretly terrified by the thought that we might not be able to perform well enough. Much more than we realize, we servants of the Lord are trapped because of our disbelief. We are trapped and hiding because we equate drawing near and receiving the presence of God as a goal that is too high and lofty for us. That we think of drawing near to God as a goal means that we believe receiving His presence is something we have to achieve. This view is pride and a blinding sin.

It is far too easy to accept the feeling that we should have to deserve God's presence before He draws near. Our disbelief is a sin that keeps us in deep bondage. As the verses say above, our "ears are open, but none hears." It is time to take action that gets our hearts to hear and believe about God coming to us according to His grace.

We know God is holy, but we act like we have to achieve purity apart from Him. We are wrong. We need to come to the place where we trust the power of the cross and God's ability to cleanse us enough to find freedom to draw near. We need Him to draw near as armor that keeps us from temptation (Rom.

13:12–14). It is time for the church to repent of having to punish ourselves until we feel like we have earned the forgiveness of God.

Some Christians are so unaware of God's provision to cleanse us when we enter the throne room that they are afraid to draw near for fear they might die. They look at Isaiah and say along with him, "Woe is me" (Isa. 6:5). But they ignore the fact that God's solution for Isaiah was to touch him. Even worse, we ignore God's provision to touch us with His holy presence by washing us inside and out anytime we draw near (Heb. 10:19–22).

It is a sorrowful thing that our disbelief and our lack of understanding are great enough to keep us shut down inside so that God has to stay away from us. We cannot trust ourselves to be righteous enough apart from God. But we don't trust God either.

The result is that many Christians are caught in the middle between wanting to draw near to God and feeling helpless to do anything about it. We act like we have heavy weights shackling us. We tend to think that even if we did enter the throne room and draw near to God, He wouldn't give us His presence freely. Because behavior flows from our hearts, we are destroyed by our lack of heart-level knowledge (Mark 7:21–22; Hos. 4:6). Our thinking needs to change.

Salvation is vital, but even with that, it hurts when we see the many ways our humanity falls short. Without the presence of God, our humanity will never be enough. Avoiding this truth results in great and unnecessary pain. Life won't ever be perfect here on earth. Still, the main reason for the amount of pain we feel in our struggles is because of our humanity and our attempts to find substitutions for God that are ineffective and hurt us. The church today is deep into idolatry of the heart, and we are afraid to face the truth and deal with it.

It is time for the church to wake up and admit that we haven't been depending on God for the righteousness we need. It is time for the church to turn from having to jump through spiritual hoops for God to bless us with His presence. We will never be enough to quench the world's thirst, and we should stop trying to lead people to God by increasing their dependence on us.

We can solve the problem of our disbelief. We can make declarations that remove the obstacles and help us turn to God. We don't have to settle for lives of secretly hiding our disbelief and independence from God. Repentance will help you. Of course, I still have room for growth, but it took many declarations of repentance and faith for me to get my heart to turn away from wanting to pride myself on what I did to deserve God's presence. It took a lot of courage to keep making declarations about the truth before my heart could turn away from fear and let me open up and believe God's radiance upon me.

The changes in our thinking are deep and require a lot of effort to change. If you are like me, you will have to make those changes before your heart is convinced that God will draw near when you trade in your glory for His. Teach your heart to be more childlike in your faith and love of taking refuge in the Lord for security, and God will respond by drawing near. Teach your heart to open up to a safer way to protect yourself, and God will prove He can be a better God to you than you can be to yourself.

CHRISTIANS HURT EACH OTHER

The misuse of authority and power is rampant in Christian churches today. Sometimes, it is from the leadership, but often, it is from those who attend the church.

It is sad, but it happens often that one Christian's glory is another Christian's pain. When we have to quench our thirst for God by substituting glory we achieve, we easily turn on each other with a vengeance to protect the human glory we believe we have earned. It is good to honor one another, but as soon as we start thinking our human glory deserves honor, life falls apart, and human interactions become hurtful. It is sad that so many of us put each other down in order to make ourselves seem more important at church. The Bible says,

> "As for you, My flock, thus says the Lord God, 'Behold, I will judge between one sheep and another, between the rams and the male goats. Is it too slight a thing for you that you should feed in the good pasture, that you must tread down with your feet the rest of your pastures? Or that you should drink of the clear waters, that you must foul the rest with your feet? As for My flock, they must eat what you tread down with your feet and drink what you foul with your feet!' "

> Therefore, thus says the Lord God to them, "Behold, I, even I, will judge between the fat sheep and the lean sheep. Because you push with side and with shoulder, and thrust at all the weak with your horns until you have scattered them abroad, therefore, I will deliver My flock, and they will no longer be a prey; and I will judge between one sheep and another" (Ezek. 34:17–22).

It is wrong that we push each other around the way we do. Some of those who call themselves Christians feed themselves with a subtle sense of pride because of how well they hurt other people. God is watching. He knows who is being hurt and who is doing the hurting.

We don't have to develop skill at controlling and manipulating people in churches. It doesn't glorify God when we think we must dominate people to achieve what we think God wants. Man's anger will never achieve God's righteousness (James 1:20). It grieves the heart of God that we settle for so little. Because God wants us to drink from Him, it is time for us to change what our hearts believe and love about the glory of the world and about what is available to us because of the glorification of Jesus (Jer. 2:11–13; Ps. 36:7–9; John 7:37–39).

Terrible things happen when the people of the church secretly think we have to feed ourselves with the glory of our humanity. We hide behind veils of self-protection that shut us off from the glory of God. Jesus promised something much better.

It was while Jesus was praying to the Father that Jesus said, "The glory which You have given Me I have given to them, that they may be one, just as We are one" (John 17:22). It is the glory of God given freely to us by His grace that makes us one. Nothing less will keep us from hurting each other.

The next verse says, "I in them and You in Me, that they may be perfected in unity, so that the world may know that You sent Me, and loved them, even as You have loved Me" (John 17:23). It is the oneness that comes from the glory of God that will make the world know.

> Salvation is vital. But we are missing something important! If you are wearing the glory of your humanity instead of God's, how can you think you have the right clothes for the wedding feast (Matt. 22:1–14)?

It is wrong that the accepted best in the church today is that we push the glory of our humanity on other people to sell our Christianity. We say we are trying to get them to believe in God—but aren't we working hardest at how we appear to impress them into believing? It is a deep sin that is rampant and unchecked in the church today. You don't have to settle for so little.

Repent and believe the grace of God. Today, the church is crying for God to pour His presence out onto us. We would do much better to draw near to God by trusting Him to draw near to us here—in abundance (James 4:8). God is waiting for you to repent and believe that He is coming even now. Draw near to God by trusting Him to draw near to you here.

OUR PRIDE KEEPS US AWAY FROM GOD

We have difficulty believing God because of human pride. We don't want to live by faith in God because we have grown too comfortable living by faith in ourselves (John 5:44).

A lifetime of practice has made us skillful at manipulations that serve to build and maintain our pride. Relentlessly, we work at finding and feeding on evidence of our human power. We quench our thirst with what we know—not the truth that we have the mind of Christ (1 Cor. 2:16). We pride ourselves with our acts of kindness. We get angry when the evidence in our relationships suggests we are not sovereign. Instead of finding delight in the beauty and majesty of God, we puff ourselves up with the glory of how we appear.

Photo by Yoal Desurmont on Unsplash

Photo by Diana Simumpande on Unsplash

Faith in ourselves is what we seek first—not the kingdom. Our bondage to self-protection is deep enough to greatly damage our faith in God to draw near to us so we can drink from Him. Make declarations with joy until your heart believes it is safer to rely on God to draw near than to trust yourself.

We are in such bondage that often we think that we have earned the right to drink from earthly sources. When we have finished some big project or earned someone's approval, we think we should be able to pride ourselves on subtle internal praise. We should not think this way! In so doing, we go after empty human and prideful self-esteem and we forfeit filling our desires with God's presence and esteeming Him (Jer. 2:11–13). Our love for God has grown cold because of it (Rev. 2:3–5).

It is a disease of epidemic proportions that we Christians try to quench our thirst for God by pride in what we earn and achieve. Seldom, however, is it diagnosed as a problem serious enough to warrant great concern. We are in such

bondage to self-effort that we are rendered almost incapable of coming to God and quenching our thirst by His grace. Doing so is unthinkable for most.

In our present state of being, the thought of receiving the presence of the Holy Spirit by faith in God's grace alone seems wrong because we think we should be spiritually deserving before receiving anything from God. Our thinking is so backward in this. It is not selfish of a child to need their parent to be close enough to protect them. In the same way, it is not selfish of us to think of God that way either.

Rather than humble ourselves and delight in God's abundant grace, we prefer to pride ourselves on how well we deserve His presence. Trust me that you have a lot of declarations to make before your heart will soften enough to hear and believe a different way of thinking. Keep making declarations with joy until you get your heart to believe it is right for you to delight yourself in an abundance of the Holy Spirit being showered upon you from God.

Embrace that in a worldly way of thinking, it won't seem right to receive God's presence when you feel spiritually dirty. But take those thoughts captive and speak to your heart until your thinking changes. You never will deserve that much glory. When you draw near by trusting Him to draw near to you, God washes your heart and your body (Heb. 10:19–22).

God has chosen us to receive His presence into this realm so that He can take over where evil has done so much damage. Will you humble yourself from pride enough to become more childlike in your faith so you can help? Enjoy that as you open up to receive His presence like a child, He comes because He delights to exercise lovingkindness, justice, and righteousness in the earth (Jer. 9:24). Great motivation is yours when you are intentional to enjoy that your childlike dependance on God to draw near brings Him delight and pleasure (Heb. 11:6).

Though we are Christians, our human pride keeps us making the same mistake as Israel and Judah: "For as the waistband clings to the waist of a man, so I made the whole household of Israel and...of Judah cling to Me,' declares the Lord, 'that they might be for Me a people, for renown, for praise and for glory; but they did not listen' " (Jer. 13:11). We don't listen or cling to the Lord because we are too busy trying to cling to earthly glory sources. We need to rest from our labors by repentance that changes the thinking and affections of our hearts.

Dear Christian, it is our birthright as Christians to enjoy the presence of God and the kingdom of Heaven around us here. Doing so should be the norm in the church today. But we will have to approach God on the basis of His delight to freely give us His presence, not on the basis of anything about who we are.

> We are to think of ourselves rightly, and what God thinks of us is important. But it is easy for religious pride to take over and dictate a belief that we deserve God's presence. If your starting point is spiritual pride about what God thinks of you, then you will be able to receive God's presence easily from time to time. But you will not be able to abide when suddenly attacked. For that, you will have to think of yourself as a needy child and God as your Father who wants to be God to you here. If your basis for worth is anything about who you are, twenty-four seven abiding is difficult.

You have to make declarations that teach your heart to think differently; no one else can do that for you. The Lord is God, not us (Ps. 46:10). Our self-effort to find reasons to boast, apart from the presence of God, has resulted in great bondage to disbelief and distrust toward God. Many Christians actually want to stay away from God and are afraid to get close. Even though we are believers, we act like we don't want to waste our efforts in pursuit of God.

To me, it seems that most Christians have learned to feel hopeless about God's presence. We don't believe God can or will quench our thirsty desires in an ongoing and practical way. Doing that seems unrealistic to us. The whole world suffers because of our disbelief and hard hearts.

The Bible talks about "your pride of power" (Lev. 26:19; see also Ezek. 24:21). We pursue earthly power because of the pride it makes us feel. It is pride that keeps us wanting to pursue anything and everything except God. The problem is that God "fully recompenses the proud doer" (Ps. 31:23). The Bible talks about how we sometimes are "asserting in pride and in arrogance of heart" (Isa. 9:9). But it also tells of how God is going to destroy "the pride of all beauty" (Isa. 23:9). Another place it says that God is going to make "the pride of the strong ones cease" (Ezek. 7:24). Wanting what makes us feel pride is what keeps us from wanting to believe it is right for us to drink from God and depend on Him to draw near.

When our hearts are turned toward pride as a means of filling our desires, we resist God because we think we are sufficient in and of ourselves. The Bible says, "God is opposed to the proud, but gives grace to the humble" (James 4:6). We are resisted because we resist Him. You don't have to live like that! Learn to worship God with declarations of thanks and praise for the truth so you can humble yourself into trusting grace and you can freely receive God's presence.

How do we know when our faith is in our own efforts to pride ourselves? We are living by self-effort when we try to hold up evidence to God that we are righteous enough to deserve to be given His presence. We are living according to our works and self-effort if we have even subtle concerns that we are not enough and that God doesn't want to pour His Spirit upon us abundantly and freely. Even though this is not about your salvation, your thinking needs to change so that God drawing near to you physically is the only thing that can make up for your humanity falling short.

Think of a young child in a threatening situation where their older brother suddenly shows up. We are like the young child, and God is like the older brother. God is the strong one who is worthy, and when He draws near, we feel strong and worthy because of His nearness and our delight about His greatness. How well we perform doesn't add or take away from the grace of God to draw near to His people. It is all about humbling ourselves to the place of thinking like that needy younger child.

It is all about God's grace and our willingness to believe it, apart from what we do or don't do. It is all about our willingness to involve ourselves in God's plan for filling the earth with His glory. Drinking from God instead of ourselves is way bigger than drinking from God to benefit us. Of course, drinking from God benefits us! It also benefits and honors God in what He is trying to do in our day.

The problem is with us, not God. The force with which we demand to have pride in ourselves results in a strong disbelief that prevents us from experiencing God coming to us freely without hindrance: "For the Lord God is a sun and shield; / The Lord gives grace and glory; / No good thing does He withhold from those who walk uprightly" (Ps. 84:11). We are the ones holding back, not God.

Sadly, in churches all across this land, our pride has made intimacy with God irrelevant to coping with life. We have lost hope in God. The glory of our earthly pursuits tastes just enough like what we long for that we keep looking in all the wrong places. We stay away from God because the surface worldly appearance of our neediness is so driving that we can hardly imagine a better way to fill our longings and desires.

OUR FEARS KEEP GOD AWAY FROM US

Earthly sources are undependable, and they hurt us. But because we think God is irrelevant to our neediness, we set ourselves up for despair and hopelessness. We should learn from the regularity with which we get hurt when trying to quench our thirst by earthly means. Pain from earthly sources should teach us to turn and trust God to draw near.

That hardness of heart results in an overgrown jungle of complex fears and subtle forms of self-protection. We ask, "What if God doesn't accept me? What if God doesn't love me enough? Why should God want to forgive me again?" Fears and distrust toward God result from being hurt so often by human ways of trying to reassure ourselves, find confidence, and feel secure. You must learn to speak to your fears with gratitude and praise for the truth about God being a better God to you than you can be to yourself.

Some are honest enough about life that they don't believe they have reasons to feel pride. That much is good, but they shouldn't stop there. They need to humble themselves from wanting to achieve enough human glory to deserve pride. When we can't have pride, many turn to despair and try to find refuge in that. If this is you, what you are doing is just as bad as those whose love for God is cold. Muster all your courage to speak with bold declarations about what your heart needs to believe.

When we were young, we were more trusting and more open. When we got hurt, we held our blankets close. If we were fortunate, our mothers held us. But then, as we grew older, life got more complicated. We found that life hurts and circumstances seldom cooperate. Fear increased. Inside, we closed up by hardening our hearts.

Deep patterns have developed that affect our relationship with God much more than we realize. The Bible says, "Today if you hear His voice, / Do not harden your hearts" (Heb. 4:7). But do you trust the cross's power and God's forgiveness? Or would you instead punish yourself until you can trust that you have felt bad for long enough? Ask yourself honestly, Have I learned to protect myself by closing up inside and hiding underneath a hardened heart? Self-hatred and condemnation shut us off from the kingdom of God by keeping the Holy Spirit from coming to us freely (Matt. 23:13). The new covenant is a ministry of righteousness with more glory (2 Cor. 3:9–10).

We can't keep holding to lies that protect us from letting God come to us freely and continuously (1 John 1:7). The Bible says, "It is better to take refuge in the Lord / Than to trust in man" (Ps. 118:8). Listen to yourself making joyous declarations that it is good and safe for you to trust God and take refuge inside Him drawing near to you here. Rather than self-protection that hardens your heart toward God, direct your heart into becoming like a child again (Matt. 19:14).

Photo by Jon Tyson on Unsplash

PAIN IN OUR RELATIONSHIPS

Early in our marriage, I read several books on husband-wife relationships. Most addressed the importance of loving our spouse by meeting their needs. That information was good as far as it went. But I somehow understood it was right to depend on my wife to meet my needs. I was expecting my needs to be met at a deeper level than what is possible apart from God. My expectations created a lot of unnecessary stress in our home and hurt our relationship. Years later, I learned my dependence on her was selfish and idolatrous. I had to believe and trust God more deeply than I had ever considered possible.

It is right to love your spouse and meet their needs as best you can. But the needs we have to be loved and feel secure are symptoms of our need for God. As a result, meeting your spouse's needs to the full extent is far beyond the ability of any human being. We can only give our spouse a little taste of what it is like to have those needs met by God.

Without drawing near to God and wrapping ourselves in His love, without enjoying His presence as our security and strength, subtle forms of selfishness run rampant in relationships. Without depending on God to meet our own needs, I don't know how it would be possible to love others as we should. Our own unmet needs would be too great for us to love others without hurtful kinds of self-protection.

PAIN FROM ALL OF HEAVEN

Many people became Christians because they wanted something more. They knew something was missing. And, to a large degree, God *has* filled that void. But do you slow down sometimes and get quiet enough to hear yourself cry out for something even more? Do you hurt inside? The truth is that something is wrong, but you're not alone.

We have considered parts of this verse previously; now see it in context:

> "Has a nation changed gods
> When they were not gods?
> But My people have changed their glory
> For that which does not profit.
> Be appalled, O heavens, at this,
> And shudder, be very desolate," declares the Lord.
> "For My people have committed two evils:
> They have forsaken Me,
> The fountain of living waters,
> To hew for themselves cisterns,
> Broken cisterns
> That can hold no water." (Jer. 2:11–13)

When we try to quench our thirst with earthly sources, God says the heavens should be appalled and shudder.

When we have not yet turned toward the fountain of living waters, we feel the pain of Heaven inside us as a result. The heavens are appalled and shudder when we drink from earthly sources that don't hold water. Deep inside, we feel Heaven's pain, and we, too, are appalled because of it.

Don't interpret the pain you feel as rejection from God! God loves you and doesn't want any of us to keep hurting. You can confidently trust God to give you an abundance of His presence. He wants you to trust He is drawing near you so you can drink from Him. God wants to keep you feeding on Him rather than having to substitute your human glory for His presence. God is good, and He is a radiant fountain of His glory. Teach your heart to have the freedom of a child because you only have to believe you are close to the fountain to get wet.

We drink from God for salvation (1 Cor. 12:13). But Heaven is "appalled" that God's people drink from worldly things instead of God (Jer. 2:11–13). Is a life lived without regard for God as a radiant fountain after salvation the same as forgetting and forsaking God (Jer. 17:13)? The radiance of God must play a central role in our everyday living or we are missing the point of how God wants to be God to us and how He wants to use us to help Him accomplish His will.

Be assured that you can find ongoing meaning and joy without having to define success in terms of exalting yourself. You will find meaning and deep joy when you believe your childlike dependence on God honors Him as God in the heavenly realms.

You can change from quenching your thirst by faith in your works. You can change to quenching your thirst by trusting you are before the Lord and that you can freely drink from the fountain of His glory by faith in His grace to come to you here.

Photo by Shane Rounce on Unsplash

11

IN CONCLUSION

LET'S REVIEW

My goal for this chapter is to do a review that ties everything together and to make some points that have yet to be said.

Because God is seeking worshipers, He designed us so that our human glory falls short of His glory. The result is what the Bible calls a thirsty need for God. Rather than learning to drink from God, our hearts have learned patterns of thinking, by countless repetitions throughout our lives, about how and what to drink from to ease our sense of falling short apart from God. But without satisfying ourselves with an abundance of God's power, glory, and holiness close to us, even the twisted glory from rebellious sin becomes attractive.

Christians who attend church every week can still be distant from God in terms of dependence on Him in everyday living. Many who have received Christ for salvation have yet to learn how to depend on God in ways that satisfy them. The result is that we have watered down the power of the gospel to where we say that Jesus died to save us from sin, but we make excuses for our lack of heart-level purity. The Christian life should not be one of simply trying harder to be good. The gospel includes salvation, the kingdom of Heaven, and the glory of Christ. All are important because the purity you can experience when God's holy presence and kingdom are upon you is far greater than what is possible otherwise.

When you praise the glory you earn and achieve to feel good about yourself, all you get is pride that hardens you from being able to depend on God like a child. Christians can stay in bondage their entire lives and not realize they are settling for something far less than what God offers.

God wants us to make Him our God by opening up like a child who drinks from the radiant glory around Him so we can abide in His presence every moment and praise Him as our God. The new thing He wants to do in our day is to give drink to His people (Isa. 43:19–21). Because the Father has glorified Jesus, we can drink and receive His Spirit's presence as He comes to us from the radiant glory that pours out from Him (John 7:37–39; Acts 2:33). When life gets difficult, listening to ourselves make declarations of praise about the glory and grace God gives (Eph. 1:6, 12; Ps. 84:11) helps to transform our thinking (Rom. 12:2; 10:9–10) so that our hearts can turn away from bondage to drinking from the glory of earthly sources (John 5:44) and toward increased faith in God as our God (Ps. 31:4). Listening to our joyful declarations removes obstacles of fear and helps us to dwell in the presence of God: "I will say to the LORD, 'My refuge and my fortress, / My God, in whom I trust!' " (Ps. 91:2).

The benefits to us are that we feel good about ourselves. We feel confident, bold, secure, protected, and worthy. The benefits to God are that we love Him more, and His kingdom comes to earth. Our behavioral and heart-level purity increases greatly. We also feel significant and powerful because what we drink from Him comes down from above, crushes evil under our feet, and establishes the kingdom of Heaven on earth more fully.

Because our hearts learn best by repetition accompanied by emotional benefits from drinking from something, the most effective way to repent is by repetitious declarations with joy that change our thought patterns, heart-level beliefs, and loves about what we treasure for quenching our thirsty needs.

Please remember to think of repentance as worship with declarations of thanksgiving and praise that change what our hearts believe and treasure while trusting God that He is cleansing us so that we don't have to condemn and shame ourselves in order to improve. If our repentance is not a joyous act of thanksgiving and praise about what pulls us toward God, condemnation will take over, and our repentance will shut us down instead of setting us free.

When we repent by changing what our hearts believe and love about filling our emotional needs, our behavior changes because our behavior is driven by what flows out of our hearts in terms of easing our sense of falling short (Rom. 3:23). When we repent by listening to bold confessions from our mouth about the truth, our hearts eventually hear and believe what we are saying (Rom. 10:9–10). When our hearts hear and believe the truth that we are able to open up and receive the presence and kingdom of God, practical righteousness increases because God comes to us as cleansing and a strong shield that burns the demonic anywhere around (Acts 3:19; Heb. 12:22–24, 28; Rom. 6:4; 13:12–14; 1 John 1:7).

I have written this book and those that follow to show you that you need to repent and how to do it by repetitious declarations with joy.[18] Start your repentance now by using the diagrams I showed you in chapter 6 as a guide for helping you to make your joyous declarations. Thank God for the many ways you don't have to feed yourself apart from Him. Then, thank Him that you can drink from Him and keep thanking Him until your heart hears it, believes it, and opens up to what pours out from God as the protection, security, significance, confidence, and worth you so desperately need in your life.

Don't get bogged down with each individual idol, trying to determine whether you are living in sin. Trust you are standing in the cleansing radiance of God (1 John 1:7). Then use the idolatry listed in the diagrams to joyfully make declarations about the many ways you can turn your heart from works to grace. This way, the idols in the diagrams become tools for repentance that help you aim your declarations at the underlying cause of the idolatry.

All of this is directly related to God's desire to plant us in His presence (Ex. 15:17). By this, Heaven's tabernacle can come to earth in more significant ways (Heb. 12:22–24, 28; Rev. 21:3), and we can drink from God easily because we are standing before Him and His radiance as a kingdom priest with our physical body here. Eventually, the tabernacle of Heaven will be fully established on earth because God's people will have readied themselves by turning their hearts from earthly glory sources and toward receiving more of Heaven here (Rev. 21:2).

Allow me to fit some Scriptures together so we can align our application of the Bible with the new thing God is doing in our day (Isa. 43:18–20). More and more, God is enthroned on earth (Ps. 22:3) when we receive the mountain of God, the kingdom of Heaven, and angels with the faith of a child (Mark 10:15; Heb. 12:22–24, 28). By this, we put on the armor of light and avoid sin (Rom. 13:12, 14) because we enjoy the presence of God with us instead of the emotional benefits we gain from sin (Ps. 103:2). These things are important for us today because all of it is related to how we can meet the conditions in 2 Chronicles 7:14 so that God can heal our land.

---

[18] More details come in a later book.

When we enter before the Lord with our physical bodies here as kingdom priests (Rev. 5:10), we can stand before the Lord as the priests did in the Old Testament and as we are told to do in the New (2 Chron. 29:11; Rom. 12:1). When we stand before Him and stay open to the radiance that shines on us from His face (2 Chron. 7:14), we can more easily drink from Him like a child who makes Him their refuge (Ps. 36:7–9). We can also more easily trust that we are looking at Him (Ps. 123:2) and praise His name close to us here (Ps. 75:1). The tabernacle of Heaven here is the place where God protects us in difficult times (Ps. 27:1–6). It is also where we help God fill the earth with His glory and crush evil by what we drink and receive from Him (Num. 14:21; Rom. 16:20; Ps. 84:11).

When you enter, remember that the opening-up muscle inside your chest is like hands inside you that normally extend toward earthly sources (Ps. 44:20–21). Instead of reaching out from you for earthly glory and then losing your protection (Ps. 63:8), teach your heart to believe you can extend those same hands briefly above you so that the edges of the torn veil between Heaven and earth are laid back, and Heaven can come down and wash your body here (Heb. 10:19-22). Learn to feel yourself opening up inside and trust you are opening the edges of the torn veil like heavenly gates that flop to the sides above you. Then let your heart believe the weight of the mountain of God is pushing through the opening and is coming down upon and going past you as it brings Heaven and angels with it here (Heb. 12:22–24). Then trust that you are resting before the Lord by holding on to the top of the mountain on either side of you down by the floor in the throne room here. Rejoice that Heaven is all around you and praise the name of the Lord as you declare the greatness of His nearness around you here. Resting in the Lord like this, without reaching, is vital for protection that helps you avoid temptation and advance the kingdom of God on earth.[19]

Receiving Christ for salvation is only where our life with God begins. Before that, our hearts learn to depend on earthly sources. After salvation, we grow in Christ as we read the Bible and pray and as the Holy Spirit teaches us. But that kind of growth can take a lifetime. If you want to grow at a faster pace, you have to change your thinking by declarations that help you become more childlike in your faith so you can turn from earthly glory, open up to God, and keep on receiving God's radiant glory and cleansing upon you here (Col. 2:6; 1 John 1:5, 7).

It is not selfish to depend on God to be God to us so we can enjoy Him in childlike ways. Based on how God defines idolatry, He wants us to love Him as our God so His kingdom can advance on earth and we can benefit both practically and emotionally from our relationship with Him (Deut. 32:37–39; Ps. 36:7–9; Hab. 1:11; Jer. 17:5–8; 2:11–13; Isa. 41:16–18). Becoming more childlike as an adult is a step up in our growth.

---

[19] If you enter like this and you start to feel dizzy, make sure you aren't pressing into the second heaven while trying to receive here. Look around at your physical environment and then apply faith to entering again. In contrast, if your head feels full, it is likely that the presence of God is increasing and you need to enter while believing you are receiving for a larger area around you. Another good problem can be that if you enter and are trusting you are before the Lord but are feeling too hot, God is giving His Spirit to you, but you need to practice releasing more. Practice releasing first though your hands, then your arms, and after that, release what God is pouring into you out through the rest of your body. Eventually, you will be releasing all the time, and those funny, sudden, violent jerks will stop. If you are vibrating too much to sleep, trust you are moving to a different part of the throne room that isn't as close to the river coming down from before the throne.

Photo by Emmanuel Phaeton on Unsplash

With the delight of a child in your tone of voice, listen to yourself as you keep declaring, "My soul will make its boast in the Lord; / The humble will hear it and rejoice" (Ps. 34:2), "The nations will bless themselves in Him, / And in Him they will glory" (Jer. 4:2), and "Glory in Christ Jesus and put no confidence in the flesh" (Phil. 3:3). Eventually, your heart will hear it and believe. By this, you will become freer and more childlike in your faith and love for God.

TRADE UP

Are you one who struggles to live the Christian life and is more acquainted with failure than victory? The failure you experience is because your thirst for God is strong, and you haven't learned how to drink from the Lord yet.

Even though your thirst may be focused on earthly things, God is drawing you to Himself by the strength of your thirsty desires. The desperation to fill your neediness is part of what God wants to use to help you turn to Him.

Christians are living far below the level of what is realistic. God is with us. He lives in us and never leaves us. But the Bible also says that when we draw near Him, He will draw near to us (James 4:8). More is always possible.

The Bible says that unbelievers have exchanged the glory of God for the glory of earthly things (Rom. 1:23). It also says something similar about God's people.

> "Has a nation changed gods
> When they were not gods?
> But My people have changed their glory
> For that which does not profit.
> Be appalled, O heavens, at this,
> And shudder, be very desolate," declares the Lord.
> "For My people have committed two evils:
> They have forsaken Me,
> The fountain of living waters,
> To hew for themselves cisterns,
> Broken cisterns
> That can hold no water" (Jer. 2:11–13).

Disbelief is so rampant in churches today that most Christians have resorted to quenching their desire for God in earthly ways. The problem is that most Christians don't realize the underlying dependencies that keep them in undetected bondage. The Scripture above says that by quenching our thirst with earthly sources, we have "changed gods." We have forsaken the "fountain of living waters" and are trying to drink from rain barrels that can't hold water. According to the Scripture above, Heaven feels pain because of our idolatry.

Unbelievers have exchanged God's glory for earthly things. But after salvation, most Christians have changed back to other gods.

> Even Christian leaders fall to sin when they don't understand how to drink from God in practical and ongoing ways.

The good news is that you can turn away from your other gods and drink from Him.

God has made a promise to quench our thirst. Cooperating with God on this is about learning to trade earthly glories for an abundance of God's presence by your delight in what He is giving. It is a promise similar to trading an old, broken-down car for a shiny new one—for free. God promises that you can trade in your earthly ways of trying to drink from earthly sources and quench your thirst with Him:

Ho! Every one who thirsts, come to the waters;
And you who have no money come, buy and eat.
Come, buy wine and milk
Without money and without cost.
Why do you spend money for what is not bread,
And your wages for what does not satisfy?
Listen carefully to Me, and eat what is good,
And delight yourself in abundance (Isa. 55:1–2).

Let your heart hear His promise. Thank Him that this promise of abundance is for you.

In verse 3 of that same chapter, it is significant that God's promise to quench your thirst is a covenant "according to the faithful mercies shown to David." In Psalm 63:1, David said that his soul was thirsty for God in a "dry and weary land where there is no water." But he didn't stay like that. The next verse says, "Thus I have seen You in the sanctuary, / To see Your power and Your glory" (Ps. 63:2).

David quenched His thirst for God by entering the heavenly sanctuary of God and looking at God's power and glory with his eyes of faith.

David tells us that drawing near and looking at God's glory quenched his thirst. In the same psalm, he wrote, "My soul is satisfied as with marrow and fatness, / And my mouth offers praises with joyful lips" (Ps. 63:5). Declarations of repentance and faith can help you find the freedom needed for drinking from God with the simplicity of a child (Mark 10:14–15).

Do you remember how freely David danced before the Lord (2 Sam. 6:14)? Like David, you too have to become more childlike in your freedom and faith to be able to enter the sanctuary easily. Make joyous and bold declarations until your heart hears what you are saying and believes that you can satisfy yourself with the closeness of God's power and glory. The path you must take requires that you humble yourself from fear, self-protection, and pride. One reason I dance before the Lord is because it helps to humble my pride.

God is a covenant-keeping God. He was faithful to quench David's thirst and be his God. The covenant of God includes you. You too can follow King David's example and God will quench your thirst for Him in the same way as David (Ps. 34:2). Thank God often that more is possible. Let your heart believe enough to find the courage to direct your faith and affections away from earthly and human glory.

Thank God He has made a covenant—a contract in His blood—to quench your thirst with His presence. Then, take steps to enter by faith so you can praise His nearness enough to help your heart believe and find freedom to open up and drink from Him freely.

A TIME FOR ACTION

Remember that Jesus warned, "How can you believe, when you receive glory from one another and you do not seek the glory that is from the one and only God?" (John 5:44).

Our problem is that receiving glory from earthly sources prevents us from believing and trusting the availability of God's glory to us here. It is time to take action. When our hearts hear us make joyous declarations of thanksgiving about being able to cut off earthly and human glory sources, we won't have any other option except to depend on God, and faith for receiving from Him comes to us a lot easier.

God is reaching out to all of us passionately. He wants to help us. The problem is that we don't realize how forcibly committed we are to our earthly ways without God. While it may not be pleasant to admit, I think most of us Christians are further from God than we realize. This can change. Our problem is a systemic commitment to self-effort and the glory we earn as a reason for pride. We must turn from our self-effort and pride in our works to faith in God's grace.

Let me say it another way: The disease of pursuing earthly ways of quenching our thirst is systemic. Therefore, the cure that addresses the cause must include directing our hearts away from earning glory and toward God and His grace for glory in all areas related to what God is like and in terms of experiencing greater closeness to Himself. Faith comes first, then the presence of God (Gal. 3:14). Therefore, our declarations must aim at reducing fear so we can get our hearts to hear and treasure believing that we can turn away from the glory we achieve and that we can turn our hearts toward greater dependence on God. Our hearts must open enough to receive the glory God gives freely by His grace.

Until the glory of God becomes visible to people (Isa. 60:2), the glory of earthly sources is easier to see. With God, we must believe His presence is close. Then, we must intentionally love enjoying His presence as our strength, protection, significance, and worthiness, and as we do this, God draws near.

If we keep our focus on changing our behaviors directly, we will never be changed deeply enough. Since behavior flows from what is in our hearts, it is the thinking of our hearts and what our hearts treasure that have to change (Ps. 119:11). The fastest way is to repent in diligent ways that remove obstacles and build our faith (2 Peter 1:5–6; Isa. 57:14). Let your declarations of repentance and faith be worship that honors God about Him being a better God to you than the little gods of this world.

TROUBLESHOOTING CAN BE HELPFUL

The fastest path toward growth in Christ requires that we be as specific as possible in changing the ways we find glory from the world so that we can direct our hearts away from that and to the place of receiving Heaven here like a child so we can stand before Him and seek His face like kingdom priests (2 Chron. 7:14; 29:11). But those ways aren't always obvious.

Even if the path seems long, it is helpful if you look at your behavior and do your best to recognize the underlying need you are trying to fill. By this, you will have direction about where to focus your declarations so you can turn your heart more fully toward God.

Consider our need for power and perfection and how twisted these God-given needs can get. Ask yourself, "What is the underlying need I am trying to fill when I use shame or condemnation or try to control someone in a hurtful way?"

Troubleshoot your idolatry by asking yourself, "What God-given need am I trying to fill through these unwanted behaviors?"

Some have twisted self-directed shame, condemnation, and control into idols to help them deal with their disappointment about their human imperfections and powerlessness. We want power and control. We want perfection and righteousness because all these things soothe and reassure us. It is deeply damaging when we try to fill our God-given needs for power and reassurance by way of religious shame, condemnation, and control (Col. 2:23; 2 Cor. 7:10). But if you learn to observe these kinds of things in yourself, you can be more specific in your declarations of thanksgiving and praise about what you are turning from and toward.

When you react to your failures with shame and condemnation, aren't you trying to motivate a perfect performance the next time? We need perfection! But we make human mistakes. Why not embrace your humanity without making excuses for bad behavior? Why not present your failure before the Lord together with the people you may have hurt and trust that God is washing the whole thing with His holiness, perfection, and healing power? When your heart learns to love the closeness of the perfection of God, you can live your life, doing what you must do as best as you can, and still give yourself room for a less-than-perfect performance. Self-acceptance is easier when God's perfection and holiness are close and touching you.

People need a sense of power and control. But when we find glory from power in how well we condemn and shame ourselves or others, we only slow our growth and create more obstacles for ourselves and them. Shame keeps us from wanting to try it again next time because of fear.

What if your declarations aim to eliminate the option of finding power and control by how well you condemn and shame yourself? When you cut that off, you are left with the needs that still must be filled. Then a clean slate, in terms of learning a better way to fill those needs, comes into view. This is why you must make declarations of repentance and faith together.

You can respond to shame by holding back from God, or you can make declarations that cut off the hard shell of shame as your preferred way to protect yourself. When your declarations help you to reject shame as a means of finding protection, power, and control, it will be much easier for you to turn to the sovereign God, open up to Him, and trust that His holiness, perfection, and sovereignty are drawing near and washing away all your reasons to feel shame.

REMOVE THE OBSTACLES!

Remember that the path to making these things simple in everyday life is to become more playfully childlike in our faith. Keep thanking the Lord with joy for the truth of the Scriptures until your application feels simple and uncomplicated.

Don't be discouraged when considering idolatry more deeply. Hidden idolatry in our hearts is a vast topic. All of us struggle at these levels. God designed us with emotional needs that drive us to try and meet those needs. You can remove the heart-level obstacles. You can become more childlike in your faith, which lets you open up to let God draw near.

But the truth we know in our heads isn't enough to change the behaviors that flow from our hearts. Our hearts have to believe and love a different and better truth for us to grow as God desires. Moving what you know in your head into your heart requires repetition. Make declarations that direct the beliefs and treasures of your heart away from having to depend on earthly and human glory sources. Use declarations to blast away at your fears until you can get your heart to hear and joyfully believe that it is safer to turn to God and trust Him to draw near.

We must fully embrace where King David said his physical body yearned for God (Ps. 63:1–2, 5). The Bible says that "the Lord is for the body" (1 Cor. 6:13). So it is right for you to receive the presence of God and His kingdom here. When God draws near, we give our body a pure form of what we long for most. When we enjoy God's closeness near our humanity, we find it easier to turn away from earthly sources and sin and toward God with joy.

A lot of the discouragement and hopelessness you can feel in these areas is being pushed onto you by the demonic (Eph. 6:12). If you let God draw near, they have to leave, and they don't want that. Take it by faith that much of the pressure you feel to avoid God gets pushed onto you from the demonic.

Don't let the demonic turn you into a reason for them to feel pride! Make declarations that build your faith about receiving the presence of God and His kingdom in ways that punish them for trying to hurt you. Audibly teach your heart to enjoy the power of the holiness of God around you that burns them. Teach your heart to believe the Scriptures about receiving Heaven here so that the peace of God and His holy mountain can decisively crush evil and witchcraft under your feet.

Photo by Ben White on Unsplash

As soon as you start to feel discouraged or overwhelmed by the amount of heart-level idolatry you see, trust that you are walking inside the light that shines from God and that the blood of Christ is washing over your physical body, washing away your shame and your feelings of discouragement and being overwhelmed (1 John 1:5, 7). Direct your heart into bold faith about trusting you are in the radiance that shines from God and that you are presenting your physical body before the Lord (Heb. 4:16). By this, any demonic or witchcraft that might be trying to mess with you and your faith gets burned and crushed (Isa. 4:4; Rom. 16:20).

USE YOUR EMOTIONAL NEEDS AS MOTIVATION

It is possible to receive Christ as your savior and not know His presence in a practical way that makes Him your God. Because of God wanting to be God to us by our drinking from the radiance of His glory, it is right for us to use the benefits to us emotionally and practically and the benefits to the kingdom of God as motivation that helps us want to direct our hearts away from the world and toward God as our one God (Deut. 32:37–39; Ps. 36:7–9; 18:1; 73:28; Hab. 1:11; Jer. 17:5–8; Ex. 15:2; John 7:37–39).

Salvation is vital, but ultimately, God is also trying to establish His kingdom on earth, and what He is trying to establish is outside our physical body, not inside us here (Rev. 21:3). Our application of the Scriptures should align with God's purposes for salvation and His ultimate plan to bring Heaven to earth.

When we believe the kingdom of Heaven is drawing close, and we enjoy the presence of God with boastful praise, our emotional needs are satisfied and Heaven comes. When we love God's presence and the closeness of His kingdom, God is greatly honored as our God and His kingdom is advanced because our abiding is more aligned with the pattern of God's design.

By learning to be more childlike in our love for God, we can glory in the closeness of God and His kingdom, where our emotional needs become the motivation we need for holiness and for letting God bring Heaven to earth.

Do you hate the damage evil does to people and our world? Do you want your life to be significant and full of meaning? Because filling our emotional needs requires that we receive glory from something, satisfying our emotional needs with the nearness of God fits perfectly into His desire to see evil crushed under our feet and with His ultimate desire for Heaven to come to earth. When we drink from God to fill our emotional needs, His presence comes to us, and we love Him with praise. When we humble ourselves enough to become playfully joyful about receiving the kingdom of Heaven and God's presence as our refuge, strength, and glory, then we praise the nearness of God, our emotional needs are satisfied because of God Himself, and His throne is more fully established on earth.

DO YOU NEED HELP WITH DELIVERANCE?

Pushing us to find refuge, strength, and glory apart from God are principalities and powers that are demons who close our eyes to the availability of God's radiant glory because they want to keep us in bondage to idols (Eph. 6:12; 2 Cor. 4:4). They want to keep us in bondage because the idols listed in the diagrams together with various sins are the very things they pride themselves about when they can keep us going after the glory in those things instead of what comes from God. If you feel hopelessness, fear, or shame about letting Heaven come and standing before the Lord, demons might be pushing these emotions onto you to keep you holding back. Don't let yourself be a victim of their pressure and lies.

The Bible speaks of Christians shrinking away in shame when Jesus appears because they haven't prepared for His coming by abiding in Him (1 John 2:28). Even though this is talking about the second coming of Christ, it very much applies to how well we can receive Heaven here so we can present our bodies before God and abide in Christ by standing in His radiance upon us here. God is our safe place as believers. But our hearts have to believe and love that as truth before our experience of God can come into alignment.

Even if there is only a possibility that demons might be causing you to hold back, loosen their grip and punish them for hurting you by making declarations that help you cut off any reason you might have for holding back from God. Listen to yourself as you make declarations that get your heart to believe and treasure that the nearness of God to your physical body is the strong place of safety that you love (Ps. 91; 27:1–6; Rom. 12:1). Based on the referenced Scriptures, your place of safety is to abide in Christ, where the heavenly tent of God's presence is around your physical body here twenty-four seven. Focus on directing your heart into a fully assured faith that makes you confident about the cleansing of God that comes onto your physical body when you enter the holy place by receiving Heaven here (Heb. 10:19–22; 12:22–24, 28).

Let me be direct. Do you feel terror or shame when you think of receiving Heaven here and standing before the Lord? The emotions you feel can be so demanding that it feels like all you can do is hold back from God. But those emotions may not be coming from you! You may be feeling the terror, shame, and fear that a demon is feeling, and they are putting those emotions onto you to control you and keep you from presenting your body before Him. How should you respond to this?

Drop the mountain of God on them. Open up the gates above you, and trust the mountain is dropping down hard. Find refuge in the mountain of God and the kingdom of Heaven while you make them suffer because of the peace of God and His holiness that you receive into this realm. Bind their power to fight back or run, and enjoy that our God is a heavy rock that crushes our enemies. Thank God that His angels are coming to fight and win decisively.

Where you have learned to treasure earthly substitutions for God's protection and strength, you may have put on things like depression, fear, lust, shame, or helplessness as a twisted form of reassurance, power, and security. If that's true, then you may be carrying around a demon with claws sunk into your human flesh. When they ride you like that, it is more than just you wanting to hold back from God. Demons push us to stay away from God and stay in bondage to idolatry and sin.

Don't be afraid of their tactics. Listen to yourself making joyous declarations that teach your heart to treasure the presence of our holy God as your reassurance and security instead of the sin that holds you back. Rather than cowering and trying to hide, muster all the courage you can find and trust with bold faith that you are presenting the demon and the unwanted emotion you are feeling before God. Then let yourself enjoy trusting that God is pouring His holiness over all of it, burning the evil away, and washing you clean.

Argue with any disbelief or hesitancy you feel by listening to yourself make declarations about the greatness of God's holiness and power coming down upon you here. Audibly tell yourself to have courage, and then, as soon as you can, run toward God rather than away. Where the kingdom of Heaven has come upon you, deliverance only needs a flick of God's finger to drive doubts away (Luke 11:20).

Remember the diagrams you saw earlier about what we don't have to depend on? Why would demons push us so hard to get us to avoid that kind of repentance with joyful gratitude and praise? It may be that the diagrams about idolatry are so central to what they pride themselves with that when we joyously repent of those things, they hate it almost as much as they hate God Himself. If that is true, shouldn't we enjoy receiving the mountain of God with the kingdom of Heaven and angels for protection even more while also praising God for what hurts them most?

But what if that doesn't seem to work? If the pressure to sin remains in these areas after you pray like that, you may need help with deliverance. Needing help is common, and there are many Christians in churches who have insight for helping with deliverance.

Just don't think you can have lasting deliverance without also turning your heart away from treasuring the thing that has had you in bondage. The more you fall in love with earthly and human glory, the more likely it is that a demon is clinging to you and pushing you to stay in bondage to the idolatrous sin.

Repent with joyous declarations that change what your heart believes and loves so you can turn to God more easily and receive from Him instead of your area of bondage. Bind the power of witchcraft and command the demons to go. When your heart learns to treasure the closeness of God's holiness and power, any demonic being clinging to you gets burned and can't stay because the presence of God gets too intense. By this, your deliverance will be lasting whether or not you need help.

LOVE OTHERS BY HELPING THEM TO DRINK FROM GOD

Jesus spoke of His followers as sheep. He said that if we love Him, we should feed His sheep (John 21:15–17). Related is where God says, "Do not call to mind the former things, / Or ponder things of the past. / Behold, I will do something new.../

To give drink to My chosen people" (Isa. 43:18–20). All those who love God's people as sheep should be trying to shepherd people in ways that lead them to the Lord so that He can feed them with what pours out from Him (Ezek. 34:11–16; Jer. 17:13; 31:14).

In contrast, the Bible speaks of shepherds who feed themselves with the sheep without feeding the sheep at all (Ezek. 34:2). Shepherds who feed themselves with the sheep aim to pride themselves on how well they impress people with how much they know about the Bible. In extreme cases, shepherds feed the sheep with force and severity and domination (Ezek. 34:4) instead of leading them to feed on God Himself.

Shepherds in today's churches must repent and turn their own hearts to drink from God. Then, they must help teach the people to do the same. If not, eventually, God will tear the sheep out of the mouths of the shepherds so that they can't feed themselves with the sheep anymore (Ezek. 34:10).

In our day, the loving thing is for all of us believers to become shepherds like Moses, who went to Pharoah to demand that he let the people of God go free (Ex. 5:1). Instead of settling for the old Christian paradigm being good enough (Luke 5:39), the loving thing is for us to courageously direct our hearts into the place of believing the Scriptures so we can receive the kingdom and drink from God in ways that bring enough of His holiness and peace to force the demonic to let people around us go free from their bondage to glory from earthly things (Isa. 42: 22–23).

God is enthroned on earth when we receive the kingdom of Heaven with the faith of a child and we praise His name close to us here (Ps. 75:1; Mark 10:15). But Christians today are living far beneath their means because they have been blinded by the devil so that they can't see the light of the gospel of the glory of Christ (2 Cor. 4:4). We must fight with our disbelief and fear until we humble ourselves into the place of being more playfully childlike in our faith for receiving the kingdom and drinking from God with gratitude and praise.

When we seek reasons to praise our human glory, we enthrone ourselves with pride and our love for others is damaged. People around us get hurt when our sense of well-being depends on maintaining pride. When we praise God's glory close to us, we humble ourselves from pride, but we still feel more secure, worthy, and significant. When we drink from the radiance of God and praise the greatness of His closeness, we are far less encumbered in our love for other people.

As long as our glory is what we love, unity in the church will be impossible. Only God's glory brings unity (John 17:22). We must learn to love others by giving them the glory of God rather than our stale and fault-filled human glory.

If we wear the pride of who we are as our identity, that is the thing we try to give to people when we minister to them. Don't let pride make you think you have to feed people with yourself! When God is our I Am, we can lead people to turn to God and drink deeply from the radiance around Him.

When you enter by receiving Heaven here and trust that angels are coming, thank God that He is assigning the angels to help you with the fruitfulness that comes as a result of abiding in Him while helping others to do the same (John 15:5; Ps. 103:20). As you apply these verses in public places while believing that angels are helping, you will be much more consistent at remaining mindfully looking at the Lord while continuing to receive on behalf of the people around you (Ps. 123:2).

The best way for you to win people to Christ is not by your kindness and the smile on your face. These things are important. But why not combine your smile with consciously believing in God for the rain of Heaven upon them? When you do this, your life will be much more fruitful.

It is right that we help people with physical needs because Jesus told us to give food, drink, and clothing to those who need it (Matt. 25:35–40). We should not neglect these things. But what could be more loving than to help people clothe themselves with the kingdom of Heaven so they can drink from God (Ezek. 34:15)? By this, we are helping them to feed themselves with God's presence rather than with glory from worldly sources that can only hurt them.

Love others by helping to stop their well-hidden suffering. Love yourself and others by receiving more of Heaven here until God's living and loving peace and the presence of His holiness increase enough to take over and force evil to stop making people suffer.

Draw near to God by trusting Him to draw near to you. Enter before the Lord by letting Heaven come down and settle around you so you can stand before the Lord with your physical body. Stop the suffering evil is causing on earth by receiving more of the mountain of God and Heaven with angels here. Love yourself and others by doing your part to fill the earth with God's glory so that the tabernacle of Heaven can come more fully.

LOVE OTHERS BY DOING YOUR PART TO STOP THE SUFFERING

How do we motivate ourselves to be more loving toward other people? Jesus learned obedience through suffering (Heb. 5:8). You can learn obedience about abiding through suffering. Let me explain.

The pain from your suffering because of sin and the evil around you should motivate you to receive Heaven here so you can abide before the Lord and stay protected in His presence. Receive so you

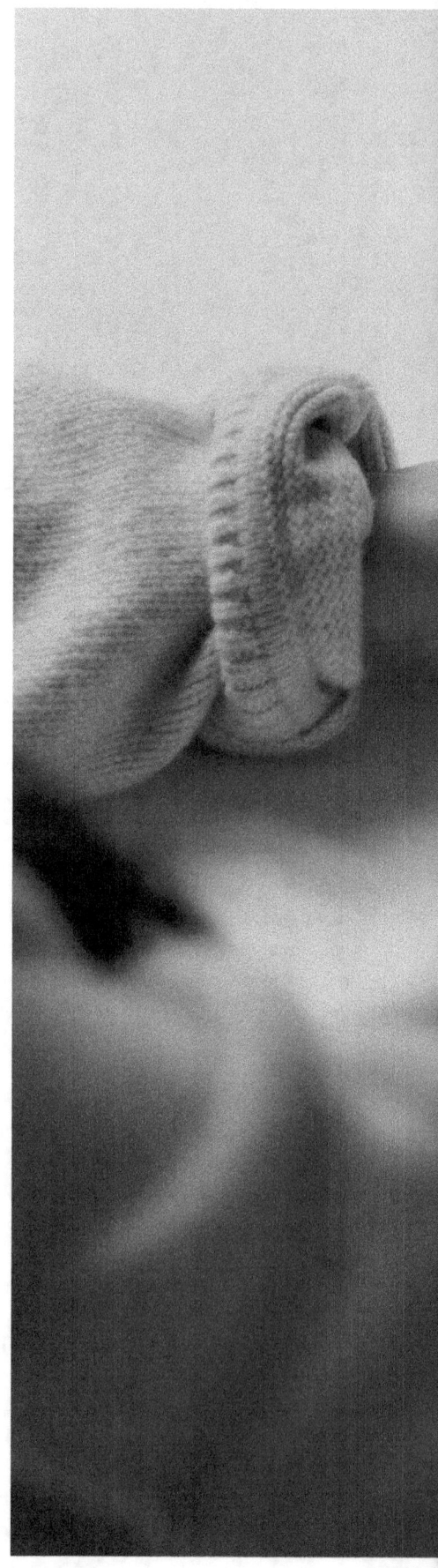

Photo by Priscilla Du Preez on Unsplash

can rest by holding onto the top of the mountain of God on either side of you near the floor. Then teach yourself to stay open so you can keep receiving.

Do you want our world to improve? Stop the suffering by dropping the mountain on evil. You can do your part.

> If we don't teach ourselves and others to humble ourselves from idolatry so we can believe better and abide by receiving Heaven here, nothing will change! Unless we learn to abide in Christ, the evil in the world will go unstopped, and the suffering will continue. Let the suffering in your life and the lives of those around you be a constant reminder to learn faithfulness to stay open to God and be active in your faith about receiving Heaven into this realm.

May God make you so deeply uncomfortable with the suffering you see around you that you can't stand by and do nothing. May God teach you, through the suffering you see in others, to keep receiving Heaven here so you can keep looking at the face of our Father while trusting that the radiance that pours out from Him is coming down like rain upon the people around you (Ps. 123:2; Hos. 6:3). Your attitude should be to punish evil by playfully drinking enough from God that you overwhelm the demonic trying to hurt people. By doing this, you protect yourself in God as your refuge while also demanding that evil influences let people go free so that they can drink and feed themselves with God instead of from idolatry and sin (Jer. 2:11–13; Matt. 11:12).

How is my love for others? I would say it is okay but improving. At times, I get discouraged about abiding because my message often seems so different from what I hear in churches today. One of the biggest helps is reminding myself of the suffering I see around me. Then I try to remember God's promise to pour out His Spirit on all people in the last days (Acts 2:17). Since we receive the promise of the Spirit by faith, I am convinced we must apply faith actively to receiving in an ongoing way (Gal. 3:14; 1 John 1:5, 7). This helps to protect me from demonic attacks. It also helps me with

Photo by Chang Duong on Unsplash

When God becomes our God at playfully deeper levels, He is honored and worshiped as God, we love Him more, and everything else falls into place. You get dangerous to evil when you direct your heart away from the world's glory and into a place of standing before the Lord in ways that help to fill the earth with the glory you receive from God.

When God sees us loving the closeness of His glory and the goodness of His power, that is how He finds the true worshipers He is seeking (John 4:23).

Let me use the verse again where Jesus asked, "How can you believe, when you receive glory from one another and you do not seek the glory that is from the one and only God?" (John 5:44). Jesus is telling us that receiving earthly and human glory damages our faith for receiving the radiant glory of God to the point of the whole thing seeming impractical and unbelievable to us on an everyday level. Repentance with joy changes our patterns of dependence and receiving.

It is not enough to stop ourselves from receiving earthly and human glory. We must also direct our hearts into a place of receiving the presence of God from the radiance around Him (Acts 3:19; Jer. 17:13). Our repentance must change what we are receiving from.

> When you embrace your emotional need for God in a childlike way, your openness to God increases because your in-the-moment emotional neediness becomes central to why you can receive Heaven here easily, quickly, and abundantly.

Listening to ourselves make ongoing, repetitious declarations of repentance is necessary because the ways we receive glory from other people, ourselves, and

motivation to do my part to help stop the suffering. I want to love people more, but nothing will change unless I stay before the Lord and keep receiving Heaven into this realm until God's holiness, peace, and goodness overwhelm the evil, crush it, and make it stop.

LIFE IS A TEST

The greatest human need is to find glory we can praise and own as ours. God designed us this way because He wants to be God to us here. Beyond food and water, finding a sense of glory and power is the underlying essence of all human motivation. But He also gave us a choice. When we find glory from worldly sources and praise ourselves for what we have gained, the result is pride, and we depend on ourselves as god and become our own idol.

> Rather than embracing pride for our sense of well-being, we must embrace humility and God as our God—not by cowering and staying weak but by being strong because the living God is with us here.

worldly things are many and well-hidden, and our thinking patterns are not easily changed in these areas. More than that, receiving glory and praising the glory we receive is how we are most naturally made to feel worthy, confident, reassured, and secure. Therefore, we cling tightly to the successful patterns of receiving earthly and human glory and don't easily give these things up.

Ongoing joyous repentance by declarations changes our patterns of dependence and thinking so that we can more easily turn to God and depend on what we freely receive from Him in an ongoing way instead of what we can only hope to gain from the world.

But don't miss this: Zealously joyous declarations are not for twisting God's arm into coming to us. Don't let yourself think you can make declarations to earn reasons for God to do something for you. You can't manipulate God!

> Ongoing repentance with joy must be adopted as central to our worship and praise or living the integrated big-picture gospel will forever seem unreal. Changing our thinking by listening to ourselves make repetitious and joyful declarations of repentance and faith helps us to go against the most natural tendency that wants to receive glory from people, ourselves, and the world—and it must be repentance with joyous gratitude because that is what helps us to strip away the pride and be more playfully childlike and unhindered in our faith and love for God as the one God we are turning to receive from.

Have other Christians hurt you? Satan often tries to use that to keep you bitter so that you are closed off from being able to be childlike in ways that freely let you receive the kingdom of Heaven here. Forgiveness makes the bitterness stop, but after that, your heart still needs to be directed into a place of faith and taught what to believe and love about receiving the kingdom of Heaven around you here (1 Sam. 7:3; Heb. 12:22–24, 28)

The reason there are so many relational problems among Christians is that even after salvation, most of us are still unknowingly bent on receiving idolatrous glory from the world and other people. Glory to one Christian is often that of controlling others and demeaning them. Glory to another is that of how powerfully they can put themselves down. A Christian's glory should not come from what causes pain in themselves or in another! God's people need to repent of idolatry and sin. We also need to repent in ways that build our faith so we can apply the Scriptures as God desires.

FITTING THE PRACTICAL PIECES TOGETHER

Remember that the kingdom of God and the kingdom of Heaven are used interchangeably in Scripture (Matt. 13:11; 18:3; Mark 4:11; Luke 18:17). Therefore, we are to enter the throne room with our physical body by receiving the kingdom of Heaven here with gratitude (Rom. 12:1; Heb. 10:19–22; 12:28), without hesitation, with the playful faith of a child (Matt. 19:14), and with delight about the abundance of what is available to us when we trade earthly glory for what is heavenly (Isa. 55:1–2).

> But to have that kind of childlike faith, we have to turn our hearts away from having to earn earthly glory and toward God and faith in His grace. The difficult part is that we have to cut off earthly glory and start turning to God before we have any experiential guarantees that God will be there when we turn to Him.

In hope, without hope, we have to listen to ourselves make joyous declarations as we take one step at a time, reassuring our hearts with the truth and turning from earthly sources and toward God. I can promise that you will find it easier to open up and believe God in ways that seemed impossible before you cut off earthly sources.

Again, it is helpful to use the diagrams I showed you earlier in this book to be specific in your thanks and praise toward God for the many ways you don't have to fill up on pride to ease your sense of falling short. Practical repentance uses declarations of thanks and praise for the earthly glories you can turn away from by changing your patterns of thinking and dependence. You must also follow up your joyful declarations of repentance with declarations of gratitude and praise that build your faith and help you turn more fully toward opening up to God so you can receive His presence and kingdom here. By making declarations of repentance and faith together, you can decrease the time you spend moving your dependence from earthly glory to God's.

As you begin to enter, trust that God tore the veil separating Heaven and earth when Jesus died on your behalf (Mark 15:38). Praise Him with gratitude (Ps. 100:4) that because of the tear in the veil, you can open up to God and Heaven above you by believing you are easily swinging the edges of the torn veil back with the inner hands that you normally extend toward earthly and human idols (Ps. 44:20–21; 24:7–8). By opening up to God and Heaven above you, the heavenly gates easily swing open instead of you opening up to earthly and human glory.

Delight your heart about the weight of God's mountain dropping down with Heaven and angels all around you and those you are praying for. Dropping the mountain on people you love is good for them. It clears the air around them and crushes witchcraft and demons bothering them.

> With practice, you will be entering to stand before the Lord in just a few seconds, even when you are half-asleep.

Remember again that the throne room of Heaven is on the mountain of God. Enter before the Lord by staying focused on keeping the gates above you open while believing with resolve that the mountain of God is coming down until you can rest in God's presence. Trust that when the mountain of God comes down, it goes past you until Heaven is all around you, and then you are standing before the Lord with your physical body and with angels all around you here.[20]

Once you believe you have entered and are before the Lord, trust by faith that your eyes are looking at Jesus and the face of your Father (2 Chron. 7:14; John 14:6; Matt. 18:10; Heb. 12:2; Acts 7:55). With your eyes on the face of God, trust that He is being gracious toward you regarding whatever help you are asking Him for (Ps. 123:2).

While believing that angels are coming, remember that they are ministering spirits sent to provide service and care for us as believers. Angels come so they can serve us in fulfilling our God-given calling. They also come to perform the word of the Lord (Heb. 1:14; Ps. 103:20).

Be sure to trust God as you thank Him that angels have come and that they are helping you or those around you in some specific way.[21] I have recently begun thanking God that angels are coming and that because of my abiding, they are helping me to produce fruit that glorifies the Father (John 15:4, 8). Don't be afraid to assign them to helping you or those you are praying for.

When you hear the Lord and you speak His Word, the angelic hosts of Heaven do the work on earth that accomplishes what God has said, even as you repeat what He said with your mouth. Enter by receiving Heaven here, then trust that you are teaming up with angels. We do the work of receiving and resting. They battle with evil.

---

[20] In his book *The Final Quest*, Rick Joyner calls this "going up through the middle of the mountain." But I don't think of it that way for many reasons. Among those reasons are that we are told to seek the kingdom and to receive it like a child (Matt. 6:33; Mark 10:15; Heb. 12:22–24, 28).

[21] I am still learning! As I finish this book, I am finding right now that applying that last sentence about involving angels is particularly helpful.

AVOIDING REOCCURRING SIN

To avoid reoccurring sin, thank God often that it is holiness and purity that you love. Without trying to condemn yourself into conformity, remind yourself that you are miserable with anything less than purity in your behavior and your heart.

Learn to troubleshoot the legitimate emotional need you are trying to meet apart from God. Then turn from idolatry and sin by repetitiously thanking God that you don't have to fill your emotional needs that way. Direct your heart with declarations that thank God about loving His closeness as what you enjoy above all else for filling that need. Then pause to think of God filling that need because of His nearness, and be intentional to enjoy Him in that way. Teach your heart to believe the closeness of God's glory, power, beauty, and love is greater than what you could ever get from any sin. Teach your heart to enjoy the greatness of God's presence as what relieves boredom better than sin.

The Bible says we are to cling to the Lord (Deut. 13:4; Jer. 13:11). One of the most important things I can tell you about avoiding sin is that you need to direct your heart into believing you are receiving Heaven here so you can enter, stand before the Lord, and rest in His presence by clinging to Him.

To understand what it feels like to cling to God, think about what it is like to hug a child across the room who has just hurt themselves. Take that same holding on you do inside to express compassion toward a hurt child, but reapply it to God. Rest in God's presence by trusting you are clinging to the top of the mountain and the lower edges of His heavenly tent around you here. Apply that same hug that you do out of compassion for a child to holding on to the kingdom of Heaven with your inner hands resting near the floor behind or to the sides of you. Rest this way, and remember not to lower the walls around you by letting yourself reach and extend those hands toward other glory sources or sin (Ps. 44:20–21; Prov. 25:28).

If we believe Jesus died to save us from sin and that He was glorified, we should not lessen the wonderful truth about being able to cling to Him. Where there is a reoccurring sin problem, we need forgiveness and should not make excuses for continued failure. Neither should we pile condemnation and shame on ourselves because those things are ineffective and damaging. Entering by receiving so you can take refuge in the Lord and rest in Him by holding tight to the top of the mountain (Isa. 57:13) near the floor is helpful because it is harder to reach out for glory from idols or sin.

Rather than simply trying harder next time, we need to adjust our application of the Scriptures to prevent sin from happening. The changes I have made continue to be effective. I am intentional about enjoying the closeness of God as what satisfies me emotionally. I also put on the presence of God and His kingdom as armor around me that keeps temptation away and punishes the devil when temptation does get through. The more I enter by receiving Heaven here and trust by faith that I am looking into the face of the Father, the easier it is to stay in purity without any sense of evil coming to taunt me, even in a small way.

THE MOST REPEATED PROPHECY AND THE BRIDE MAKING HERSELF READY

One of the most repeated prophecies in the Bible is that God will be God to us and we will be His people (Lev. 26:11–12; Ezek. 37:26–28; Jer. 24:7). By salvation, the Spirit of Jesus lives inside us. But with these prophecies, God also says that His dwelling place will be with us and that He will walk among us here (2 Cor. 6:16).

It is not a coincidence that one says that we will say to God that He is our God (Hos. 2:23). By listening to ourselves declare that He is our God instead of other sources and sin, we remove obstacles of idolatry that can keep these prophecies from being more fully true (Isa. 57:14).

As time progresses, the bride will make herself ready. By receiving Heaven here, we put on the presence of God as our wedding dress. We make a highway for God (Isa. 40:3–5) when we remove obstacles and turn away from earthly glory and toward God. By this, the tabernacle of Heaven is more fully established on earth (Ps. 27:4–5; Rev. 21:2–3; Heb. 12:22–24, 28). Along with a fully assured faith that we have entered the throne room by receiving Heaven here (Heb. 10:22–24), it is the boldness and strength of our joyful and childlike praise that establishes the throne of God on earth (Ps. 22:3; Matt. 21:16).

Remember again that to "walk in the Light as He Himself is in the Light" (1 John 1:7), it helps our hearts to hear and believe when we intentionally enjoy and thrill ourselves with the fact that God wants us "covering Yourself with light as with a cloak, / Stretching out heaven like a tent curtain" around us here (Ps. 104:2).

Evil is rampant in our day, but we aren't to wrestle against flesh and blood (Eph. 6:12). The good news for us includes that "righteousness and justice are the foundation of [God's] throne" (Ps. 89:14) and a river flows down from before Him (Rev. 22:1). Related is that our God delights to use lovingkindness, justice, and righteousness in the earth (Jer. 9:24). But He tells us to "let justice roll down like waters / And righteousness like an ever-flowing stream" (Amos 5:24).

By receiving the mountain of God with Heaven and angels here, we can boast in the Lord, present our bodies to God (Rom. 12:1), and give thanks to our God who is exercising lovingkindness, justice, and righteousness as He sees fit because of what we are receiving here. Humble yourself into receiving Heaven here so you can boast in the Lord and praise His name as you believe He is drawing close to you and making your revengeful enemies cease (Ps. 8:2). By this, God can heal our land because we have identified with Him as our God to the point of turning from our sin and becoming those who are "called by [His] name" (2 Chron. 7:14).

IN CLOSING

By the time this book comes out, additional help will be available on the web at hearttrainingministries.com. There, I will be giving help with joyous declarations of repentance and faith, but I will be calling it "Heart Training."

Don't let yourself be among those whose love for God grows cold because lawlessness has increased in these last days (Matt. 24:12). God made an "everlasting covenant" to be God to us (Gen. 17:7; see also Gal. 3:29).

By listening to ourselves make joyous declarations of repentance and faith, we can become childlike in our freedom and faith enough to open up and receive God's kingdom with His lovingkindness, justice, righteousness, and peace that crush evil under our feet (Rom. 16:20; 14:17). Surround

> Don't get bogged down in your joyful repentance. Be thorough by using the idols listed in the diagrams! But keep it as simple as possible. Repent from dependance on your works aimed at earning glory as reasons to praise yourself and feel pride. Repent toward dependance on the grace of God and His willingness to freely draw near with His kingdom and presence so you can boast in the greatness of His nearness with joyful praise.

yourself with the kingdom of Heaven as your refuge, and satisfy yourself by intentionally enjoying the nearness of God's greatness instead of sin.

In these last days, you can be among those who "display strength and take action" (Dan. 11:32). Bind the power of witchcraft and evil (Matt. 16:19). Courageously direct your heart away from hopelessness and fear until your faith becomes more childlike (Mark 10:15) and you find yourself opening up and receiving the cleansing of God as He comes with the mountain of God, Heaven, and angels (Heb. 12:22–24, 28; Isa. 57:13). Loose the mountain God and Heaven with angels so that these come down hard enough to crush demonic opposition and that God's will can be done on earth as it is in Heaven. Be courageous in cutting off the option of holding back and staying away from God. Believe that your opening up is allowing Heaven to come to a wide area around you. As you do this, practical purity will greatly increase. You will help fill the earth with the glory of God (Num. 14:21). Truth, lovingkindness, justice, and righteousness will prevail over evil (Jer. 9:24). The will of God will be done on earth as it is in Heaven (Matt. 6:10).

The world is a mess because sin and idolatry are rampant. God's presence and kingdom are far better. Will God's people take the lead by going the path of repentance with joy (Pro. 28:13; Isa. 55:1-2; Rev. 3:19; Jer. 26:3)? Together, let's direct our hearts to believe the Scriptures until we can turn away from idolatry and toward childlike freedom and faith. Together, let's praise God with playfully bold gratitude that Heaven is coming to earth more and more, and that God is pouring out His Spirit on all flesh as He promised. Let's keep looking at Him before us here until He is gracious toward us and heals our land.

Photo by Grayson Neill on Unsplash

www.ingramcontent.com/pod-product-compliance
Lightning Source LLC
Chambersburg PA
CBHW080755120626
46557CB00006B/1274